THE SOVIET STATE

The Domestic Roots of Soviet Foreign Policy

THE SOVIET STATE

The Domestic Roots of Soviet Foreign Policy

Edited by
CURTIS KEEBLE

Routledge
Taylor & Francis Group
LONDON AND NEW YORK

First published 1985 by Westview Press, Inc.

Published 2019 by Routledge
52 Vanderbilt Avenue, New York, NY 10017
2 Park Square, Milton Park, Abingdon, Oxon OX14 4RN

Routledge is an imprint of the Taylor & Francis Group, an informa business

Library of Congress Catalog Card Number: 84-52147

ISBN 13: 978-0-367-29605-6 (hbk)
ISBN 13: 978-0-367-31151-3 (pbk)

Contents

Contributors

Archie Brown, St Antony's College, University of Oxford
David Dyker, School of European Studies, University of Sussex
Peter Frank, Department of Government, University of Essex
Curtis Keeble, H.M. Ambassador to Moscow (1978–82)
Stuart Kirby, Senior Associate, St Antony's College, University of Oxford
David Lane, Department of Sociology, University of Birmingham
John Lawrence, Keston College
Malcolm Mackintosh, Cabinet Office, London
Alastair McAuley, Department of Economics, University of Essex
Edwina Moreton, *The Economist*
Alec Nove, Centre for Development Studies, University of Glasgow
Hugh Seton-Watson, School of Slavonic and East European Studies, University of London
Alan Smith, School of Slavonic and East European Studies, University of London

Editor's Acknowledgements

This work had its genesis in an invitation by David Watt, at that time Director of the Royal Institute of International Affairs, to contribute to the Institute's series of studies on Soviet foreign policy. A more detailed outline for the study was then developed in collaboration with William Wallace and Adeed Dawisha, as a result of which we were able to start with a general scheme which remained largely unchanged throughout the later stages. At those first meetings it was particularly helpful to have the benefit of advice from Hugh Seton-Watson and the late Leonard Schapiro. It was a cause of particular sadness to all the members of the group that Professor Schapiro could not take part in the later stages of our work.

A volume such as this is the product of many hands. It is of course the individual contributors who have made it, not only by their own essays, but by the constructive spirit in which, at the meetings of the study group, they discussed and developed the initial drafts. To them and to the other participants in the study group I am deeply grateful.

The organizational support of Chatham House was invaluable. We owe much to the cheerful readiness of Ann De'Ath to tame the untidiest manuscript, to the firm and meticulous hand of Pauline Wickham at the publication stage and above all to the wise and patient guidance of Geoffrey Goodwin.

June 1984 C.K.

1 Introduction

Curtis Keeble

The conduct of relations with the Soviet Union has caused difficulty to successive Western governments from the time of the October Revolution to the present day. The experience of Soviet diplomacy over two-thirds of a century leaves us with the essentials of the problem unchanged, its significance sharpened by the rise of the Soviet Union to a nuclear superpower. Is Chernenko's Soviet Union Lenin's state writ large, with its policies firmly rooted in the political philosophy of 1917? Does it really see the world order in terms of a struggle between socialism and capitalism, in which socialism will inevitably triumph and in which the task of Soviet foreign policy is to ensure that the transition is accomplished tidily and safely? Has the old imperial Russian drive been absorbed into the new philosophy to create a force, uniquely malign in character, whose relationship with the West is, by its own choice, one of hostility, modified only by expediency? Or is this major power now guided more by its practical interest than by its ideology and so beset with its internal and imperial problems that it has more to gain from stability than from conflict? Has it now become a power with which the West can create a relationship necessarily characterized by ideological confrontation, but, for all that, safe, stable and on occasion, mutually beneficial? To pose the problem in these terms is, of course, to over-simplify it at the outset. There is in reality no simple choice among all-embracing policy concepts. In the real world, policy is the product of a multitude of separate acts, often with no clear linkage to an underlying philosophical concept, often uncoordinated and not infrequently conflicting. Yet, ultimately, in all their facets, the policies of Western governments towards the Soviet Union turn upon certain assessments, conscious or instinctive, about the nature and objectives of the Soviet state. It may, of course, be argued that there is nothing very remarkable about Soviet policy; that, in its essence, it is merely the policy which is to be expected from a continental imperial power, newly risen to superpower status and faced with the need to consolidate the areas under its control, to sap the strength of its opponents and to develop the means for world-wide projection of its power. This it is. But it is more. Our objective in this set of studies has been to look beneath the external manifestation of Soviet policies to the roots from which they spring.

Through their history, their political structure, their economic resources, their geographical location, their beliefs, through a whole range of mutually interlinking factors, states develop the characteristics which make each of them unique as an international personality and unique in reaction to any given set of external circumstances at any given time. It is only too easy to judge international problems in terms of their observable elements and to underrate the psychology of the protagonists. 'What kind of people do they think we are?' said Churchill. We paid heavily for failure to understand in time what sort of state Nazi Germany was. We are still paying for the failure of successive British governments to understand in time the mood of post-war Europe and the psychology of the founders of the European Community. Lord Franks' report on the events which led to the Falklands war offers yet another illustration. Officials and ministers recognized a situation which was moving towards armed confrontation, studied it with care and reached a reasonable conclusion on the basis of the observable evidence. Their conclusion, as Lord Franks observed, 'proved to be a misjudgement' and prominent among the reasons was the fact that 'sufficient allowance was not made for the possibility of Argentina's military government, subject to internal political and economic pressures, acting unpredictably'. It is only too easy to overlook the fact that those who form policy in any country, no matter how great their political power, are constrained to an extent which they themselves may not realize by the political, social and ideological climate in which their own ideas have developed; by the geopolitical situation of their country; by the military and economic resources they can deploy; and by the individuals and institutions through whom they must operate. Dearly though we have paid for past misjudgements, the price of error in relations with the Soviet Union is of another order of magnitude.

It was with these considerations in mind that our group gathered in the autumn of 1983, under the auspices of Chatham House, to examine not so much the nature of Soviet foreign policy as the nature of the state and the society from which it stems.

There is a substantial volume of authoritative literature on most aspects of the Soviet Union and it is constantly being added to. Within the compass of the studies we envisaged, it would not be feasible to deal comprehensively and in depth with any individual aspect. There are also many excellent personal accounts by journalists, politicians, diplomats and others who have grappled in this century with the reality of the Soviet Union as their predecessors over the centuries grappled with imperial Russia. Yet, for all this wealth of study, the essence of Soviet international behaviour is by no means clear. It seemed to us that we might best help to bring some of the main aspects into view by a group of studies which are in no sense exhaustive treatments, but rather selective illustrations of some of the main features of the Soviet state as it is today. Each contribution represents the personal view of a contributor on an aspect of the life of the Soviet Union in which he has specialized and each of which is relevant, in one way or other, to the kind of foreign policy which we may expect the Soviet state to deploy. Each reflects a different personal experience and professional discipline. Our studies fall into three broad groups, each of which was made the subject of a separate Chatham House conference, the first on history, ideology and society, the second on the economy and the third on the policy-making institutions. The individual papers have been revised in the light of these conferences and on most of the essentials they reflect the very broad measure of agreement among the members of the group. There are, however, still some differences of opinion and of emphasis and it is inevitable that there should be. Certainly, on a subject as complex as the Soviet state, none of us would venture to lay claim to a full and definitive understanding. The reader will find not so much a posed portrait as a series of views from different angles. We hope they will add to the understanding of the whole. We may have raised more questions than we can answer. If, in so doing, we have inspired others to fill the gaps and seek the answers, we shall be content.

In looking to the domestic roots of foreign policy, we may seem to be at one with Soviet theorists on at least one point. The official history of Soviet foreign policy, edited by Gromyko and Ponomarev, states squarely on page one, 'The policy of any state is determined in the final analysis by its economic and social system.' But even in relation to the domestic roots of policy this Marxist analysis is scarcely adequate. It is therefore, as a Soviet writer might put it, 'not by chance' that our first section begins with an analysis of both the historical and the ideological roots of Soviet policy, followed by a consideration of some of the problems of contemporary society. In a single-party state, where those who rule seek to base their legitimacy on their role as heirs to the revolution, with no more than the post facto justification of an alleged popular mandate, ideology has a special force. Whether one agrees with those who see it as the dominant factor in Soviet foreign policy or with those who assign to it a lesser role, there can be no doubt that in the view of Soviet theorists, it is the ideology which makes Soviet foreign policy different in character from that of the Western democracies. The ideology must, however, be seen in a historical perspective, both Soviet and Russian, and this, within the limitations of space, is what we have sought to do. We have not dealt separately with the geopolitical background to Soviet policy. The unique geography of the Soviet Union, its vast size, its open land frontiers, its few warm water ports, its terrain and its resources have powerfully influenced its policies, as they did those of Tsarist Russia. They were an essential background to our studies rather than material for separate and specific treatment. In the later chapters of the first section we consider some of the broader trends in the changing structure of Soviet society, before turning to two specific sources of potential internal strain, both with implications for foreign policy, nationalism and religion. To our regret we were not able to include a separate study of the cultural scene, an area where the cross-currents of Marxist–Leninist ideology, national temperament and artistic independence produce a pattern of peculiar complexity in relation to domestic and external policy.

It is probably the case that, in so far as any order of priorities can be established, economic policy has come second only to the security of the Soviet state as a factor in Soviet foreign policy. The natural resources of the Soviet Union give it the potential to be uniquely independent. It has been the dream of Soviet leaders to realize that potential and exploit the resultant power. Lenin, for instance: 'Once we solve this problem [the economy], we shall have certainly and finally won on an international scale.' Yet, despite all the achievements in this field, the inefficiency of the Soviet economy and the need for structural reform were still unresolved problems when Chernenko came to power. In foreign policy terms, it is remarkable how little the economic considerations have changed since the need for trade links with the capitalist world was debated in the 1920s, and it is in this area that the West still finds one of its major unresolved policy problems. In a world of nuclear arms, where war between the major powers has become unrealistic as the ultimate arbitrament for disputes, the search for means by which a nuclear power may be constrained to honour its obligations has led to renewed consideration of the use of economic sanctions. At the time of the Afghan and Polish crises there was no clear Western view about their appropriateness or effectiveness as a means of influencing Soviet policy. In the longer term, it is far from clear whether the dominant influence upon Soviet foreign policy will be the potential for autarky, or the benefit to be derived from closer cooperation with technologically sophisticated economies. We examine separately the problems of Soviet industry, agriculture and international trade, before turning to two specific questions, the relationship between Soviet economic capabilities and defence needs and the special influence on Soviet policy of Siberia, its main reserve of natural resources.

State policy is in the last resort a matter of practical application and that, in any country, must reflect the character, power and interrelationship of the individuals and organizations responsible for its formulation and implementation. The Soviet Union is, above all, institutionalized bureaucracy on a superpower scale. In any bureaucracy, institutions and those who staff them become factors in their own right in the formation of policy. In the Soviet Union they are more than normally difficult to study, for, in proportion as it is zealous in proclaiming its doctrine to the world, the Soviet leadership is secretive about the internal processes by which that doctrine is put into effect. The roles of the party organizations, the military, the KGB, the institutes and the media, even of the Foreign Ministry itself, are not easy to disentangle. Nor is it easy to draw a clear line between those organizations where policy may be said to be rooted and those which are concerned only with its implementation. Together they determine the manner in which the Soviet Union projects its power beyond its boundaries and they form the subject matter of the third main section of our study. Throughout it we have been forced to rely heavily upon reasonable inference from scanty published Soviet material, but the picture which emerges, of effective control by the tight central core of the party machine, is an unsurprising one. Much is said in the West about the influence of the army on Soviet policy and we devote a chapter largely to this question. There can be no denying the massive burden which military requirements place upon the Soviet economy or the absolute priority given to the defence of the Soviet state, but we see no sign that the army is challenging or is likely to challenge the top party leadership. It has no need to do so.

The outcome of this set of studies cannot be a set of predictions about the likely evolution of Soviet foreign policy. For that, not only would the internal factors themselves need to be more clearly observable than is frequently the case, but, more important, they would need to be matched against the external factors with which the Soviet leaders are likely to find themselves confronted. Policy is the product of their interaction. To complete the study in this way would take us far beyond the reasonable confines of this book. We have, however, thought it right to attempt, in a final chapter, to bring together the separate studies into a sketch of the characteristic features of the Soviet Union as it is today and to suggest some ways in which such a political entity may be expected to conduct itself on the international scene. There can be no tidy summing up. It will suffice if we have added a little to the understanding of the background against which Soviet foreign policy is formed and helped to lessen the risk of future misjudgement on this account.

PART ONE: IDEOLOGY AND SOCIETY

2 The Historical Roots

Hugh Seton-Watson

Discussion of the historical roots of Soviet foreign policy can best begin from the well-known fact that the Soviet Union is both the heir to the geographical position of the Empire of the Tsars and the homeland of the Bolsheviks, of the 1917 Revolution, the Communist International and its successors.

Marxism-Leninism and legitimacy

This is no place to discuss at length the principles of Marxism, or of the version which became known as Leninism, or to consider such theoretical refinements or modifications as have been introduced by Soviet ideological specialists since Lenin died in 1924. It must suffice that Marxism-Leninism is officially regarded in the Soviet Union as an exact science, a 'correct grasp' of which makes possible a scientific understanding of the past, present and future of the human race; that the decisive stage of humanity's social development, namely the advance to socialism, began with the Bolshevik seizure of power in November 1917, always referred to as the Great October Socialist Revolution (GOSS); and that the model of socialism which was subsequently built up in Russia is the model for the future socialist order for other countries and peoples – even if it is conceded that there will be some minor variations from region to region. The development is inevitable, because the inexorable laws of Marxist science predict it, and the inexorable forces of 'history' are at work. Nevertheless Lenin insisted that it was the duty of Marxists to do all they could to accelerate the process: merely to sit back and wait for 'history' was a grave dereliction of duty. The organization through which active Marxist revolutionaries must work was a communist party, based on the principles summarized in the Twenty-One Conditions of the second congress of Comintern in 1920.[1] This basic doctrine has been constantly reiterated by Lenin's successors. A mere sixty years have passed, during which the revolutionary cause has had its fluctuations. Soviet government has sometimes actively assisted communist movements elsewhere, at other times been passive. When Stalin proclaimed the doctrine of 'socialism in one country', his opponents in the CPSU[2] accused him of abandoning the cause of world revolution; but subsequent history seems rather to have shown that prudence caused him to postpone but not to abandon.

There were moments when the pursuit of revolution conflicted with the political-strategic interests of the Soviet state (in Germany in 1923 and in China in 1927), but in later years Stalin succeeded fairly well in simply identifying the revolutionary cause with the state interest: what was good for the Soviet Union was good for all communists. Persons who revolted against this proposition were not real communists at all.

There is no need here to summarize the history of communist successes and setbacks; but there is one aspect of communist doctrine which requires brief mention. This concerns the legitimacy of the Soviet system. Most forms of government have some type of legitimacy. During most of the recorded history of organized and civilized polities, the legitimizing doctrine has been some variant of the divine right of kings (medieval Christian rulers, Caliphs of Islam, Sons of Heaven in China, descendants of the sun-goddess in Japan). In recent times this kind of legitimacy has been challenged by alternatives based on some form of popular sovereignty, expressed through some form or other of representation for smaller or larger sections of the people, or for the whole people. It is true that there have often been, and still are in some parts of the world, governments based on mere force, personal dictatorships whether military or civil, but these do not usually last long.

Soviet spokesmen claim that their regime is based on popular sovereignty, and can point to their series of very democratic written constitutions. But this is not the essence of Soviet legitimacy. Rather this is based on the achievement of The Great Lenin, who made the GOSS and handed down his wisdom through the successive members of the Central Committee of the CPSU.

If one asks, how do we know that the events of November 1917 were not merely the forcible seizure of power by one small socialist faction from a weak government of other socialists, but were the GOSS, the answer has to be: 'Lenin said so'. If we ask, how do we know that Lenin and his comrades possessed an exclusive 'correct grasp' of Marxist science, the answer is the same. If we ask, how do we know that the members of today's Central Committee of the CPSU, led by its First Secretary, possess that grasp, the answer is that these are comrades chosen by elder comrades, who were chosen by persons who were chosen by Lenin. We have thus a principle of legitimacy based on (non-divine) revelation and subsequent recruitment by laying on of hands.

There is at this point a certain difficulty. In the Great Purge of 1936–9 three-quarters of the members of the Central Committee were removed from their posts, and most of these were 'unmasked' as 'enemies of the people', some being allegedly agents of the British or French or German or Japanese secret services, or of several or all of these at the same time. If indeed these men were such traitors, confidence in the scientific infallibility of the system of appointment is shaken. If however they were, as Khrushchev was tending to show by his speech to the Twentieth Congress of the CPSU in February 1956, innocent comrades and victims of a monster, Joseph Stalin, then again confidence in a system which enables such a monster to achieve sole power is shaken.

The Great Purge is a *damnosa hereditas* with which, despite Khrushchev's brief brave attempt, the Soviet rulers have not yet come to terms, and which still haunts them. Those who have ruled the country for the last twenty years are persons who rapidly advanced their careers through the Purge, leaping up many rungs in the ladder of power at an early age by learning the technique of getting in their denunciations of their colleagues before their colleagues denounced them. There are still men at the top from that peculiar elite, of which the late Kosygin and Brezhnev were outstanding examples. The extreme sensitivity of the Soviet leaders to this issue was shown at the time of the 'Prague spring' in Czechoslovakia in 1968, when demands were expressed from both inside and outside the Czechoslovak communist party, not only that victims of the Czechoslovak purges of 1949–52 should be released and rehabilitated, but that those responsible for these perversions of justice should be punished. The Czechoslovak purge had indeed been a nasty affair, but it was a small matter in comparison with the Soviet purge of 1936–9. If judicial murder and perversion of justice were to be punished in a socialist country, an appalling precedent would have been set. Though direct evidence is lacking, it is reasonable to assume that this prospect was one of the things which most contributed to the decision to invade Czechoslovakia.

The search for security

It has often rightly been pointed out that rulers of Russia have been obsessed since the earliest times with the security of their frontiers. Russia contains no natural borders to west or east, and has frequently been invaded from each direction. The small principality of Moscow was obliged constantly to defend itself from threatening neighbours. Its success in doing so can be grasped in a moment by comparing the maps of Muscovy in 1400 and the Soviet Union today. Self-defence made it necessary to extend Russia's borders to the Baltic, the Black Sea, the Caspian, the Pacific Ocean, into the fertile valleys of Turkestan, the ruins of Königsberg and the islands of the Sea of Okhotsk. Russian obsession with defensible frontiers looked rather different to the inhabitants of the intervening lands, and can hardly be a source of much comfort to the Soviet Union's neighbours in Europe or Asia. At the same time there still remain areas where Russia has been vulnerable in the past, and which still escape Russian control: the Belt and Sound, the Iceland Gap, the Black Sea Straits, Iran, the Amur river.

The defensive mentality is an undoubted fact, and it has not militated against expansion, but rather has promoted it. In the last years however a new note has been heard. The Soviet Union has been nominally one of two superpowers at least since the early 1950s, but in reality only since the late 1970s. Its achievement of that status results from its catching up with, and possibly in some fields surpassing, the military power of the United States; and a symbol of this is the presence of Soviet naval forces, and of harbours controlled by subservient governments on adjacent land, in all the oceans of the world. This assumption of the role of world power is the Soviet answer to the 'encirclement' with which it has long seen itself threatened, first in the alleged tendency of all capitalist states to combine against it, and more recently in the *entente* between the United States and China. The professional deformation of the historian inevitably recalls the case of an earlier Power which sought to combat *Einkreisung* by a great ocean fleet, and to make itself felt in Venezuela, Morocco and Kiaochow. It also makes him wonder whether Admiral Gorshkov has studied the career of Admiral von Tirpitz. History of course does not repeat itself, not even as farce echoing tragedy, but historical precedents can provide warnings. The names of Afghanistan, Aden, Ethiopia, Angola and Cuba are linked with a process of worldwide expansion which differs in many ways from European expansion in the late nineteenth century but also resembles it, not least in the fact that its exponents genuinely see themselves as defending themselves against encirclement.

The whole problem of security acquired a new dimension with the appearance of the intercontinental missile. The concepts of strategic positions and buffer zones and overseas bases, as understood by previous ages, were no longer adequate. That is not to say that they have been made obsolete: the Soviet leaders, who did rather well in these traditional terms in 1945, and have kept up their search for these assets with some success, certainly do not regard them as obsolete. However it is true, as it was not in any previous age, that no state can possess security as long as a single state exists in the world, independent of it, in possession of intercontinental missiles. Complete security can be achieved only by sovereignty over the whole world.

At a long-term theoretical level Marxist-Leninist science can provide a confident answer. In the long term the whole human race will advance to 'socialism'; the only true 'socialism' is the system devised in the Soviet Union, and requires of all who adopt it allegiance to the Soviet leaders; and when this happy state of affairs has been achieved, ideology and security will alike have been satisfied.

In practice it is rather silly to assert that the Soviet leaders 'are out for world domination'. It is extremely unlikely that any of them consider this a realistic aim in the predictable future. However, ideology and security seem normally to convince them that, whenever any crisis occurs anywhere in the non-Communist world, they must do what they can to exploit it and if necessary exacerbate it, mainly in order to harm their American and Chinese adversaries, but also – if circumstances permit – to give a helping hand to local communists. If they decide that they can do nothing, they do nothing. If they can do something to damage a Western interest, but at the cost of accepting the suppression of local communists, they will settle for that. In a nuclear age, undue risks must not be taken, and the risk of direct superpower military conflict is an effective constraint. The retreat from Iran in 1946, and the decision not to invade Yugoslavia after 1948, are well-known examples of Soviet caution, as more recently is the relative self-restraint shown by the Soviet government in the Middle East. There are, however, no grounds for thinking that this restraint implies abandonment of long-term Soviet aims in the region. Subject to these important limitations, the Soviet leaders will always seize any opportunity to extend their area of domination.

What they have in practice been very reluctant to do right up to now is to cooperate with other powers to calm a crisis. This is not to say that the Soviet leaders can never cooperate with another independent power of equal or greater strength: such cooperation has been seen in the past, but only at the expense of a third party, a common enemy. Outstanding examples are cooperation with Germany against Britain and France (1939–41), and with Britain and America against Germany (1941–5). Another is the Soviet-Japanese treaty of April 1941 – arguably Stalin's most brilliant diplomatic success – which saved the Soviet Union from a two-front war, and diverted Japanese aggression against the western powers in the Pacific. In the post-war world there were no more third parties, until one appeared in the late 1960s. However, attempts to cooperate with China against the United States, or with the United States against China, have hitherto been unsuccessful. The Non-Proliferation Treaty may be seen as a rare example of cooperation in relation to which the third party was all would-be nuclear states.

The study of Soviet history, the record of the behaviour of the Soviet government, and the experience of those who have had to deal personally with Soviet officials for substantial periods, all point to the conclusion that these men are in no sense starry-eyed revolutionary enthusiasts, or indeed any sort of revolutionaries. They are extremely conservative men, resolved above all to preserve the hierarchy of power and privilege which they and their predecessors have painfully constructed, and from which they benefit. One of the principal instruments for its preservation is the revolutionary rhetoric which proceeds from the leadership, and which involves the active participation of the population. The abstraction 'the working class' is the object of unending hymns of praise; everything that is done is done in the name of the working class which allegedly holds power; and the flesh and blood workers are engaged in continuous paeans to themselves and their rulers. The real workers are at least as subordinate to their bosses in factory and in government as workers in any capitalist country, and doubtless many of them are aware of this; but still their voices swell the chorus. It is impossible to make any quantitative estimate of the contribution which this constantly mobilized assent makes to the strength of the regime, but it is a phenomenon specific to the Leninist state and its value must be considerable.

The rulers are not revolutionaries but extreme conservatives; yet in their view Revolution *is* the Leninist system, the protagonist in the world-wide class struggle *is* the Soviet leadership, and 'the interest of the working class' *is* the interest of the Soviet state.

Do the leaders really believe this? This question, often raised by western commentators, has no straightforward simple answer. There have always been, in all history, degrees of fervour in the acceptance by public figures of public doctrines. Today's Soviet leaders as small children saw the triumph of the Bolsheviks; in their early adult years they saw the regime survive the Great Purge, and then stand up to the still more terrible impact of Hitler's invasion; and during their years at the political summit they have seen their country achieve the rank of superpower, and become possibly the strongest military power in the history of the human race. They grew up in the official Leninist doctrine, they know no other, and despite the setbacks they have experienced enough successes to make them believe that the doctrine can be made to work pretty well. The leaders are not specialists in Marxist theory: the priesthood of theorists appointed by the Central Committee of the CPSU can safely be left to their job of refining theory and bringing it up to date, subject to some broad directives from the Politburo. But the doctrine in a simple potted form, suitable to daily working needs, is accepted, and serves to uphold political morale, to maintain implacability towards the outside world, and to reinforce the comforting conviction that 'History' is on their side, and that the future belongs to them. It provides them with that impenetrable carapace of self-righteousness, perhaps somewhat more intellectualized than that of the Victorians, in which they are firmly encased.

The Soviet leaders are a successful upstart elite (whether a 'new class' or a 'caste' is debated by western non-Soviet Marxists with an erudition to which this essay lays no claim), full of self-admiration, boastful bullies as they face the outer world, yet inwardly resentful that they are not accepted as equals by older elites – or perhaps, it would be more correct to say, resentful that they do not receive from those other elites the same adulation that they can extract from their own subjects. The postures of these men strikingly recall those of the new elites of Europe and North America at the turn of the nineteenth to twentieth centuries. They recall the age of Joseph Chamberlain, Theodore Roosevelt and William II. They exhibit the same imperial pride and insecurity. It is not fanciful to detect in them the impatient belief that it is the turn of their country, and more especially of the Russians, to be top-dogs in the world, successors to Palmerston, to Admiral von Tirpitz and to Henry Luce of *Time* Magazine and his American Century.

Russian nationalism

It is arguable that one further element enters into the ethos of the Soviet political class, and so into the motivation of Soviet foreign policy: Russian nationalism. This requires closer examination.

The national consciousness of the Russians, and indeed the concept of a Russian nation, developed at a rather late stage in the history of Russia. The traditional objects of the loyalty of the Russian people were the Orthodox faith and the person of the Tsar. For his part the Tsar required of his subjects not that they should be Russians but simply that they should obey him.

At the beginning of the nineteenth century three historical trends, visible already earlier, came to a climax: the emergence of Russian as a standardized written and spoken language and a vehicle for a brilliant literature; the penetration of the ideas of the European Enlightenment into the educated minority and their reformulation to fit Russian reality; and the appearance of a mortal danger to Russia in Napoleon's invasion. The response of the Russians, elite and people alike, to this threefold challenge recalls the response of the English to a similar threefold challenge in the reign of Elizabeth.[3] In the post-Napoleonic era educated Russians increasingly took pride in the Russian language, and concerned themselves specifically with the condition of the *Russian* – that is, of the Russian-speaking people. This is true not only of the great poet Pushkin or the Decembrist revolutionary Pestel', but also of many conservative government officials. It was one of these – the Minister of Education Count Uvarov in 1832 – who formulated a new official doctrine of legitimacy based on three principles – not only Autocracy and Orthodoxy but also a (Russian) National Outlook (*narodnost*).[4]

In the following decades the idea that Russians, who formed roughly half the population of the Russian Empire, were more realiable, and therefore entitled to higher status, than members of other nations or tribes, gained ground in the educated class, and to some extent also penetrated downward into the lower strata. It was at first strongly resisted by the Tsars, many of whose most trusted officials were Baltic Germans or Finno-Swedes or foreigners. But by the 1890s Russian nationalism had become a strong influence on Tsars Alexander III and Nicholas II, and a policy began to emerge which became known as Russification. Essentially it aimed at compelling the non-Russian half of the population not only to learn Russian in addition to their own language, but to accept Russian culture in place of their own, and to become Russians – that is, not only to be loyal servants of the Russian *state* but to become members of the Russian *nation*. This policy was never completely endorsed by the whole government apparatus, and its application fluctuated from region to region and from year to year; but during the last three decades before 1917 there is no doubt that it increased, and was increasingly resented by those nations which already had a strong national consciousness – Poles, Finns, Germans, Armenians, Tartars – and to a growing if lesser extent by others which were at least keenly aware that they were different from Russians, and objected to being bullied into an identity which was not theirs – Ukrainians, Baltic peoples, peoples of Central Asia. Russian nationalism, in its aggressive form of Russification, positively created anti-Russian nationalism. From the point of view of its authors' aims, it was counter-productive.

Lenin utterly rejected Russification, and made 'self-determination' of nations, including if desired separation from Russia, one of the Bolsheviks' main slogans during the civil war of 1918–20. However, in reality Bolshevik victory meant forcible reincorporation of nearly all non-Russian territories of the old Empire in the new Soviet Union. The theoretical justification for this was that the proletariat of these nations desired union with the Russian proletariat, and that those Ukrainians, Tartars, Uzbeks or others who demanded separation were only unrepresentative bourgeois or feudal cliques. This may or may not have been a part of the truth: what is certain is that these peoples were never given the chance of deciding, by free elections or plebiscites, whether they desired independence or not. Those peoples who did separate were able to do so only because they had the backing of one or more European great powers, and all except the Finns were re-annexed or brought back under Soviet control in 1939 and 1944 or earlier.[5]

After the Bolshevik victory in the civil war, the main local languages were given official status, and local persons filled the lower ranks of the administration, to a much greater extent than under the Tsar; but the political and social system, as well as the hierarchy of the communist party, were extremely centralized, and the decision-makers consisted overwhelmingly of Russians. In recent years more non-Russians have risen to high positions, but in most of the republics there still remain Russians in key posts.[6] Great efforts have also been made to induce non-Russians to learn Russian, with a considerable degree of success. Inevitably the predominance of Russians has aroused the resentment of non-Russians, and awareness of this resentment has often caused Russians living in non-Russian regions to assert their predominance in a manner which to local people has appeared arrogant or aggressive. Tension on both sides has been most acute in periods of general crisis (the famine at the end of collectivization of agriculture in 1932–3, the Great Purge of 1937–9, at some critical moments in the war and in the reoccupation in 1944–5 of territories that had been occupied by the Germans). In periods of relative calm and material improvement (the later Brezhnev years) tension has been less.

To many non-Russians Soviet policies towards the 'nationalities' (as the non-Russians are officially called) have appeared a continuation of Russification, and the Soviet Union itself a mere reincarnation of the Russian Empire under another name with other political and social methods. The Soviet leaders however strongly deny that their policies amount to Russification. They explain the predominance of Russian personnel in non-Russian regions as a consequence of the lower level of culture of the other peoples. They insist that, as this level is steadily raised, Russian predominance is diminishing. In Armenia, and to a slightly lesser extent in Georgia, the role of Russians is now small; if it remains important in the Ukraine, Estonia and Latvia, this can be justified on the ground that large Russian populations have lived in their cities since long before the Revolution. As for the spreading of knowledge of Russian among the non-Russians, this can be attributed not to any desire to Russify, but simply to the necessity of having one language used by the authorities throughout the vast country: the other peoples are free to use their own languages not only in private life but also in local public business.

The sincerity of these official Soviet arguments need not be doubted. The communist leaders are not conscious Russian nationalists. They are not trying to impose traditional Russian culture on non-Russians. On the contrary, they have made great efforts to denigrate this culture, especially its religious dimension, which is of its very essence. Indeed there are Russians – forming one of several trends in the 'dissidence' of recent years – who feel that the Soviet regime has been one of domination by non-Russians, determined to trample on Russian culture. It may well be argued that Russian nationalism, which appears to have increased in recent years, and which is reflected not only in the vigour of religious communities (see Chapter 5), but also in a marked increase of public interest in Russian historic buildings and in Russia's medieval and pre-Petrine history, is a force of opposition, or at least of criticism; and it is not improbable that this critical Russian nationalist mood has its supporters within the CPSU.

It is difficult, in view of these contradictory trends and opinions, to estimate the role of Russian nationalism as a force behind Soviet foreign policy. Though the interpreters of Marxism-Leninism at the highest level, and the members of the Politburo, aim not at Russification but at the creation of a Soviet patriotism that must subsume the national cultures of the various 'nationalities', and intend to reduce them all to the level of picturesque folklore; yet the hundreds of thousands of Russians who administer the country through the medium of the Russian language, and who have grown up in a Russian environment and been through a Russian education, tend to show towards the non-Russians an attitude of condescension which is at best paternalist and at worst contemptuous.

The truth seems to be that Marxism-Leninism, the search for security, a culturally mutilated Russian nationalism and imperial ambition are all inextricably interrelated. It is legitimate to analyse them as separate factors: this is the traditional approach by western scholars to the subject, and has been used above. In reality however these four factors cannot be unscrambled. They have been fused together into a chemical compound which is more than the sum of its parts.

How far this official ethos, propagated through the vast machinery of the media and the schools, is accepted and shared by the population as a whole can only be a matter for conjecture. Though the more abstract aspects of Marxism-Leninism may not arouse enthusiastic interest, and the repetition of sacred formulae may be something of an empty ritual, one can hardly doubt that the terminology and rhetoric of the omnipresent mass-mobilizing media affect the thinking processes of Soviet citizens. It also seems likely that the strength of the Soviet state, and its imperial expansion as a world power, are a source of pride – perhaps stronger among Russians than among the 'nationalities'. There is certainly a contradiction between the xenophobia of official propaganda and the natural hospitality and curiosity of Russians towards foreigners. It is arguable that when western public attitudes to the Soviet Union stiffen, this enables the Soviet rulers to strengthen their hold on the people, arousing patriotic xenophobia and making 'the imperialists' a scapegoat for all the hardships and frustrations of Soviet life; whereas in periods of relative mutual politeness between West and East, Soviet citizens, being able to taste the forbidden fruits of western contacts, have more opportunity to develop critical thoughts.

'Cold war' and 'détente'

The basic political outlook towards the outer world of the Soviet leaders, derived from this evolving public ethos, has changed very little in sixty years. Soviet policy has adopted from time to time varied tactics, which have been represented by Soviet spokesmen as being different forms of the 'class struggle'. The two best-known phrases used by Soviet spokesmen in the post-Stalin era are 'peaceful coexistence' and 'détente'. Both are commended as methods of unremitting struggle against the class enemy. Consequently, just as the interest of the working class is identical with the interest of the Soviet state, so all governments not subject to Soviet control are potential enemies. The Soviet government sees itself as in a state of political struggle with the outside world. This is a statement of fact, not an attribution of guilt or virtue. This state of affairs was described, soon after the end of World War II, by western journalists as 'cold war'. This rather useful and vivid expression denoted a situation, not a policy. However, semantics are a field in which Soviet political warfare is highly skilled, and these two words came to be used, not only by Soviet but increasingly also by western writers, to denote policy, and solely western policy. 'Cold war' has come to mean a western, principally of course American, policy of hostility to the Soviet Union short of shooting. Cold war is something which is directed against the Soviet Union. Soviet policy, by contrast, disinterestedly pursues peace. This statement, which is often proclaimed by Soviet propaganda, is seen to be true when it is understood that 'peace' is simply the Soviet code word for whatever is the Soviet specific aim at any time. Tautologies, by definition, are always true.

Détente – or 'relaxation of tension', a literal translation of the Russian expression that is its equivalent – means concessions by others to the Soviet Union but not concessions by the Soviet Union to them. In the 1930s the rather similar slogan word – 'appeasement' – then much used by western leaders in relation to the Axis Powers, was rendered in Russian as 'appeasement of the aggressors' (*umirotvorenie agressorov*). In the circumstances, this was a rather apt usage. However, it is worth noting that conciliation between any pair of mutually hostile powers has always been regarded by the Soviet leaders as anti-Soviet and aggressive, as a step towards the united front of capitalism against the land of socialism. Throughout the changing stages of Soviet foreign policy – from Popular Front to Nazi-Soviet Pact to Grand Alliance to Cold War to Peaceful Coexistence to Cuban missile crisis to Détente to post-

Afghanistan tension – despite tactical variations, the basic attitude of the Soviet leaders to the West has not changed, nor has the picture of the conflict between 'capitalism' and 'socialism', or of the evil intentions of 'the imperialists', presented by Soviet media to the Soviet public, changed.

Détente and appeasement, as understood in the West at certain moments, signifying relaxation of tension by mutual concessions and reconciliation, have been noble aims, and indeed are the essence of wisdom in foreign policy. But they have not been seen in operation in the last fifty years. The phrase 'détente is dead' is not true; the truth is that détente has not yet been born.

A case can of course be made against these arguments. During the years of détente policy in the United States there was some easing of the tone of Soviet dealings with the West – though little change in the picture of the western world presented to the Soviet public. It became easier for selected Soviet citizens to visit the West, and slightly easier for western academics to conduct research in the Soviet Union. Rather more western literature was made available to Soviet readers, and the number of tours by musical or ballet groups from either side to the other increased. There was also some expansion of trade. None of this adds up to any significant change in Soviet policy.

More important was the fact that for a time Soviet jamming of western broadcasts stopped altogether, and even recently has not been resumed on anything like the pre-détente scale. Still more important was the SALT I agreement with the United States. Yet even this should arguably be considered a pause in the Soviet march to its goal rather than any substantive change, still less any abandonment, of that goal – and in any case it only partly limited Soviet rearmament.

The basic difference between the Soviet Union and other states remains. Conflicts of interest, and community of interest, arise frequently between governments of all states; but Soviet interests – as seen by the Soviet rulers – include both the promotion throughout the world of 'socialism', and of 'liberation movements' (that is, anti-western armed actions), and the achievement of complete security for the Soviet Union (that is, steady expansion). Moreover the Soviet Union has not only permanent interests but permanent enemies – all 'capitalist' and all schismatic 'socialist' states – and systematically works to undermine them. Westerners need not be unduly disheartened by this fact; it is perfectly possible to live with it for many years yet, and in time it, like all phenomena of human history, will cease to be a fact. But today it is a fact.

Western misconceptions

In the pursuit of its interests the Soviet Union is much assisted by, and perhaps consciously makes use of, certain western perceptions, which may be called 'either-or fallacies'. Some of these should be noted here.

The most widespread is the controversy between those who see 'ideology' as the main force behind Soviet policy, and those who give this place to 'security'. It is our case that the two are inseparable, and there is no need to repeat the argument. Arising from this misleading 'either-or-ism' is the dispute, perhaps even more widespread, as to whether Soviet policy is 'expansionist' or 'defensive'. It is both. Obsession with protection of frontiers and of strategic positions leads to expansion, and each successful act of expansion creates new positions to defend. From the point of view of those who are expanded on to, it makes no difference, and those against whom it is more distantly directed ought to be aware of this.

Another controversy, more frequent among American than British commentators, debates whether successive crisis situations in Third World countries – especially in tropical Africa and Central America – are due to Soviet subversion *or* to local social unrest. The truth is that both may, and often do, operate simultaneously, and wise observers keep their eyes open to both. To take only two, in both Nicaragua and Angola bitter local discontents of national (anti-Portuguese or anti-North American) and of social (anti-landlord, anti-capitalist) origin were at work, but it was also true that sustained subversion and intervention by Cubans, stage-managed by the Soviet Union, played a major part.

Still more widespread and pernicious is the false choice between defence programmes and diplomacy as means of coping with Soviet power. Defence and diplomacy are always necessary all the time. The fact is that, however hostile the polemics on either side, there will always be matters on which it is necessary to negotiate. There are those in the West who argue that when foreigners behave badly, you must stop talking to them, and there is a delusion that once both sides sit down to talk round a green baize table a marvellous spirit of conciliation will gradually grow, and conflicts will disappear. One related 'either-or-ism' deserves a mention. This may be called '*either* politeness *or* confrontation'. As long as we negotiate with the Soviet Union, it is argued, we must refrain from denouncing or insulting them. The Soviet leaders have never thought that negotiations precluded simultaneous hostile propaganda and subversion. All the time that they are negotiating they pour out the steady flood of hatred of the West, directed to their own peoples and to their worldwide propaganda audiences. Yet when, from time to time, western statesmen have denounced Soviet behaviour, drawing attention to the nature of the Soviet system and its empire in Asia and Europe, the cry of 'cold war' is raised. The comparison between the two records, and between the two results for each side, is hardly conducive to western complacency, but compels respect for Soviet effort. The massive continuous world-wide hate campaign against the West, and the similar campaign among Soviet citizens, are a most important part of the conduct of Soviet foreign policy, and a major internal source of strength. Unfortunately the very vocabulary of this subject, in most if not all languages, is laden with emotion. For this reason, not a few academic students of the Soviet Union, seeking clinically clean, 'value-free' judgements, shy away from it. But to leave this out of a discussion of the domestic sources of Soviet foreign policy is to present 'Hamlet' without the Prince of Denmark.

This brings us finally to a dimension which, for the same reasons, is almost always left out: the moral dimension. Western commentators have a healthy dislike of moralizing; are still haunted by the shades of Victorian hypocrites; and have no wish to impose 'bourgeois morality' – which in any case they reject for themselves – on other people. This sceptical attitude has much to commend it; yet the fact that the official morality of the Soviet Union, manifested through the whole publicity machine, is radically different from the range of moralities prevalent in the West, is an important fact; and if it is left out of the picture, the picture will mislead its beholders.

Soviet doctrine repudiates all universal morality, and maintains that the only supreme criterion is the interest of the working class. In practice, the interest of the working class is simply equated with the interest of the Soviet Union, and the interest of the Soviet Union is what the infallible exclusive possessors of scientific wisdom in the Central Committee of the CPSU, led by its General Secretary, at any particular time say it is. This is of course the claim for total power – for the concentration of all political, economic and spiritual leadership and power in the same hands. In practice the claim has never been made effective, not even at the climax of Stalin's power. Loyalty to family, to religion, to national (Russian or other) culture and even to personal friendship were never eliminated. Since Stalin's death much less effort has been made to achieve total power; but the claim is still there. Although in practice most Soviet citizens are still deeply affected by what we may call the traditional Helleno-Judaeo-Christian or Irano-Judaeo-Muslim outlooks, the elevation of the will of the leader (or collective leadership) of the CPSU to supreme criterion of morality has never been revoked.

One more pernicious 'either-or-ism', deeply rooted in western mass democracies, needs mention, as a severe impediment to understanding of the forces behind Soviet foreign policy. This is the belief that if a foreign state is an enemy, its people must be wicked; and conversely, if its people are demonstrably no more wicked than one's own compatriots, but a normal human mixture, then the state cannot be an enemy. Historical truth is that conflicts between states – with or without bloodshed – have been between good and good, and bad and bad, at least as much as between good and evil. This is something which democratic politicians and democratic public opinion have found very hard to understand. Yet they need to grasp three truths: that there are profound conflicts of interest and aims between the Soviet Union and the western democracies; that the Soviet leaders operate according to moral and intellectual criteria profoundly different from theirs; and that most Soviet citizens are decent, fallible, sinful and well-meaning folk like themselves.

If the arguments of this essay are sound, then the reality is bleak, and prospects for the predictable future are bleak. The Soviet leaders are unlikely to change their view of the West, or to be converted to western concepts of democracy, but they will be influenced in their practical foreign policy by the political actions of other governments. Whilst sensitive to the overriding need to avoid nuclear war, they will expect, and seek, further short-term gains, further expansion wherever a weak point in enemy defences appears which it is not dangerous to seize; and they will continue to believe that the cumulative effect of these successive gains will be the disintegration of western power, or as they would put it, the collapse of 'the imperialists' and ultimately of 'capitalism'.

There is no need to take an apocalyptic view of this. It is perfectly possible to live with these realities, perfectly possible to accept implacable Soviet enmity as a fact, to refuse to feel equivalent enmity towards them, to respect, even admire them, but also to maintain effective defence of the West (by diplomacy, industrial power and propaganda no less than by military strength, for none of these four pillars of the western edifice can be neglected). It is perfectly possible to hope that if such is and remains the western posture, the condition of cold war (in which we have been, by Soviet choice, ever since the October Revolution) will one day come to an end. It would be foolish to assume that the new generation which will soon take over the Soviet Union will be easier to live with than the present. They may, but the possibility is not one we can rely on. Yet Soviet enmity does not mean that the Soviet Union is the incarnation of evil: the Soviet leadership and the Soviet peoples probably include as high a proportion of honourable and virtuous persons as the leaderships and peoples of western countries, but the unilateral enmity remains. Neither miraculous solutions nor apocalyptic catastrophies are likely, and there is no alternative to realism and patience.

Notes

1 Comintern, founded in 1919, was dissolved in 1943. Since then there has been no single supreme organ of 'international communism', but Soviet leaders have not for that reason ceased to consider the Soviet Russian model to be valid for all societies advancing into socialism.

2 The party in 1917 took the name 'Russian Communist Party (Bolshevik)' RKP(b); later, after the state became a Union, it was changed to 'All-Union . . .' VKP(b); and later still to Communist Party of the Soviet Union (KPSS, in English CPSU), by which name we shall here call it.

3 The corresponding elements are the emergence of a great English literature, both sacred and secular, the ferment of ideas in the Reformation, and the threat from Spain.

4 This slogan was formulated in a report submitted by Uvarov to the Tsar in December 1832 through the Minister of Education Count Lieven. It was the result of an inspection of Moscow University which Uvarov had been appointed to undertake, and on the strength of it he was then appointed Minister in place of Lieven, and held the post for sixteen years.

5 Armenia, Azerbaidjan and Georgia separated in 1918, but were reconquered in the early 1920s; Estonia, Latvia and Lithuania were independent states from 1920 to 1940; Romania acquired eastern Moldavia in 1918 and lost it again in 1940; Poland has remained a nominally sovereign state but has been at the mercy of the Soviet Union since 1945.

6 The usual pattern in the Muslim republics has been for the first secretary of the CPSU at republican and *oblast* level to be from the indigenous nation, but the second secretary to be a Russian. Similar situations have also existed in the Baltic republics amd Moldavia, but patterns have varied and still vary.

3 The Societal Dimension

David Lane

When we speak of the 'societal dimension' to Soviet foreign policy, we usually refer to the underlying social structure and social trends. More precisely one has in mind the size, division and dynamics of the population stock, the emergence or maturation of class and social groups, the growth or decline of major social supports, the appropriateness of ideology, changes in the nature of values and beliefs, developments in science and technology and the viability of organizational forms to contain, sustain and innovate. While such factors undoubtedly influence the formation of foreign policy, I would emphasize that even the most profound knowledge of the changing social structure cannot be translated directly into policy choices. Social developments may lead to a variety of alternative responses by the political elites. Politics has its own peculiar dimension and shapes the articulation and aggregation of demands thrown up by the changing social structure. The political experience, outlook and mentality of the political leadership is crucial in the interpretation and mediation of social trends and political demands. A variety of alternative responses is possible. The justification for a focus on social trends is that it brings to the fore some of the important factors which limit or constrain foreign policy decisions and which may play a part in policy formation.

Papers are included in this symposium on nationalities, religion, the economy and ideology. In this chapter I shall consider a limited number of topics: population trends, developments in the formation of the working class and 'intelligentsia', social mobility; in addition, brief reference will be made to forms of social dislocation and dissent. At the conclusion of each section of the paper I tentatively suggest how the topic under consideration may influence foreign policy.

Population

It is widely recognized both in the USSR and the West that the Soviet Union is facing a number of demographic problems. There is firstly a decline in the coefficient of population reproduction and secondly severe imbalances between regional (and their associated ethnic and class) rates of population growth.

The population decline is indicated by data in Table 3.1, which shows

Table 3.1 Number of births per year per thousand women, by age group

Age	1958/9	1969/70	1978/9
15–19	29.2	30.4	39.4
20–24	162.2	163.9	174.6
25–29	164.8	128.7	125.6
30–34	110.1	88.1	72.1
35–39	66.6	48.5	31.9
40–44	24.1	15.3	11.7
45–49	5.0	2.9	1.6
15–49	88.7	65.7	69.9

Source: V.I. Perevedentsev, 'Vosproizvodstvo naseleniya i sem'ya'. *Sotsiologicheskie issledovaniya*, no. 2, 1982, p. 83.

the average number of births per thousand women in three time spans (1958/9, 1969/70, 1978/9).

The average decline indicated in the table (from 88.7 to 69.9) is even greater than the figures suggest, for during this time the average age of marriage of women declined (the period of required compulsory military service was reduced, thereby boosting early marriage). The coefficient of net reproduction rate steadily fell from 1.26 in 1958/9 to 1.03 in 1979/80. One obvious effect of these changes is that the number of people of working age in the USSR may be predicted to fall absolutely during the years 1986–90, after which it will recover somewhat, but will remain well below the increases of the last fifteen years (1971–85). The statistics are shown in Table 3.2. In addition, the number of aged dependants (born in the early 1930s and not depleted by war losses) will grow and become an economic liability.

The figures are further complicated by regional and ethnic imbalances. The Western European areas, and especially the Baltic states, face a serious decline in births. The gross coefficient of reproduction is

Table 3.2 Increase in the USSR's working-age population

Year	Millions of people	Percentage
1971–1975	8.5	7.0
1976–1980	13.8	10.6
1981–1985	7.7	5.4
1986–1990	–1.0	–0.6
1991–1995	4.2	2.8
1996–2000	1.5	1.0

Source: *Politicheskoe samoobrazavanie* 1981, no. 8, p. 5. Cited by Perevedentsev, p. 81.

Table 3.3 Gross coefficient of reproduction of the population, 1978/9

RSFSR	0.93	Moldavia	1.16
Ukraine	0.96	Latvia	0.91
Belorussia	1.00	Kirgizia	2.15
Uzbekistan	2.48	Tadzhikastan	2.91
Kazakhstan	1.47	Armenia	1.20
Georgia	1.12	Turkmenia	2.57
Azerbaydzhan	1.70	Estonia	0.98
Lithuania	1.01		
		USSR	1.11

Source: *Politicheskoe samoobrazovanie* 1981, no. 8, p. 50. Cited by Perevedentsev, p. 85.

a statistic which measures the number of female births to women of child-bearing age. It is shown for the republics of the USSR on Table 3.3. These figures refer to republics and should not be confused with ethnic groups whose boundaries are not coterminous with republics. Such statistics may be supplemented by data on the nationality of births. Table 3.4 shows the average size of family by the nationality of both parents. These data show that nationality groups may be demographically grouped into two. First, nationalities with a low reproduction rate – Estonians, Latvians, Russians, Ukrainians, Belorussians and Lithuanians; these are European ethnic groups. A second grouping consists of Asian nationalities with very high birth-rates: Kazakhs, Uzbeks, Azerbaydzhanies, Kirgiz, Tadzhiks and Turkmens.

Let me make some tentative suggestions as to how these developments may affect policy, other things being equal:

(1) The Soviet army will have fewer men and a greater rank and file membership of non-Europeans.
(2) The economy which has depended for growth upon increasing labour power will need to improve labour productivity.

Table 3.4 Size of family by nationality of parents (1979 census)

Russians	3.2	Moldavians	3.5
Ukrainians	3.2	Latvians	3.0
Belorussians	3.2	Kirgiz	5.7
Uzbeks	6.2	Tadzhiks	6.5
Kazakhs	5.5	Armenians	4.5
Georgians	4.0	Turkmens	6.3
Azerbaydzhanies	5.5	Estonians	3.0
Lithuanians	3.3		

Source: *Vestnik statistiki*, no. 5, 1983, p. 74.

(3) Defence and other industries may compete for manpower.
(4) There may be some relocation of industry to areas of population surplus such as Central Asia or population may shift to the West. There is likely to be a greater ethnic mix.
(5) The ageing population will mean that the production of services and goods will have to be done by fewer workers.
(6) Demand for labour saving capital goods from the West may enhance East-West cooperation and hence détente.

The class structure

As far as the occupational structure is concerned, there has been a long-term tendency of the USSR to follow a similar trajectory to that of Western Europe. The proportion of labour in agriculture has fallen, and that of the industrial workforce has risen; this has been followed by the development of the service sector. The number of manual workers has increased absolutely but its percentage rate of growth has fallen. In 1982, 39 per cent of the workforce was in industry and building (23 per cent in 1940), 20 per cent was in agriculture (54 per cent in 1940) and 41 per cent was in the service industries (23 per cent in 1940).[1] In quantitative terms the Soviet Union has the largest employed manual working class in the world: in 1979 it numbered 77.7 million and in 1982 80.4 million (non-manuals totalled 32.9 million and 34.8 million for the respective dates).[2] The industrial manual working class is also becoming more differentiated: levels of skill and education have risen. In Leningrad in 1976/7, in the machine-tool industry, unskilled workers had an average 7.7 years of schooling (6.5 years in 1965), and the most highly skilled manuals had 9.1 years (8.7 in 1965).[3] The number of manual workers with seven years of education has risen from 40 per cent in 1959 to 76 per cent in 1979, though the total for full secondary and above was only 45 per cent.[4] The skill profile of industrial manual workers has also changed: in 1962, 38 per cent were 'low and unskilled', 49 per cent were 'semi-skilled and skilled' and 13 per cent were 'high-skilled', by 1979 the comparative figures were 26, 51 and 23. (The large 'semi-skilled' group includes what are effectively unskilled machine operatives.) While standards have improved, the workforce of Soviet industry still comparatively lags behind the advanced countries of Western Europe and the USA. In the USA in 1965, of all manual workers only 15 per cent were 'low and unskilled' and 44 per cent were 'high-skilled'.[5]

In the last twenty years, the manual working class has improved its position in relation to that of non-manuals in two ways. Income differentials have fallen and the proportion of manuals in the party has risen considerably. Work conditions have also improved: the hours worked

Table 3.5 Earnings of manual workers in industry, agriculture and building, 1940–81

	1940	1965	1975	1981
Industry (roubles)	32.4	101.7	160.9	190.2
As % of ITRs	46.6	68.5	80.8	88.7
As % of non-manuals	90	118.5	122.5	128.3
Agriculture (roubles)	20.7	72.4	124.7	152.6
As % of specialists	41.1	52.3	69.5	82.4
As % of non-manuals	66.6	88.0	109.4	124
Building (roubles)	31.1	108.4	180.3	215.8
As % of ITRs	41.3	67.5	87.1	99.7
As % of non-manuals	67.9	105.9	123.7	143.2

Source: *Vestnik statistiki*, no. 4, 1983, p. 64.

in coal-mining have declined from 47.6 hours per week in 1955 to 35.6 in 1981, while in industry as a whole the working week has shortened from 47.8 hours to 40.6 between the two dates.[6] It is not being argued that the real income of manuals is 'equal' to that of professionals, managers or the political elites. When family income is taken into account it is skewed in favour of non-manuals.[7] The trend, however, is for money income to become more equal. Money wages for manual workers have had a steady upward rise. The ratios of earnings of manuals to specialists and other non-manuals are shown on Table 3.5. Payments in kind to managerial and executive staff have not increased proportionately more over time; on the other hand, the growth of a (black) market for services outside official channels (repairs) and for goods (especially in agriculture) has probably increased the proportion of extra income earned by manual workers and some collective farmers. The prevalence of corruption in distribution may have led to some people making large incomes, but this is compensated by some lowly paid employees in retail trade receiving 'under the counter' incentives. As a proportion of turnover, illegal dealings are relatively small and do not significantly alter the pattern noted above. Rises in prices have been low (under 5 per cent) and real income, even taking account of suppressed inflation, has shown a steady rise. The index of consumption rose to 176 in 1982 (1970 = 100). In the early 1980s, however, there has been a stagnation in consumption levels; the index of consumption (1980 = 100) was 104 in 1981 and the same in 1982. Also, some products declined in number: the index for meat fell from 100 in 1980 to 92 in 1982, that of woollen goods declined to 78.[8] As one can assume that expectations were of a rising standard of living, one might assume that frustration and grumbling were on the rise in the early 1980s.

In 1956, just under a third (32 per cent) of party members were manual workers; by 1983, the number had risen to 41.1 per cent (i.e. nearly 8 million).[9] Since the mid-1960s, manual workers have increased their share of new admissions to the party's ranks: from 52 per cent in 1966–70, to 57.6 per cent in 1971–5, to 59.0 per cent in 1976–80.[10]

Despite the fact that the authorities are confronted with many difficulties in the industrial workforce (discipline, turnover, incentives, mismatch of demand with supply), they can count on the loyalty of the labour force. The political leadership has tried to enhance the status of the manual working class and regards it as a major support. The Soviet industrial worker has had his immediate demands fulfilled by the political leadership and by his employers. Permanence of employment, a relatively easy work routine, and a rising living standard are important features of Soviet life which contribute to social stability. There is a vast Western literature on dissent in the USSR.[11] The literature, however, is like a large sail on a very small boat. Unlike in Poland, where Solidarity represented a popular movement, dissident groups in the USSR have been small, obscure and localized.[12] The movement (excepting some religious groups) is largely intellectual in composition. 'Free Trade Unions' in the USSR (the Association of Free Trade Unions of Workers and the Free Interprofessional Association of Workers) have been relatively insignificant and have been easily broken up by the authorities.[13] Legitimacy, in the sense of psychological attitudes of loyalty to the regime by the working class, is ensured in the USSR.

More important than legitimacy crises, on the Polish model leading to political collapse or upheaval, are problems of political and economic output. Can the regime continue to fulfil the expectations of the working class for a higher standard of living? Can it provide the type of work required by the more demanding working class? Can expectations for education be fulfilled? There is a dilemma here between the maintenance of loyalty through full employment with slack labour discipline and the need for economic efficiency. (This will be discussed in Part Two of this book, the section on the economy.) The working class like other strata in Soviet society has consumerist aspirations and there has been a contagion of Western values, not only of the consumer market expressed in desires for jeans and disco-music but also even for Western political models, and many of the ideals of Marxism-Leninism have been eroded among certain strata.

Influences on foreign policy are likely to be indirect and contradictory. If one assumes that the greater representation of the industrial worker in the party is translated into political pressure, what policies are likely to be favoured? The working-class party member may be less likely to accept compromises with the West, he may support more traditional hard line attitudes and respond to a chauvinist militarist position. As Hedrick Smith rather anecdotally has put it, 'At factories, farms or power projects . . . workmen or farmers or construction engineers speak proudly of their own chief as "a strong boss" . . . they like feeling that someone above them is firmly in charge.'[14] On the other hand, the maturation of the working class, its higher levels of education, its settled urban base, its need for a higher standard of living may create demands for relaxation of East-West conflict and an ensuing decline in military type expenditure and a rise in Soviet imports of Western technology. As far as social pressures coming from outside the political stratum are concerned, there are likely to be significant regional differences. Western organizations studying public opinion in the USSR have found that Soviet citizens in the Baltic and in the Transcaucasian Republics are 'more favourably disposed to *samizdat* than people from other areas of the USSR'; people from these areas, for instance, had more 'positive views on the aspiration of Polish strikers' than did Soviet citizens from other areas.[15] Such views, however, are exceptional, and one can confidently predict that the Soviet industrial working class, unlike that in Poland, is likely to remain a reliable stanchion to the present regime.

The 'intelligentsia'

The 'intelligentsia' is a crucial social group, both for political support and to ensure the development of the economy. By 'intelligentsia' I refer to a social group distinguished by higher or specialist secondary education performing a complex technical, executive or administrative work role.[16] The functions of the Soviet intelligentsia are fourfold; it is concerned with: (i) the organization and development of productive forces; (ii) the transmission of culture; (iii) the critical theorization of social experience; and (iv) the maintenance and renewal of the political system.[17]

The Soviet intelligentsia in past years has grown enormously in size. Let us take as an index the number of people with higher education. In 1939 there were only 1.2 million people in the Soviet Union with complete higher education (i.e. 8 per 1000 of the population aged over 10). By 1982 the number had risen to 17 million (76 per 1000) (see Table 3.6). In employment, the number of people with higher education rose from 3.545 million in 1960 to 12.6 in 1981, and those with specialist secondary qualifications from 5.24 million to 17.2 million.[18] Census data for 1979 on the numbers of employees in positions of responsibility and leadership have not yet been published: in 1970, however, these numbered 3.547 million (see Table 3.7). One can infer with certainty

Table 3.6 Population of USSR with higher and specialist secondary education

	Total (000s)			Per 10,000 population aged over 10 years		
	1939	1959	1982	1939	1959	1982
Total number of people having higher and secondary (including incomplete) education	15.9	58.7	149.2	108	361	670
Of which:						
Complete higher	1.2	3.8	17.0	8	23	76
Incomplete higher	—	1.7	3.4	—	11	15
Secondary specialist	—	7.9	25.8	—	48	116

Source: *Narkhoz 1922–82* (1982), p. 42.

that this number has grown somewhat and that the levels of competence and education have risen.

All commentators on the Soviet scene acknowledge the enhanced role of professional groups in society and politics. Many Soviet writers advocate greater decentralization of decision-making as a consequence of the scientific-technical revolution. They see the Soviet intelligentsia providing support to and being in harmony with the political leadership. The growth, specialization and greater competence of the intelligentsia is simply another aspect of the more highly developed division of labour. Academic credentials have become necessary for the political leadership (in 1981, 90 per cent of the Central Committee of the CPSU had higher education). The intelligentsia is regarded as playing an important participatory role on advisory committees.[19] At the other extreme are views of dissident writers, such as the Hungarians, G. Konrad and I. Szelenyi.[20] Such critics envisage a significant change in the structure of political power. Soviet-type societies, they argue, are 'directed' ones. Guiding society becomes a complex business and planning is the prerogative of a range of technical, social, economic and political experts. The 'intelligentsia', however, does not simply replace the political class which led the revolution and economic and social development consequent to it. The ruling class changes in composition. It is constituted by three main groups: the ideologue (party secretary), the police (KGB) and the technocrat.[21] This view seems to me to overlook the differences in outlook between various strata of the 'intelligentsia'; it also belittles the mass of intellectuals who are outside of the political leadership and the ways that these groups shape their own demands.

Table 3.7 Groupings of persons having positions of responsibility and leadership (thousands)

Chiefs of organs of government administration and their structural sub-divisions	210.8
Chiefs of party, Komsomol, trade unions, other social organizations and their structural sub-divisions	194.9
Chiefs of enterprises, collective farms and their structural sub-divisions	1570.1
Chiefs in research and teaching istitutions (excluding primary schools	633.2
Chiefs and their assistants in publishing	39.2
Directors in culture and art	20.7
Directors and chiefs in trade and catering	463.3
Heads of planning, finance and economic institutions	85.8
Chief doctors and other leaders in medicine	57.7
Leading specialists among engineering-technical employees	282.2
	3557.9

Source: *Itogi vsesoyuznoy perepisi naseleniya* (1970) Vol. 6, Table 2.

There can be no doubt that the rise of a class (in a general social sense) of urban non-manual personnel with higher levels of education has great significance for the political culture of the USSR. In the last twenty-five years a 'critical mass' of 17 million people with a complete higher education has evolved. They have higher levels of expectations, a more sophisticated view of the world and more political demands.

The implications for foreign policy seem to me to be threefold. First, the role of experts and specialists in foreign affairs has undoubtedly increased. The complexity and consequences of modern international politics are such that expert knowledge needs to be brought to bear to guide decision-making. It is likely that the various committees on foreign affairs, defence, and the armed forces increasingly 'make' decisions which are 'taken' by the Politburo. Secondly, such specialists do not present a 'united front' to the political elites. (The Institute for the Study of the USA has a different world view to that of the Army Chiefs of Staff.) The Politburo performs a crucial role in interpreting advice. The personalities of the leadership themselves are important. It is likely that Chernenko heeds the advice of specialists more than the shoe-thumping Khrushchev did. Third, the 'intelligentsia' is not a homogeneous group. 'Intellectuals' from the constituencies of the arts, sciences, administration, economy, police and Party have different goals and images of the world. These groups have distinct ways of thinking and acting as well as heterogeneous life styles. The presence of such a large middle class will in time change significantly the Soviet political culture. It is likely to move from a subject-political culture to a subject-participant one. By this I mean that until say 1956, the Soviet population was one which was required and tended to accept the guidance of the political leadership. It was a 'centralized authoritarian structure' in which citizens' expectations mostly coincided with the political structure.[22] Since then, the expectations of the leadership and population have led to a mixture of passive attitudes to government and more articulate groups with activist orientations.[23] The maturation of the Soviet Union involves economic, social and political development. In practical political terms notions of individual (and group) rights are linked to modernization. In capitalist countries, Hans Park has shown that economic rights (physical quality of life) are positively correlated with level of gross national product and also this is the case in Marxist-Leninist states (correlations of 0.77 and 0.64 respectively).[24] In capitalist countries, there is a positive quantitative relationship between physical quality of life and political rights (0.6). The index is positive, but lower in Marxist-Leninist countries (0.2). It seems most likely that with the cumulative processes of modernization in the USSR claims for individual and group rights will increase. If one assumes that the leadership is dependent on the loyal support and creative activity of these groups, it seems likely that as they grow in size and maturity their opinions will be taken into account in the foreign policy field. This would lead to caution, to marginal changes and to conservatism rather than activism in foreign policy.

Social mobility

Social mobility, or the movement of individuals and their children between statuses and occupational positions, is a major component in securing social stability or fomenting unrest. As Sorokin has put it: 'the open doors of a mobile society offer a great chance for the majority of leaders and ambitious persons to rise. Instead of becoming leaders of a revolution they are turned into protectors of social order'.[25] Underlying the approach that sees upward mobility as solidifying of the social order is the assumption that an increase in social contact between social classes or strata reduces their internal cohesion. The fulfilment of aspirations for social betterment for an individual or his/her offspring may be achieved through rising within a given social order, rather than questioning or changing the social structure. By the same token, considerable downward mobility may create frustrated individuals who may attribute the cause of their unfulfilled ambitions to an illegitimate

Table 3.8 Composition of Soviet population by class, 1913–82

	1913	*1928*	*1939*	*1959*	*1979*	*1982*
Manual and non-manual workers	17.0	17.6	50.2	68.3	85.1	86.7
Of whom manuals	—	12.4	33.7	50.2	60.0	60.9
Collective farmers and cooperative handicraftsmen	—	2.9	47.2	31.4	14.9	13.3
Independent peasants and handicraftsmen	66.7	74.9	2.6	0.3	0.0	0.0
Bourgeoisie	16.3	4.6	—	—	—	
	100.0	100.0	100.0	100.0	100.0	100.0

Source: *Narkhoz v 1978g* (1979), p. 9, *Vestnik statistiki*, no. 4 (1983), p. 60.

social system. For political purposes, the quantitative measures of social movement have to be related to the subjective aspirations of various strata.

A major characteristic of Russian and Soviet society since the mid-nineteenth century has been rapid and extensive economic growth. This has entailed major changes in the occupational structure, which has induced upward mobility. The factory system has created large numbers of skilled and unskilled manual jobs, and the expansion of commerce, science, education and social services (widely considered) has entailed a massive expansion in non-manual and professional occupations. Table 3.8, in rather crude terms, quantifies these changes.

The social trends following such structural changes are twofold. First, from the late nineteenth century to about the mid-1950s there has been a massive inflow of peasants from the countryside to the towns. There was little downward social mobility. The increase in number of non-manual occupations reflects the recruitment of socially mobile sons and especially daughters of peasant urban immigrants. The urban working class has experienced upward mobility even into the professional strata. The urban professional groups themselves have, for the whole period of Soviet power, been self-generating. In 1938, for instance, 47 per cent of the student body was composed of the offspring of non-manual parents.[26] The upward mobility was structurally induced – it resulted from an increase in the number of statuses – rather than being characterized by 'exchange' mobility (i.e. an exchange of statuses between fathers and sons).

The second phase, since the mid-1950s, is associated with a reduction in the rate of economic growth and the rate of formation of new

Table 3.9 Social composition of young entrants of the working class (molodogo popolneniya) of different areas of the USSR (%)

	Area		
	Moscow	Chelabinsk	Ufa
From manual worker background	55.8	56.2	58.1
From collective farmer background	15.2	18.7	36.4
From unskilled non-manual background	19.6	16.2	1.8
From professional (*spetsialistov*) background	5.4	8.3	3.3
Others	4.0	0.6	0.4

Source: *Sotsial'naya struktura razvitogo sotsialisticheskogo obshchestva v SSSR* (Moscow, 1976), p. 183.

occupational positions. From that time till the present there has been a similar tendency towards the inheritance of their parents' social status by non-manual sons and daughters. In the 1970s, the manual working class was, for the first time in Soviet history, largely self-recruited from its own ranks. It even included a sprinkling of people from the ranks of specialists. This is illustrated by Table 3.9.

We may make three general conclusions about interstratum mobility in the 1970s and 1980s. First, the sons and daughters of non-manual families inherited their parents' social position. As Inkeles remarked over thirty years ago, 'as stratification has become institutionalized there has been a noticeable tendency for social mobility to decline and for the system to become less an open class structure'.[27] Second, manual working-class and peasant sons and daughters still have a good chance to enter the non-manual strata, though the rate of mobility has declined. Pravda, in generalizing on the opportunity for upward mobility remarks that 'perhaps one in three blue-collar workers has been able to take up a non-manual career . . . Only one in ten at most end up as professionals.'[28] Third, the major way for social advance is now through the educational system. The initial placement in the occupational sphere which is determined by educational background is now of much greater consequence for further social advance than hitherto.

Education

All commentators on social mobility in the Soviet Union agree that admission to specialized and higher educational establishments is secured by a greater proportion of non-manuals' children than those of

Table 3.10 Distribution of social background of students in higher educational institutions, various years (%)

	USSR[a] 1965	Sverd-lovsk[b] 1968	Kazakh-stan[b] 1970	USSR[a] 1973	Sverd-lovsk[b] 1974	Kazakh-stan[b] 1974
Children of workers or workers	—	44.6	43.2	—	49.7	48.8
Children of workers	36.5	—	—	43.1	—	—
Children of collective farmers or collective farmers	—	4.9	16.5	—	5.2	9.8
Children of collective farmers	19.7	—	—	18.0	—	—
Children of non-manuals or non-manuals	—	50.5	40.3	—	45.5	41.1
Children of non-manuals	43.8	—	—	38.9	—	—

Sources: [a] *Sotsial'noe edinstvo sovetskogo obshchestva* (Moscow, 1980), p. 217.
[b] *Sotsial'naya struktura razvitogo sotsialisticheskogo obschestva v SSSR* (Moscow, 1974), p. 191.

manuals and collective farmers. The kind of data used to make such inferences are illustrated in Table 3.10. Pravda has calculated ratios of access of various social groups to full-time higher education (i.e. 'the relative weight of the social group in the student body divided by the group's weight in the population as a whole'). The 'disparity of access' is an index of the difference in opportunity of non-manuals over manuals; it is obtained by dividing the index of access for white-collar children by that of workers' children. Thus an index of 1 gives parity of access for both groups, an index of greater than 1 shows relative advantage to non-manuals' children. Pravda's calculations yielded the following indices 1960: 3.51 (for USSR, all students in full-time higher education); 1969/70, 3.69 (USSR, first-year students); 1975/6, 2.84.[29] The difference is greater in the more prestigous institutions (in Moscow University in 1973 it was 5.25, in medical faculties in the RSFSR in 1978 it was 5.97).[30]

While one may not doubt the inequality of 'life chances', political dissatisfaction cannot be equated with the statistics so far considered. A grievance may be nurtured only if a given stratum's expectations fall far short of the system's ability to meet them. There are reasons why I think that a significant feeling of social deprivation will not be experienced. First, the level of educational opportunities in quantitative terms will rise. In 1966, over a third of the appropriate age cohort was admitted to *vuzy*, and another third to specialized secondary schools. By 1980, the percentage admitted fell to just over 20 per cent for *vuzy* and 30 per cent for *ssuzy*.[31] This proportion is still high on any criterion. When one takes account of the decline in birth-rate, the proportion of each cohort admitted is likely to increase. For middle-class families, taken as a whole, there is likely to be no problem about admission. The reproduction rate of Slavic middle-class stock is falling, and is certainly lower than that of the Slavic manual working class. Data cited by Pravda and others do not take account of regional imbalances between cohort size and educational provision. The European areas of the country, particularly in the larger 'closed' cities, have a more preferential access to education than the southern and central Asian areas with a younger population profile.[32] Secondly, changes in the educational system that have taken place in the 1970s have led to a tempering of levels of expectations. Margaret Thatcher and Keith Joseph in the mid-1980s in Britain are following Brezhnev's lead in upgrading and emphasizing vocational education. Enrolments in full secondary trade schools have increased and demand for them is also improving. Manual workers' sons are increasingly seeking better paid skilled manual, rather than non-manual, jobs.[33] Vocational education is being taken seriously since the 1970s in the USSR, and aspirations are not as great as they once were. Thirdly, there are many 'alternative routes' in education. There is an extensive network of part-time and correspondence courses. They are significant in providing an opportunity for those who fail in the competition for a full-time place to continue their education. In the Soviet educational system, study for higher qualifications may take place for a very long time; competitors who experience failure can always try again. In such a way failure is considered to be a personal attribute, and is not projected onto the political system. Also, of great importance, politically, is the party's own educational system which provides opportunities for its own members to improve their qualifications and thereby gain promotion within the hierarchy of the party.

The implication of the pattern of social mobility for foreign affairs is indirect rather than direct. Policy is likely to be made in a society without serious internal social and class conflict. Given a continued moderate rise in living standards, people's expectations are likely to be met. The decline in population of the Slavic groups and the growth of the service sector will ensure that the children of non-manuals inherit their parents' social status – and probably improve on it. The offspring of manual and collective farm workers should also experience a modicum of structural upward mobility. In the areas of high population growth, it is possible that there may be unfulfilled levels of ambition unless facilities are improved. Overall, the Soviet Union is, in my view, unlikely to experience any *major* dislocation with respect to people's life expectations. In this context, foreign affairs are unlikely to be utilized as a source of political mobilization or contrived solidarity. The objectives of leadership are likely to be to minimize international conflict, and to reduce areas of stress, in order to secure increases in living standards.

Conclusions

The 'societal dimension', it should be emphasized, is only one input to foreign policy. It may not be the most important one. But there are a number of long-run trends in the social structure which undoubtedly affect the decision-making process. First, Russia and the Soviet Union during the past hundred years has been subject to a process of modernization. Structural differentiation is part of this process of change. The population is more differentiated, more highly educated and more specialized. The traditional subject political culture is gradually being replaced by a more participant one. The views and reactions of the 'intelligentsia' and the mature working class are taken more account of in the making of decisions. Second, the legitimacy of leadership is conceived of in terms of its success in meeting internal needs. The chiliastic or utopian aspects of ideology now have less salience than social demands. The claims of domestic consumers come into competition for resources required to fulfil foreign policy goals. The latter are safeguarded by the authoritarian political system, but social stability and loyalty are also prized by the political leadership, and defence spending is likely to be increasingly closely scrutinized as the population becomes more demanding. Third, internal changes in population and social structure do not seem likely to lead to serious problems of political legitimacy. The political leadership is likely to be able to rely on a loyal if critical working-class and intelligentsia. More crucial problems are associated with political 'outputs', particularly the need to satisfy consumer demands. Fourth, in the foreign policy field, internal social changes are likely to have an indirect, rather than a direct, effect on policy-making. Social developments are likely to lead to a cautious, conservative foreign policy, to one of cooperation rather than confrontation with the West.

Notes

1. *Narodnoe khozyaystvo SSSR v 1982g* (hereafter *Narkhoz*) (1983), p. 362, and *Narkhoz 1979g* (1980), p. 385.
2. In 1940 the figures were 23.9 million and 10.0 million. *Narkhoz 1922–82* (1982), p. 399, and *Narkhoz 1982g*, p. 364.

3 N.P. Konstantinova *et al.*, 'Changes in the social characteristics of workers under developed socialism', *Soviet Sociology*, Vol. 17, no. 4 (1979), p. 15.
4 *Vestnik statistiki*, no. 4, 1983, p. 66.
5 Data cited by A. Pravda, 'Is there a Soviet working class?', *Problems of Communism*, Vol. 31, no. 6, Nov-Dec 1982, p. 5.
6 *Narkhoz 1922–82* (1982), p. 407.
7 See data in Pravda, pp. 8–10. On equalization, see Janet C. Chapman, 'Recent trends in the Soviet industrial wage structure', in A. Kahan and B. Ruble, *Industrial Labor in the USSR* (New York, Pergamon, 1979), pp. 151–83.
8 *Narkhoz v 1982g*, pp. 408–9.
9 *Partiynaya zhizn'*, no. 15 (1983), p. 21.
10 *Partiynaya zhizn'*, p. 18.
11 See R.L. Tökés (ed.), *Dissent in the USSR: Politics, Ideology and People* (John Hopkins University Press, 1975).
12 On the human rights movement see David Kowalewski, 'Human rights protest in the USSR: statistical trends for 1965–78', *Universal Human Rights*, Vol. 2, no. 1, Jan–March 1980, pp. 5–29.
13 See A. Karatnycky *et al.*, *Workers' Rights, East and West* (Transaction Books, 1980).
14 H. Smith, *The Russians* (Sphere Books, 1976), p. 305.
15 *SAAOR Analysis Report* 9–77, p. 10, and 8–81, p. 6. Cited by E. Teague, RL (Munich), 109/83, pp. 5–6.
16 The lower level white-collar workers (*sluzhashchie*) are excluded here, though Soviet writers often include them in the 'intelligentsia'. See V.S. Semenov, 'Ob izmenenii intelligentsii i sluzhashchikh v protsesse razvernutogo stroitel'stva kommunizma', *Sotsiologiya v SSSR* (1963) Vol. 1.
17 See L. Churchward, *The Soviet Intelligentsia* (Routledge, 1973) p. 93.
18 *Narkhoz 1922–82* (1983), p. 407.
19 This line of approach has been taken by Western writers such as Jerry F. Hough.
20 *The Intellectuals on the Road to Class Power* (Harcourt Brace Jovanovich, 1979).
21 Ibid.; see especially p. 148.
22 G.A. Almond and S. Verba, *The Civic Culture* (Princeton University Press 1963), p. 21.
23 Ibid.
24 Hans S. Park, 'Human rights and modernization: a dialectical relationship', *Universal Human Rights*, Vol. 2, no. 1 (1980), pp. 91–2.
25 P.A. Sorokin, *Social Mobility* (New York, Harper, 1927), p. 533.
26 *Kul'turnoe stroitel'stvo SSSR* (M. 1940), p. 114. Cited by A. Inkeles, 'Social stratification and mobility in the Soviet Union, 1940–1950', *Amer. Soc. Rev.* Vol. 15 (1950), reprinted in A. Inkeles and K. Geiger, *Soviet Society* (1961), p. 572.
27 Ibid., p. 571.
28 Alex Pravda, 'Is there a Soviet working class?', *Problems of Communism*, Vol. 31, (Nov-Dec 1982), p. 17.
29 Ibid., p. 13.
30 Ibid.
31 A *vuz* (*vysshee uchebnoe zavedenie*) is a higher educational institution, and a

ssuz (*srednee spetsial'noe uchebnoe zavedenie*), sometimes called a technicum, is literally a secondary specialized educational establishment giving students a technological education of higher technician status. For empirical data, see Ellen Jones and Fred W. Grupp, 'Modernization and ethnic equalization in the USSR', *Soviet Studies*, Vol. 36, no. 2 (1984, p. 169.)

32 Ibid.

33 See Soviet data cited by W.D. Connor, *Socialism, Politics and Equality* (Columbia University Press, 1979) p. 188; Pravda, 'Is there a Soviet working class', p. 16.

4 Nation and Nationalism in Central Asia

Alastair McAuley

The Soviet population is made up of more than a hundred language-and-culture groups. Some of these communities are located wholly within the frontiers of the USSR, others extend across the country's borders. These facts require Moscow to adopt a nationality policy or set of policies; and this in turn will have implications for Soviet foreign policy. A complete study of the influence of nationality on Soviet foreign policy should therefore start from an account of the position and experience of the major ethnic groups within the USSR; it should also discuss the ways in which communal interaction and the state's domestic policies have constrained or facilitated particular foreign policies; it should, finally, consider how these interrelated factors are likely to evolve over the next couple of decades. Such an analysis is clearly beyond the scope of an essay like the present one. My aims in this chapter are more modest in two respects. First, discussion is limited to the experience of a subset of Soviet language-and-culture groups – those who inhabit Central Asia (See Appendix). Second, discussion is focused on a particular issue – the existence and consequences of political nationalism. Certain other aspects of the broader topic are dealt with in Hugh Seton-Watson's and John Lawrence's contributions (Chapters 2 and 5); fuller consideration of the remainder must be deferred to another occasion.

The decision to concentrate on Central Asia has been dictated by a number of factors. The region constitutes a distinct part of the USSR with its own history and its own social conditions. Its prospects may differ from those of the rest of the country. It thus calls for a separate analysis. But the same argument could be advanced in respect of the Ukraine or the Baltic states and I have not chosen to deal with them. Here I must claim personal interest; I have done more research on the republics of Central Asia than on those in other parts of the USSR. And it can also be urged that the position and problems of Central Asia are likely to be of growing importance in Soviet domestic policy-making in the next twenty to forty years; the region may also come to exert a greater influence on the formulation of foreign policy than it has up to now.

Similarly, the decision to concentrate on the issue of political nationalism has been prompted by my research and can be seen as a reaction to the work of others. Although Soviet Central Asia has not been the subject of extensive academic study in the West, a number of books and articles published in the last ten or fifteen years have dealt with the region's nationality question.[1] From these studies it is possible to distil what may be called the West's conventional wisdom on the topic. This may be summarized as follows:

> Central Asia and its population pose significant political problems for the government in Moscow, and these problems are likely to become increasingly acute in the coming decades. A major source of these problems has been the inability of the Soviet government to devise a set of policies which would break down the web of allegiances that make up the distinct self-identity of the Central Asian population. This distinctness is demonstrated, *inter alia*, by differences in demographic behaviour (birth-rates are far higher and the incidence of divorce is far lower in Central Asia than in most other republics); it is also demonstrated by social exclusiveness (so far as one can tell, the incidence of inter-marriage between the European and Central Asian populations of the USSR is negligible); finally, it is shown by the unwillingness of the Central Asian population to learn Russian and to migrate to other parts of the country. This set of attitudes is identified as nationalist. Thus it is argued that although the government in Moscow may have been able to contain or suppress open manifestations of nationalism, it has been unable to eradicate the sentiment itself. The Central Asian population is intensely nationalistic.
>
> The differences in demographic behaviour which reflect differences in national consciousness will result in radical changes in the ethnic composition of the Soviet population in the medium term. The share of Central Asians will rise, that of Europeans fall; ethnic Russians may cease to be a majority of the population by the end of the century. This can only aggravate the problem of nationalism.
>
> The reason why Central Asian society has shown itself impervious to Soviet social engineering is that the core of the population's self-identity is Islam. This Muslim national identity has the potential to unite the region even though language and culture may divide it. Central Asian nationalism is thus more threatening to Moscow than it would have been if it had consisted of Uzbek, Tadjik, Turkmen nationalisms and so on.
>
> The existence of this nationalist 'timebomb' in Central Asia means that the government in Moscow must adopt policies to contain or defuse it. These possibly oppressive policies will affect the Soviet Union's image abroad, particularly in the third world. They may also

constrain Soviet foreign policy. The fact that the core of this nationalism is Islamic makes these consequences more likely. It means that Central Asia provides fertile soil for the propagation of fundamentalist ideas from the South. This imposes on the Soviet government the need to adopt a policy which will insulate the region from such contamination. In turn this will limit Soviet policy options towards the Middle East.

In the rest of this essay, I argue that this 'conventional wisdom' about Central Asia is based on false premises. In particular, those who advocate it too often are guilty of what may be called the nationalist fallacy. As a result, the inferences that are drawn from the available evidence are frequently misleading if they are not mistaken. But before developing these arguments in detail there is a more general point that needs to be made. I am very much aware of how little western scholars know about Soviet Central Asia. The evidence on which I base my arguments (and, for that matter, the evidence adduced by such writers as Bennigsen or Rywkin) is very flimsy.[2] This can in part be explained by the fact that few western scholars have studied the region, few can read or speak the local languages, few have spent extended periods of time there. But it is also, in part, a feature common to all Soviet studies. Censorship, official secretiveness and, possibly, cultural distance, mean that we know less about the USSR than we do about the countries of Western Europe; they mean that less information is available; they mean that opportunities to undertake enquiries designed to confirm or refute particular hypotheses are extremely limited.

The fact that we know so little about Soviet Central Asia, however, does not mean that we cannot apply the methods of social analysis which have been used to investigate problems in other parts of the world. Indeed, analogy and the comparative method may allow us to draw inferences with more certainty than the evidence itself would warrant. Rather, general ignorance about the region, its population and their political attitudes requires us all to be flexible, to be willing to listen to new arguments and to be ready to revise our conclusions.

The remainder of this chapter is organized as follows: in section 1, I set out a model of the determinants of political nationalism. This model directs attention to the sorts of evidence that are relevant to the discussion of Central Asian nationalism. It suggests a series of questions whose answers will put the issue into a more appropriate perspective. In sections 2–4, I put forward a set of answers, and the chapter ends with a brief discussion of the relevance of nationalism to the formulation of foreign policy and a reminder that arguments which are valid in relation to Central Asia may not apply in other parts of the USSR.

1. Nationalism in political theory

Broadly speaking, the term nationalism is used in two overlapping ways. It can be used to describe the feeling of belonging to a cultural community whose members constitute a 'nation'. It can also be used in a more explictly political sense. Nationalism is the political principle which asserts that the political and national unit should be congruent. Finally, in this sense it is also usually extended to cover the sentiments of those who feel anger when the nationalist principle is violated and satisfaction when it is fulfilled.[3]

It is important to recognize that these two concepts of nationalism are distinct. This means that it is possible for individuals (or groups) to be nationalistic in the first sense without necessarily subscribing to nationalism in the second sense. (But, those who are nationalistic in the second sense will also be nationalistic in the first.) This, in turn, implies that evidence that particular groups are aware of cultural solidarity cannot be used to infer that they have espoused the doctrine of political nationalism. Separate and explicit information about political beliefs must be adduced. Here, of course, I address this latter question of whether there is widespread support for the doctrines of political nationalism in Central Asia, since it is nationalism in this sense that has the most constraining effect on the formulation of Soviet foreign policy.

What I have called the nationalist fallacy consists in assuming that the definition of nationalism given above is unproblematic. Nationalists believe that there is little or no ambiguity about what constitutes a nation; they believe that nations are a persisting feature of human social organization; they believe that men have always been conscious of their nationality and have always attached considerable importance to it.

Comparative and historical studies show that all these propositions are false.

> Nations as a natural god-given way of classifying men . . . are a myth; nationalism, which sometimes takes pre-existing cultures and turns them into nations, sometimes invents them and often obliterates pre-existing cultures; *that* is the reality . . .[4]

That is, nations are created by nationalists rather than the other way around. Moreover, nationalism is an intellectual response to particular economic and social conditions rather than being a permanent feature of man's political consciousness. Finally, in constructing a national identity, the nationalist may well pervert and distort the pre-existing cultural tradition to which he appeals.

If we accept this analysis, if we accept that nationalism is a political philosophy which appeals in particular economic and social circumstances, the first question we must ask is: what evidence is there for the existence of nationalism in Central Asia? We cannot automatically assume that a separate cultural identity implies latent (or repressed) nationalism. Second, if the available evidence suggests that nationalism exists in the region we should ask what it is that constitutes the core of this crystallized national identity? Is it Islam? Is it pan-Turkism? Or is it one of the narrower and somewhat artificial language-and-culture groupings imposed upon the region after 1924? Third, given the existence of nationalist sentiments and in view of their precipitating factors, what grounds are there for believing that such an ideology will become more widespread? Or will it gradually fade away? Answers to these questions will permit a more soundly based characterization of nationalism in Central Asia. This in turn will allow us to decide whether or not Central Asian nationalism at present poses serious political problems for the government in Moscow – and whether it is likely to do so in the future. It will also allow greater clarity of thought about the influence of nationalism on foreign policy and vice versa. These are the issues addressed in the remainder of this essay.

2. Nationalism in Central Asia

According to recent interpretations, nationalism is the product of specific social and economic conditions. Indeed, most theorists, suggest that it is not a concomitant of modernization or industrialization.[5] I do not intend to reproduce such theoretical models here, nor will I elaborate my own model. But I will present one analysis in schematic form. This suggests that nationalist sentiments should be rife in Central Asia. I go on to argue, however, that there is little convincing evidence that this is the case and the section ends with a discussion of the factors that may have impeded the growth of these beliefs.

In a paper that was in fact devoted to the question of nationalism in Central Asia, Immanuel Wallerstein proposed the following model.[6] The world economy, though interrelated because of the division of labour, can be divided into two components – core and periphery. The core consists of countries with industrialized economies and highly developed, articulated social structures. The populations of core countries usually enjoy a relatively high standard of living. The economies of countries in the periphery are much simpler: a majority of the population is engaged in agriculture; there is a limited social structure. Living standards for a majority of the population are relatively low. Differences between core and periphery result in differential manifestations of ethnic conflict.

In peripheral countries the agricultural labour force often belongs to a different language and culture group from the managerial elite. This is true by definition in colonies and was frequently the case in other agrarian societies. In such circumstances, resistance to exploitation (itself the product of pressures from the world economy) or political action to increase the share of resources at the disposal of the agricultural labour group usually takes on a nationalist form. In core countries, on the other hand, nationalism is more often to be found among minorities seeking to protect areas of privilege or to expand opportunities in the face of encroachment from the majority. (In this category, according to the Wallerstein model, one would place such phenomena as the recent upsurge in Welsh nationalism.) In so far as core countries rely upon the recruitment of labour from the periphery to undertake the least skilled work of their economies (the *gastarbeiter* phenomenon) and to the extent that these people are not incorporated into the traditional institutions for the defence of labour, this too can give rise to a second form of nationalism in the core.

Whether or not we assume that the USSR forms part of the world economy (and with the growth of Soviet foreign trade in the post-Stalin period it seems increasingly plausible to assume that it is) it is possible to argue that Central Asia is located in the periphery. The Wallerstein model therefore predicts that the native population of Central Asia should find nationalism an attractive political ideology.

If the Central Asian population is in fact nationalistic, we might expect to observe in the cities of the region manifestations similar to those that are to be found in other peripheral countries. Although there are accounts of isolated incidents, such is not the case. It seems to me that there are three possible explanations for this.

First, it could be argued that the outside world is ignorant of the manifestations of nationalism that occur in Central Asia either because it has no observers there or because the observers who are there look at the wrong things. Oriental society is closed and secretive; the bases of its political activity will not be accessible to Europeans. (This, I think, is what Bennigsen would claim for the dervish orders of the Caucasus.[7]) Second, it could be argued that although the population of Central Asia thinks in nationalist terms, the repressive organs of the Soviet state have been successful in preventing open demonstrations of that fact. Neither of these explanations strikes me as particularly plausible. We are aware of nationalist activities and nationalist demonstrations in other parts of the USSR. This shows that the Soviet police are not always successful in suppressing overt nationalism. There is no reason to believe that they would devote more time and effort to its suppression in Central Asia than in the Ukraine or in the Baltic states. Also, there is no *a priori* reason to believe that nationalism should take a different form in Soviet Central Asia from that elsewhere in the Middle East. And, indeed, we do have accounts of 'bazaar riots' and similar incidents in the region; it is just that they do not seem to happen very often. This suggests that the third explanation is most plausible: there are few nationalist manifestations in Soviet Central Asia because nationalist feelings are not widespread among the native populations of the region.

If this proposition is accepted, it gives rise to the following question: why do conditions which have given rise to nationalism in other parts of the world, according to the Wallerstein model, not result in nationalism in Central Asia? The answer lies in a proper understanding of the region's experience under Soviet rule. (I should point out that Wallerstein himself offers a different explanation to the one given here; Mary McAuley provides yet another explanation.[8])

One interpretation of the Wallerstein model is that it predicts a nationalist response when pressure from the world market leads to an intensification of exploitation and the consequent disruption of traditional agricultural society. Now it is certainly true that Russian colonization in the nineteenth century followed by the imposition of Soviet rule in the 1920s and collectivization in the 1930s resulted in the destruction of certain features of traditional agrarian society in Central Asia. But Soviet rule was not followed by a calamitous decline in peasant living standards – or at least not on the scale that this occurred in the Ukraine or in the grain-growing areas of Russia.[9] Also, there is evidence to suggest that in the postwar period the Soviet government has protected Central Asian cotton-growers from the pressures of the world market – and so has underwritten if not subsidized living standards in the area.[10] Finally, even the Wallerstein model requires the intervention of an intelligentsia to formulate and articulate a nationalist ideology. But, for reasons that are discussed at greater length in the next section, the Central Asian intelligentsia has not (or at least not yet) undertaken this role. Thus, I suggest that despite the fact that Central Asia is located in the 'periphery' of the world economy, its relatively protected position, its relative immunity from intensified exploitation combined with the fact that its intellectuals have been 'distracted' or 'seduced' has allowed the region's population to remain pre-nationalist to a significant extent. This is not to say that there is no Central Asian nationalism. Rather, nationalist ideology does not enjoy the intensity or ubiquity of support claimed for it in what I have called the 'conventional wisdom'.

3. Nationalism and Islam

In the last section I argued that the conventional view of Central Asia was mistaken in ascribing widespread adherence to nationalism to the population of the region. In this section I claim that it is also wrong to assert that the core of this national identity is to be found in Islam – at least in the sense in which that word would be understood in other parts of the Middle East.

The imposition of Soviet rule on the region in the 1920s resulted in the destruction of the power and authority of the official institutions of Islam. In particular, the Soviet authorities abolished the system of courts that had administered religious law; in consequence only social sanctions exist to punish infractions of Islamic law. The government also abolished *vakuf* tenures; this deprived the religious authorities of their economic power. Finally, religious schools were largely abolished – and replaced by universal state-controlled educational systems. The religious authorities were thus deprived of their exclusive power to propagate the religious world-view.

Soviet control and secularization of the institutions of law and education together with state control over the economy has had a considerable impact on both the inner and outer worlds of the native population of Central Asia. First, it is important to realize that the populations of these republics are far better educated than the population of any other significant Islamic country in terms of all the standard indicators. (For example, literacy is higher as is the incidence of secondary or further education, proportion of engineers, or scientists and so on.) In addition, because the Soviet educational system is so tightly controlled from Moscow, the Central Asian population will have been exposed to a more consistently secular and scientific world-view than will have been taught in most other Islamic countries.

Second, Soviet control has provided Central Asian women with immeasurably greater economic opportunities and far stronger legal protection of their freedom than is available to women elsewhere in the Dar-ul-Islam. Indeed, Soviet law in this respect often runs directly counter to the tenets of religious law. Equality between the sexes, even if it is more often formal than actual, has brought about significant changes in social attitudes and social ethos.

Third, convention if not law inhibits the public practice of Muslim rites. The five daily prayers are not commonly recited (at least in urban areas;) the fast of Ramadan is not observed; Central Asians do not commonly make the pilgrimage to the holy places of the faith. This absence of public ritual is complemented, so far as one can tell, by private ignorance: given Soviet publishing policy and educational practice, it is inconceivable that knowledge of the Koran is widespread. Seen from the perspective of Mecca, the culture of Soviet Central Asia represents a very debased form of Islam – if it merits that name at all.

Soviet control over education has done more than change the conceptual environment of the mass of the population in Central Asia. Together with language policy and changes in orthography, it has transformed the intellectual world of the intelligentsia. On the one hand, intellectuals in the region have at least as ready an access to the world of European science and technology as those in more traditional Islamic states; indeed, given the administrative unity of the system they are probably better placed in this respect than all except those in francophone Africa. On the other hand, their literary heritage has been hidden away, replaced to a substantial extent by culture models that have been borrowed from the Russian. The result is that Central Asia now has a Westernised, secular-scientific intelligentsia and a literary culture in which Islamic elements enter more as local colour than integral parts.[11]

This is an over-simplication. In Central Asia as in most other developing countries there are traditionalist intellectuals as well as those who believe in the desirability of constructing a modern industrial society.[12] But what one may call reformism and fundamentalism represent differing intellectual responses to the tensions induced by modernization. And I believe that the more deeply modern secular-rational structures penetrate, the more developed a society becomes, the more widespread the appeal of reformism, the more restricted the field for fundamentalism. As Soviet Central Asia has achieved a significantly higher level of economic development than any of the countries in the 'northern tier' reformism will be a more prevalent ideology among the region's intelligentsia than elsewhere in the Middle East. This means, I would argue, that Islamic fundamentalists are less likely to provide intellectual leadership in the development of a nationalist ideology.

If it is correct to reject the claim that the core of Central Asian nationalism (so far as it exists) is Islamic, it is possible to resolve another problem. Although there are few reports of civil unrest in Central Asia, several of those that I know about involve what appear to be 'nationalist' clashes between different native groups. These would be more consistent with nationalisms centred around the language-and-cultural groupings imposed on the region after 1924. Alternatively, they might reflect pre-nationalist inter-communal friction.

If there is no strong Muslim (Muslim national) identity in Central Asia, why do the region's culture and society differ so markedly from those of other regions? It is not possible to answer this question fully here. But, high birth-rates and a low incidence of divorce are not an exclusively Muslim trait. Rather, they are characteristic of rural populations all over the world; and Central Asian society is still more rural than urban. For that matter, there is evidence that urbanization in Central Asia is having a similar effect to urbanization elsewhere.

Similarly, I do not believe that Central Asian unwillingness to migrate can be ascribed to Islam. On the contrary, the Muslim peasantry of Anatolia has shown itself willing to migrate to Germany and Muslims from Pakistan have been eager to come to Britain. Central Asian reluctance to move to central Russia can more plausibly be explained in terms of the absence of appropriate economic incentives. For a Pakistani or an Anatolian peasant, the advantages of migration are reasonably straightforward: higher money earnings, access to a range of consumer goods that is substantially broader than in the natal village and, not least, the prospect of accumulating money capital. For members of an Uzbek collective farm, on the other hand, or even for those who have grown up in the tenements of Ashkhabad, the balance of net advantage from a move to Siberia is not so clear-cut. It is not certain that televisions, motor cars or other 'desirable' consumer goods can be more easily acquired in Omsk than in Frunze or Dushanbe. It is not clear that accumulated ruble savings from work in the north can be used for anything more than the purchase of traditional houses back in one's home area. Since the Soviet system has, until now at least, managed to ensure full employment in Central Asia, the region's population has been exposed to neither 'pull' nor 'push' influences; it is, perhaps, not surprising that migration remains low.

Then there is the question of a 'national' refusal to learn Russian. Given the fact that a majority of the Central Asian native population live in rural areas, there can have been little incentive to master the Russian language. But urbanization and the spread of modern communications are bringing about changes – as the most recent census returns, however distorted imply. It is only in the 1960s and 1970s that television has become widely available in rural Central Asia. Many of the programmes broadcast in the region originate in Moscow. However dull Soviet television may appear to sophisticated Western eyes, it must come as a revelation, as a window opening on to a wider world, to the inhabitants of the rural hinterland of Uzbekistan. For the first time, I would suggest, the rural population of the region have been faced with a widespread incentive to learn Russian. And they are doing so.

Thus, I conclude that the Central Asian national identity is not Muslim, or rather, it is not Muslim in the sense that that word is understood in other parts of the world. Hence, at the present time the region should not prove over-receptive to the appeal of Islamic fundamentalism. But, for reasons spelled out below, this may change in the next twenty years or so. And, since nationalists often pervert or distort the cultural traditions from which they create their nations, it is quite possible than local nationalists *think* of themselves as Muslims.

4. The future of Central Asian nationalism

The conventional view of Central Asia assumes that the national question will inevitably become more acute in the decades to come simply because the population of Central Asia will grow relative to that of the RSFSR. This too is misleading. As has been pointed out by others, the power and authority of Russians within the USSR does not rest on numbers alone.[13] Nor will it be undermined by divergent demographic trends on their own.

This is not to deny that these demographic trends presage serious political problems for the Soviet government. Of course they do. But I would argue that it is only if the government proves unable to solve the economic problems that they will create that the risk of an increase in nationalism and national disaffection is likely to be high.

The argument of this essay has been that nationalist sentiments are not widespread in Central Asia because the bulk of the population has not felt itself to be economically exploited by Moscow and because the Central Asian intelligentsia has not felt it necessary to defend its privileged status against encroachment from other cultures. But the economic position of the native population has been secured by a policy of intensive cotton culture on irrigated land. It is now questionable whether a continuation of this policy will continue to ensure stable or rising living standards in the area.

First, yields are so high that it is doubtful whether they can be raised further by the application of additional doses of fertilizer. Similarly, attempts to increase the area under cultivation are likely to run into the problem of an inadequate supply of water. This means that any substantial increase in the gross income generated by agriculture can come about only as a result of the very substantial investment involved in the diversion of Siberian water into Central Asia. In a period of slow overall growth, this demand for extensive additional investment is likely to aggravate conflicts with other regions. Such conflicts might generate an increase in territorial nationalism. There is an alternative policy, however, which should permit substantial increases in net incomes from agriculture: mechanization which will result in increased labour productivity. But such a policy would produce rising incomes for those employed in agriculture at the expense of a constant or contracting demand for labour. In the face of a rapidly growing labour supply, such a policy would be very unpopular – unless the government could offer alternative employment opportunities. It too might result in the growth of nationalism. A third policy, attraction of the surplus labour of Central Asia to the industrial cities of the north, even if it could be achieved, might also result in the growth of *gastarbeiter* nationalism.

So far, the position of the native intelligentsia in Central Asia has been protected from the consequences of the growing maturity of Soviet society by the policy of *korenizatsia* – affirmative action *à la russe*. For the society as a whole there has been a marked decline in the rate of growth of white-collar jobs; this has resulted in a reduction in social mobility. In Central Asia, however, preferential treatment for members of the titular nationalities in individual republics has deferred the slow-down. But there are limits to this mechanism. As the competition for white-collar jobs becomes more acute, it is likely that Central Asian intellectuals will become increasingly attracted by nationalist ideologies. And, Soviet emphasis on education means that the number of aspirant *intelligenty* is growing at least as fast as the Central Asian population.

Thus, rapid population growth in Central Asia combined with slow growth in the rest of the economy confronts the Soviet government with a set of intractable problems. One consequence of the failure to solve them may be the growth of nationalism in the region. But even if that does occur, I still believe it more plausible that the conceptual core of the new movements will be the language-and-culture groups constructed at the inception of Soviet power and not the wider pan-Turkic or pan-Islamic ideology; that is, I believe that the new nationalism will be a reflection of the economic particularism of individual republics.

5. Nationalism and foreign policy

Before attempting to spell out the implications of this analysis for Soviet foreign policy, it may be helpful to summarize the argument. Nationalism, or acceptance of the political principle that nations should enjoy autonomy, if not independence, is not an innate characteristic of the human mind. Rather, it is the product of particular economic and social conditions. Since there is little concrete evidence of nationalism in Central Asia, this is taken to imply that nationalist sentiments are not widespread among the region's population rather than that the Soviet government has pursued a successful policy of repression. Further, it is misleading to label the sentiments that do exist Islamic nationalism; Soviet Central Asia is not strongly Islamic – at least not in the sense in which that term is used to describe Iran, Pakistan or even Turkey. The weakness of nationalist feeling in the region is a consequence of the economic policies which have been pursued there in the past half-century; it is doubtful if these policies can be maintained – or replaced by others that will prove as effective. It is likely that the region will suffer a decline in living standards relative to the rest of the country in the next few decades; this will be compounded by difficulties in finding jobs for the region's rapidly growing labour force. If this does occur, it is possible that nationalism will become much more widespread in the next twenty or thirty years.

What bearing does this have on the formulation of Soviet foreign policy? First, because nationalist sentiments have not been widespread in Central Asia the government in Moscow has not had to adopt repressive policies to contain them. Up to now, it has not thereby had to incur odium in the third world. Rather, the Soviet government has been able to make use of Tashkent as a venue for international and diplomatic conferences; it has been able to impress visitors with the range and variety of social infrastructure the Soviet system secures. But the position may change. If nationalism becomes rampant in the face of relative economic decline, repression may have to become more widespread. This may tarnish the Soviet image abroad.

Second, because the basis for nationalism in Central Asia, so far as it exists, is not Islam, the USSR has relatively little to fear from the recent upsurge in fundamentalism. Fear of contamination or of the emergence of a 'fifth column' at home should not cause Moscow to modify its policy towards Islamic states in general nor, specifically, towards those in the northern tier. But, in so far as the rural population remains pre-nationalist in its ideology, it may respond to the pressures of economic decline by a return to fundamentalism unless the reformist intelligentsia succeeds in articulating and communicating a nationalist ideology based on language-culture and ethnos. At the present time, then, I do not see Central Asian nationalism posing any particular constraints on the articulation of Soviet foreign policy. But whether or not this state of affairs will persist depends upon Moscow's ability to solve the region's economic problems. This remains doubtful.

Before finishing this essay, however, it is important to stress two further points in order to avoid misunderstanding. Discussion has focused upon the specific issue of the ways in which political nationalism in Central Asia may constrain or otherwise influence Soviet foreign policy. It has not been concerned with the character of Central Asian ethnic self-awareness, culture or material living standards and the ways in which these might affect the formulation of policy in Moscow. I have argued that, because political nationalism is not prevalent in Central Asia, it cannot have had a seriously inhibiting effect on the making of Soviet foreign policy. But this does not mean that Central Asia has not posed problems for the Soviet government. Of course it has. At the very least, the recent demographic experience of the region has faced the authorities with difficult economic problems; the changing ethnic composition of eighteen-year-old males has implications for the armed services. And such issues may even affect foreign policy. But this influence is not mediated through political nationalism.

Second, it is important to stress that the analysis of this chapter has been concerned with Soviet Central Asia. I have argued that a special set of circumstances has resulted in the virtual absence of political nationalism in the region. But those circumstances are particular to Central Asia; they cannot necessarily be generalized to other parts of the USSR. Indeed, there is evidence that political nationalism is more widespread in other republics, particularly in the Ukraine and in the Baltic region. Each of these territories merits a separate study to establish the nature and extent of nationalist sentiments and the ways in which they may have affected the determination of foreign policy. It is possible that such studies would reach different conclusions from the one arrived at here.

Notes

1 See, for example, the two volumes edited by E. Allworth, *Soviet Nationality Problems* (New York, Columbia University Press, 1971), and *The Nationality Question in Soviet Central Asia* (New York, Praeger, 1973); J. Azrael (ed.), *Soviet Nationality Policies and Practices* (New York, Praegar, 1978); H. Carrere d'Encausse, *L'empire eclaté* (Paris, Flammarion, 1978); A. Bennigsen and M. Broxup, *The Islamic Threat to the Soviet State* (London, Croom Helm, 1982); and M. Rywkin, *Moscow's Muslim Challenge* (London, C. Hurst and Co., 1982).

2 A. Bennigsen, 'Muslim conservative opposition to the Soviet regime', in Azrael (ed.), *Soviet Nationality Policies and Practices*; and Rywkin, *Moscow's Muslim Challenge*.

3 E. Gellner, *Nations and Nationalism* (Oxford, Blackwell, 1983), p. 1.

4 Ibid., p. 48.

5 For a survey and synthesis of recent work, see A. Smith, *Nationalism in the Twentieth Century* (London, Martin Robertson, 1979), and Gellner, *Nations and Nationalism*.

6 I. Wallerstein, 'The two modes of ethnic consciousness: Soviet Central Asia in transition', in Allworth (ed.), *The Nationality Question in Soviet Central Asia*, pp. 168–75.

7 Bennigsen, 'Muslim conservative opposition to the Soviet regime'.

8 Wallerstein, 'The Two Modes of Ethnic Consciousness: Soviet Central Asia in Transition', pp. 172–5, and M. McAuley, 'Nationalism and the Soviet Multi-ethnic State' in N. Harding (ed.), *The State in Socialist Society* (London, Macmillan, 1984), pp. 195–8.

9 A. Nove and J. Newth, *The Soviet Middle East* (London, Allen and Unwin, 1967), especially Chapter 6.

10 A. Khan and D. Ghai, *Collective Agriculture and Rural Development in Soviet Central Asia* (London, Macmillan, 1979), especially Chapter 2.

11 For an explanation of this point, see Rywkin, *Moscow's Muslim Challenge*, pp. 150–2.

12 These two currents in Central Asian intellectual thought are well described by Alexandre Bennigsen in Bennigsen and Broxup, *The Islamic Threat to the Soviet State*, pp. 144–7.

13 For references see the McAuley article, 'Nationalism and the Soviet multi-ethnic state'.

Appendix *Ethnic composition of Soviet Central Asia, 1979* (thousands)

	Uzbek SSR	Kirgiz SSR	Tadjik SSR	Turkmen SSR	Other Republics	USSR
Uzbeks	10,569.0	426.2	873.2	233.7	353.9	12,456.0
Kirgiz	142.2	1,687.4	48.4	0.3	28.0	1,906.3
Tadjiks	594.6	23.2	2,237.0	1.3	41.6	2,897.7
Turkmens	92.3	0.6	14.0	1,891.7	29.3	2,027.9
Kazaks	620.1	27.4	9.6	79.5	5,819.8	6,556.4
Other non-Slavs	1,572.6	329.3	188.0	166.6	44,776.6	47,033.1
Slavs	1,798.5	1,028.7	436.0	391.6	185,552.4	189,207.2
Total	15,389.3	3,522.8	3,806.2	2,764.7	236,601.6	262,084.6

Source: *Vestnik Statistiki* 1980, no. 11, pp. 65–7.

5 Religion in the USSR

John Lawrence

Soviet policy towards religion contains contradictory elements. The Leninist variety of Marxist materialism requires the elimination of all religion as soon as possible. This has been the dominant element in Soviet domestic policy, which has not shrunk from outright persecution of religion over long periods. But there have been times, notably in World War II when the Russian Orthodox Church has been an indispensable support of Russian patriotism. Moreover the persistence of large Christian and Muslim communities is useful to Soviet foreign policy, especially in connection with the Soviet 'peace' movement.

Until rather over twenty years ago evidence for the state of religion in the Soviet Union was very scanty. Since then it has become copious, if exceedingly hard to quantify. Yet there is no doubt that some very remarkable things are happening.

Evidence about religion is always open to dispute, because there are no 'windows on men's souls', and the study of religion in the Soviet Union has special problems. One difficulty in establishing the facts is that any expression of religious belief is severely frowned on, and this leads to much concealment. Another difficulty is that all official writing on religion must do lip service to the official view that religion is on the way out. Yet this makes it all the more remarkable that Soviet writing, including sociological research, testifies again and again to the vitality of religious belief of many kinds. There generally follows a sort of doxology about the decline of religious belief, which is inserted to show loyalty to the Party line, however much this conclusion fails to follow from the previous evidence.[1]

The evidence about religion in the Soviet Union comes from a number of different sources which can be checked against each other. This has been done systematically for the last fourteen years at Keston College and on a smaller scale by other researchers in Europe and America. From the material gathered by this research it is now possible to give a reliable picture of what is happening in the big cities and some parts of the countryside, but it is not yet possible to know with any certainty what is going on in large areas of the countryside or in many provincial towns.

Some evidence comes from official Soviet publications, but in order to use it one has to learn to read between the lines and to remember that propaganda is always directed to changing the thoughts of those to whom it is directed. Thus a large output of anti-religious writing is evidence that there is a good deal of religious faith to be combated. And persistent attacks on particular religious phenomena indicate that these phenomena are widespread. Other carefully filtered evidence comes from the few religious publications which are allowed to exist. Sometimes it is possible to draw conclusions from the facts of Soviet life. During the 1960s for instance the price of all types of religious books on the black market went up tenfold. Copious evidence comes from conversations with Soviet citizens. It would be risky to build much on evidence, some of which might fairly be called anecdotal, if it stood by itself, but generally it can be checked with evidence from other sources. Moreover, those who study religion in the Soviet Union very often know each other and regularly compare notes about what they have learned, heard and seen on their visits. In general, the coherence of what is learned by experienced observers is striking.

Still more copious and varied evidence comes from the vast amount of religious *samizdat* (self-publishing), which reaches the West by various means. This includes verbatim reports of trials, letters of spiritual counsel, poetry, biographies, concentration camp reminiscences, copies of appeals and protests sent to the authorities, and many descriptions of chains of particular events, as well as books of contemporary history, some of them quite long books. There are also the many underground periodicals, such as *The Chronicle of Current Events*, which while not exclusively religious contains much religious material, and other more specifically religious periodicals, such as *The Chronicle of the Lithuanian Catholic Church*. These *samizdat* periodicals are a particularly valuable source. There are also valuable books published in the West but written by people who have lived most of their lives in the Soviet Union. In this connection the chapters on religion in Solzhenitsin's *Gulag Archipelago* must be singled out. In writing this chapter I have drawn on evidence of all these kinds, but I have also checked the written sources with close personal observation of the Soviet religious scene over a period of more than forty years.

The total quantity of evidence is so vast that no one can read it all. But the researchers at Keston and elsewhere have concentrated on particular fields. Some of the substantial body of evidence available is published in *Religion in Communist Lands* (RCL) or the *Keston News Service* (KNS), but much of the highest importance lies unpublished in the Keston archives, and I am greatly indebted to all those at Keston who have helped me by criticism and by drawing my attention to valuable material, in particular to Jane Ellis.

What does the evidence indicate about the numbers of people involved in religion in various degrees? Is it few or many? The Russian Orthodox Church alone claimed to have thirty million 'regular adult worshippers' when it joined the World Council of Churches in 1961. This figure was not at variance with the little that could be gathered from other sources; for instance Archbishop Boris of Odessa told me in 1958 that by counting the candles sold in church it had been deduced that there were thirty-three million adult Orthodox believers. Since then the numbers seem to have increased, and there may be as many as fifty million firm Orthodox believers, though not all of them can get to church regularly, if only because not enough churches are open. A total community of up to a hundred million persons with some degree of adherence to Orthodoxy (as shown by baptisms and religious funerals) is sometimes suggested on the basis of studies by Soviet sociologists. This is speculative but it could be true. If the numbers of Muslims, Catholics, Protestants of various denominations, Jews and indigenous Russian sects (such as the Old Believers) are added, it would appear that something like half the total population of 270 million may have some adherence to religion.

Twenty-five years ago no one could have foretold the extraordinary change in attitude towards religion which was about to take place in the Soviet Union at the very moment when Khrushchev was preparing his savage attack on the churches, an attack which was intended to eliminate all religion by 1980. So far from this happening there has been a continuous upsurge of interest in religion, particularly among the educated classes, and especially among younger educated people. And this has taken place in the teeth of strong official discouragement, not infrequently amounting to persecution.

Recent events in Poland have now shown beyond doubt that in one country under Communist rule it would be folly to neglect the influence of religion. The Soviet Union is very different from Poland and it proved possible for a long time to hide the growing influence of religion from most Western eyes, but here, too, it would be a grievous error to underestimate the present and growing influence of religion. It is true that neither the Russian Orthodox Church nor any other religious body has yet any visible influence on policy, but it is clear from official Soviet statements that the Kremlin regards religion in the long run as a serious threat to the Soviet Union's established order.

The essentials of what has happened in the religious field can be told briefly. From about 1840 for well over a century the bulk of the Russian intelligentsia were strongly opposed to religion. And a section of the atheist intelligentsia set the tone for fifty years after the Revolution of 1917. But traditional religion continued to have a strong hold on the peasantry and it must be remembered that the working class was recruited from the peasantry. The peasant religion was despised by the atheist intelligentsia and sentimentalized by many of the educated Christians, but it was more thoughtful than might be gathered from a reading of Russian literature.[2] And from about 1850 there was in the Russian Orthodox Church a minority stream of profound theological and philosophical thought which came to a head in the last ten years before the Revolution. This *aggiornamento* was cut short in 1917 and a period of harsh persecution followed.

In theory there was no persecution of religion *as such*. By the Soviet Constitution the church is separated from the state and the school from the church. So worship within the four walls of the church building, if a believer can find one that is open for worship, is not illegal, but in practice hundreds of thousands of believers – perhaps millions – were severely punished on trumped-up charges for violations of state laws. The result was that by 1939 the visible structure of the churches had been almost completely destroyed. Only a handful of churches were open for worship. Most of the bishops and other leaders had perished in the purges or were shut away in the Gulag Archipelago. But very large numbers of people did not cease to believe just because the churches were closed, icons were confiscated and believers were persecuted. Many, indeed, fell away from the Church during this time of persecution, and among those who remained faithful there was certainly some superstition, but in the main this was a time when faith was tempered by fire and the thinking peasantry met the church intellectuals in prison and concentration camps. The type of faith which emerged is singularly robust and has little to fear from the acids of modernity.

In 1939 the Soviet Union acquired extensive new provinces on her Western border. In most of these new districts religion was strong, and in 1941 the German attack made national unity more important than ideological unity. At the same time a great part of the Soviet Union was occupied by invaders who did not in general encourage religion but nevertheless allowed the inhabitants to reopen the churches.[3] Moreover Christians played a great part in the patriotic resistance.[4] So more churches were opened, the Moscow Patriarchate was restored and, in a word, the Russian Orthodox Church was able to resume its institutional life. Other denominations, and notably the Soviet Baptists, also benefited from the change of policy.

After World War II much of the ground regained by the Church was held. The Church's loyalty was no longer suspect, and the Communist Party seems to have calculated that religion could be left to die a natural death. When the last *babushka* (literally 'grandmother') had died, there would be no Church left. In the meantime the Party must make sure, so far as it could, that no great zeal was exhibited by the Patriarch, the bishops, the priests and monks or by the laity. By 1958, however, it had become clear that religion was not dying away, that belief in Marxist ideology was at a very low ebb, that new *babushki* had replaced those who died, that a younger generation who had grown up under communist rule were being drawn to Christianity and, worst of all, that some of the intelligentsia were becoming affected by religion.

Taking fright at what they now discerned as a threat to the Party, the communist leadership under Khrushchev prepared to cut the Church down to size. So in the last years of Khrushchev's rule pressure on religion was increased once more to the point of persecution. This was not such a severe persecution as under Stalin but in some ways it was more dangerous. The methods now used could still be cruel but often they were sly and indirect. The purpose was to undermine the Church from within by placing the Party's own men in key positions and by changing the Church's legal constitution so as to make it easier to manipulate. In 1961 the parish priest ceased in the eyes of the law to be the head of his parish or to have any say in financial affairs or the control of the church building. The priests became, at least in theory, simply hired servants of the parish or rather of its executive of three, and hired for purely liturgical purposes. The Executive Committee of the local Soviet nominated its own men or women to the parish executive, not infrequently appointing known atheists to those key positions. I have myself spoken to such persons. Care was taken to ensure that compliant bishops were appointed, while more than half of the 20,000 churches then open were closed on one pretext or another. For the present purpose there is no need to go into further details of the methods employed to tame the Church, illuminating as they are. The subject is well documented from more than one source, and particularly from the so-called *Furov Report*.

This remarkable document which was leaked to the West consists of secret material submitted to the Central Committee of the CPSU by the official Council for Religious Affairs (CRA), a sort of ministry of cults whose job it is to keep all religions under control. The Furov Report is conveniently available in French as *Rapport Secret au Comité Central sur l'Etat de l'Eglise en Urss*.[5] This report, which was written at some time in the 1970s, describes a system that was introduced in 1961. There is no reason to think that any great change in the system has occurred since then. The Furov Report makes no bones about the CRA's decisive powers in Church appointments, and describes in detail the attempts made to influence the Church at all levels to refrain from doing anything to spread the Christian faith and, whenever church leaders have anything to do with foreigners, to give a favourable picture of Soviet policy towards religion. This report gives a picture of the Orthodox Church as loyal to the regime, as indeed it is. It proceeds to divide the bishops into three groups according to the degree of their cooperation with the Communist authorities, giving names in each category, which accord fairly well with the expectations of Western observers. Many of the bishops are said to 'understand' that the Party does not want the influence of religion to increase, and are said to collaborate with varying degrees of zeal to produce this negative result, partly by doing absolutely nothing and partly by slavish obedience to the Council's requests, e.g. to remove any unduly zealous priest from his parish. But the report admits that other bishops and priests are active and effective, trying from time to time to get round the Soviet legislation on religion. The final impression given is that, as the report admits, the Church is very much alive. Indeed, in spite of all the Council's efforts, a surprising number of appointments are in fact made of bishops and incumbents of important churches, who are effective leaders of their people.

It should be added that there are special reasons why the weakness of the official leadership makes less difference than might be expected. The Orthodox give strict canonical obedience to their hierarchy, but moral authority lies elsewhere. Already under Tsarism the Russian Orthodox Church had developed a charismatic leadership which conferred immense moral and spiritual authority on certain persons who had no hierarchical positions but were recognized by the faithful as *startsy* (literally elders). The greatest of these was St Serafim of Sarov, who died in 1833. The character of Fr Zosima in *The Brothers Karamazov* was partly based on a famous *starets*. Since the office of a *starets* is charismatic, it is outside the control of canonical authority. Very little has been said about *startsy* since the Revolution, but it is clear that the institution still exists, if only from the case of Fr Tavrion of Riga, who exercised an enormous influence till his death in 1978. Till then his existence was not known in the west but now important information about him has come through.[6] The Baptist Church inherits some of the traditions of seventeenth-century independence by which authority is vested in the local congregations, which are of course open to local pressure, but are not easily controlled by a central authority. As will be seen from the concluding pages of this essay, the Muslims, too, have effective ways of circumventing the weakness of official leadership. If there is evidence about whether the two million Jews or the 400,000 Buddhists in the Soviet Union have anything of the same kind, it has not come my way.

After 1956, when Khrushchev denounced certain aspects of Stalinism, the collapse of Marxist ideology began to become apparent to ordinary members of the Soviet intelligentsia. It must be difficult for anyone who has not lived in the Soviet Union under Stalin to believe to what an extent people had ceased to communicate their thoughts to each other. But the sober fact is that even members of the same family were very discreet in what they said to each other. There is a well-known story of those days which is no doubt invented but must surely have happened in real life more than once. Boy meets girl. Boy marries girl. A child is born. After three years he says to her, 'Would you mind very much, darling, if I have our son baptized? Of course it will be done in absolute secrecy.' 'That's all right, dear, I had him baptized a year ago.' This story and further accounts of this kind are mentioned in a letter written in 1967 to Pope Paul VI by *samizdat* writer Anatoly Levitin, who is now in the West.

Nearly every year since Stalin died in 1953 people have spoken a little more freely in private, if not in public. The change has been so slow that it is scarcely noticeable to those who spend only two or three years in Moscow, but it is readily apparent to anyone who has known the Soviet Union for ten or twenty years. After 1956 the pace quickened, and in 1963–4, rather suddenly – as it seemed to me from my personal observation – the cup overflowed. Then and in the next two or three years very large numbers of people realized not only that they themselves did not believe in the Marxist ideology but also that very few of their neighbours believed. Their reaction was as varied as one would expect, but most of it was very Russian.

They did not look for relief in pluriformity but began to search for a new orthodoxy. They were patriotic and therefore began to look into the Russian past and at every turn they found the Russian Orthodox Church. So quietly that many observers failed to read the signs, they began to approach the Church as it still existed among them. Many have described the sudden relief of going into a church and encountering a truthfulness and sincerity which were alien to Soviet life as it had become.[7] The worship of the Church opened to them a world that was new to them but had been familiar to their forefathers. And the help that the Christians gave each other contrasted to all that they saw around them. It was beginning to be said once more, as in the days of Tertullian, 'See how these Christians love each other!'

All this, of course, did not happen at once. Alexander Ogorodnikov has described the predicament of himself and his friends, which is typical of an important section of Soviet youth. 'My friends and I grew up in atheist families. Each of us has undergone a complex, sometimes agonizing, path of spiritual questioning. From Marxist convictions via nihilism and the complete negation of any ideology via attraction to the "hippy" life style, we have come to the Church.'[8]

In a letter to Dr Philip Potter, the General Secretary of the World

Council of Churches, the same Alexander Ogorodnikov wrote on 27 July 1976, 'Russian culture today while pushing its way out from under the rubble of terror, lies and delusions, has given birth to an intellectual ferment, which neither we nor the world expected.'[9]

It is important not to exaggerate and it would be hazardous to generalize about all parts of the Soviet Union, but when every discount is made, it is safe to say that in the last years of Khrushchev's rule there began a religious renaissance at least among the intelligentsia of the great cities, and no doubt in some other places. And this has affected members of the Communist Party as well as the rest of the population. It can still be dangerous for anyone except 'the lowest of the people' to profess a religious faith openly, but Soviet citizens are good at concealing their true thoughts.

There have been moments when the Kremlin's attitude to these developments seemed ambiguous. It is true that religious faith is to say the least not wholly compatible with the wholehearted devotion to Marxist ideology which Lenin and his followers have demanded. And experience has shown that the Church is very, very difficult for the Party to contain. Yet the Russian Orthodox Church is, and always has been, a focus of Russian patriotism, a patriotism which increases as belief in Marxist ideology decreases. There seems to have been some internal argument within the Party about the possibility of taming the Church and forming an alliance with her. And there are elements in the Russian Orthodox Church which could lend themselves to an alliance with the Soviet state in what can only be called an inverted clerical fascism. The Slavophil and even Pan-Slav ideas of the last century are very much alive and in their extreme forms could lend themselves to bizarre and sinister paradoxes.[10] However that may be, and however often the question may come up in secret discussions, it is clear that so far the decision has always gone the other way and that the regime still regards the Church as an ultimate threat to its position. At the moment of writing the most recent explanation of the paradoxes of Soviet policy towards religion come from Yuri Belov who spent fifteen years in Soviet prisons, labour camps and psychiatric hospitals, before being allowed to emigrate to the West in 1979. He writes in *Christian Prisoners of Conscience in the USSR 1983–84* (a Keston College staff study), 'The Soviet authorities cannot destroy religion just like that, so . . . they attempt to limit the church within the four walls of a church building. . . . However believers cannot . . . remove missionary or charitable activity. So it is these things which are called "crimes" in the USSR. Recently a KGB official quite openly told an arrested believer during interrogation: "Religion is a crime which we are tolerating just for the time being." '[11]

It is possible to understand the fears of the Soviet authorities, but it should be made clear that there is no evidence that Soviet religious believers are opposed to socialism, indeed rather the contrary. But they are opposed to the dogmatic atheism, the untruthfulness, and the cruelty which have accompanied the Soviet form of socialism.

At the end of Brezhnev's life drastic new measures against the Church were in preparation, and under Andropov these were put into operation. It is too early to estimate the nature of this new wave of persecution but its first objective seems to be to neutralize two of the three great surviving monasteries, the monastery of the Caves near Pskov and Zagorsk near Moscow. The spiritual influence of these places of pilgrimage is indeed enormous. And the method of destroying them now chosen by the authorities is to put their own people in the chief positions. For instance, Gavriil, the present abbot of the Pskov Caves, has all the marks of being a KGB appointment, including the fact that he gives orders to the Militia police force. He does his best to prevent pilgrims visiting the monastery. The famous catacombs are now closed to visitors and all the monastery's churches are closed except for services. The atmosphere of this monastery, which was flourishing three or four years ago, is now more that of a prison.[12] Indeed, there are now indications that it is actually used as a substitute prison.[13]

A tepid religion practised by persons of no importance would no doubt still be tolerated, at least for a time, but the indications are that any living faith is coming under increased pressure, particularly if it is practised by people with a position in Soviet society. But this does not prevent the Soviet government from using the influence of religion as an instrument of foreign policy, notably through the Prague Peace Movement and through various initiatives undertaken by the Moscow Patriarchate and other churches at the behest of the authorities, such as the religious peace conference held in May 1982 and attended by Dr Billy Graham.[14]

So far we have confined ourselves to a consideration of the Russian Orthodox Church, because this Church always lies very near to the consciousness of the Russian people, even surprisingly of some of those who are atheists. But the Soviet Union is a multinational state; and even among the Russians there are other important religious communities. Not all of them call for notice here, but the Russian Baptists and the Pentecostalists, who are sometimes united with them but more often not, are a mainly working-class movement which has important links with the World Baptist Alliance, links which give them a potential value for Soviet foreign policy.

The Russian Baptist Church has greatly increased since 1917. But it has deeper roots in Russian and Ukrainian history than is generally realized, and Baptist spirituality has more in common with the Orthodox than either side was prepared to admit until recently.[15] It recruits to a great extent among the best elements in the working class, the sort of people who in England a hundred years ago were building up the trade unions, the cooperative movement and later the Workers Educational Association. It is impossible to estimate the size of the Baptist movement in the USSR, for many reasons. For one thing it is not possible to disentangle the number of adherents of the legally permitted branch of the Baptist movement and those congregations which have no legal registration. Many believers attend churches of either branch as may be convenient. No figures are available for the unregistered Baptists, while those given for the registered Baptists may be inflated, in order to increase their importance in the eyes of the Baptist World Alliance, or too low because they omit secret baptisms, which are believed to be many. A figure of 500,000 baptized members and three million adherents, which used to be given year after year, has no basis in fact, but was taken from a speech made by Bukharin some time in the 1920s. Some figure had to be given when the Baptist Church emerged from the catacombs after World War II.[16] It seemed safer to give a figure from a Soviet source, and no doubt the true figure was unknown, for the Baptists had undergone their full share of Stalin's persecution and had only just begun to restore their shattered organization. Numbers have certainly grown since then. It would be dangerous to claim any specific figure, but Baptist influence is substantial among the working class and in some regions among the peasants.

There is no need here to go into the divisions in the Baptist community, which arose in the 1960s and turn on the question whether it is better to operate through 'registered' congregations, which are subject to the same difficulties of Party control which have plagued the Orthodox or to work through unregistered congregations which have no legal existence, with all the risks which that entails. As with the Orthodox, the Party squeezes the Baptists as much as it can at home while using their existence to further its foreign policy in every possible way.

The Russian Orthodox and other churches in the Soviet Union are required to give active support to various 'peace' movements, understanding the word 'peace' as support for Soviet foreign policy. And efforts are made to use the extraterritorial influence of the Soviet churches for the same purpose. In this the Soviet government has varying degrees of success.

The Russian Orthodox diocese of Surozh, namely Great Britain and Ireland, is an example of a diocese which accepts the canonical authority of the Moscow Patriarchate, while going its own way in political and social matters. The Russian Spiritual Mission in Jerusalem is a training ground for higher positions in Soviet ecclesiastical diplomacy. The famous Metropolitan Nikodim served his apprenticeship in Jerusalem. And since the fall of the Greek colonels, strenuous efforts have been made to build up Soviet influence on Mount Athos, that semi-autonomous monastic peninsula in the north of Greece. The means chosen for this attempt is the infiltration and control of St Panteleimon's monastery which has been a Russian monastery since the earlier part of the last century.[17] It is hard to see what tangible gain can be made that would justify the considerable effort that is being made to build up Soviet influence on the Holy Mountain, but in this case the temptation to follow a Tsarist example has proved irresistible. Until 1911 Mount Athos, with the rest of Macedonia, formed part of the Ottoman Empire, and the Russian Government was second to none in its efforts to secure a favourable position for itself and its Bulgarian client state in the eventual carve-up of that empire.

In order to use the Church for the purposes of Soviet foreign policy the Soviet government has to give the impression that religion is free. They have had some success in persuading some respected leaders of the churches in the third world that this is in fact so. But most of those Western churchmen who have studied the matter are well aware that this freedom is to say the least limited. They have, however, judged that on balance it is best to maintain official contact with churches in the Soviet Union, even if this puts some restraint on what they themselves are able to say publicly in their official capacities.

Conversely the Soviet authorities have to accept that there are limits to how far they can put pressure on the churches. If pressure goes beyond a certain point the believers will simply go underground, where it will be harder for the Kremlin to control them, as has already happened with a large section of the Baptists.

The choice before the Soviet government is unenviable. The attempt to suppress religion altogether has been made and it has failed. Any wholehearted renewal of this attempt would be likely to fail again, and would make it impossible for the Soviet Union to use religion for the purpose of its foreign policy. But if some religious freedom is permitted, the churches will continue to grow, and eventually it seems inevitable that a point will come when the Communist Party's claim to be the sole embodiment of the true will of the people will no longer be plausible. For the present it seems that we must expect a policy of vacillation, with periods of increased pressure interspersed with times of relative relaxation.

The Soviet experience of religious vitality within their own borders has now brought the Soviet foreign office to take a new and lively interest in the religious situation in other countries, including Britain. This is shown among other things by the interest in religion which is now shown by the Soviet Embassy in London.

So far our attention has been chiefly focused on the Russian churches but the religious composition of the Russian empire has always been even more complicated than its ethnographical composition. In Russia proper the old sects survive and new sects continue to grow. A century ago Anatole Leroy Beaulieu in his classical three-volume study, *L'Empire des Tsars*, devoted a whole volume to the varieties of Russian religious experience; and the situation has not greatly changed.

The Roman Catholic Church is as strong in Lithuania and certain parts of Latvia as it is in Poland, and has proved almost totally inassimilable to the Soviet system in spite of severe pressure, often amounting to persecution. The Eastern Rite Catholics of the western Ukraine were suppressed after the annexation of eastern Poland at the end of the war.[18] They have no legal existence but continue defiantly and are strong in the hearts of their believers,[19] indeed so strong that some Russians despair of ever completely incorporating the western Ukraine into the Soviet system.

The Armenian Church is in a special sense the incarnation of the Armenian nation and therefore has an influence among the large and wealthy Armenian diaspora, which Soviet foreign policy cannot ignore. Moreover, the Soviet authorities know that the Armenians are basically loyal to Russian hegemony, if only because the alternative is Turkish rule, and the massacres of World War I are ever present in Armenian memory. All this has given the Armenian Church an unusual room for manoeuvre within the Soviet system. In Armenia the system of control by the CRA is in form the same as elsewhere in the Soviet Union. But very few Russians know Armenian, and the agents of the Kremlin in Armenia may be Armenians first and Soviet citizens second. Moreover, the Armenian diaspora is able to help the Armenian Church in various ways. The number of churches open for worship is not large, but many of the churches which remain from the Middle Ages and before are so well built that they can still be used for worship even when they have for several centuries been formally abandoned. It is quite common in these churches to find signs of recent worship, though I have yet to learn that worship has ever taken place when tourists are present. All in all, since Stalin's death the Armenian Church has rebuilt its life to a remarkable extent, and has a firmly established position in the national life.

There has been a degree of religious revival among the two million Jews of the Soviet Union and there are some remarkable stories about Jewish faith under adversity, but this subject has not been sufficiently investigated. The Jewish bodies concerned for the cause of Soviet

Jewry have rather concentrated on Soviet antisemitism and on the political and social disabilities of Soviet Jews.

After the Russian Orthodox Church, the Muslims are by far the largest religious body in the Soviet Union. Estimates differ but there are about forty-five million persons of Muslim descent in the Soviet Union, and they are rapidly increasing, while the Russians are barely holding their own demographically. There is very little inter-marriage between the peoples of European Russia and the Muslims. Since 1928 the Soviet Muslims have undergone severe persecution but have kept their Muslim way of life and their faith more completely than either Christians or Jews. This is confirmed by a number of Soviet surveys which give figures showing a higher proportion of believers than in the European parts of the Soviet Union and show that a religious way of life is so strong among the Soviet Muslims that an open avowal of unbelief would lead to social ostracism.[20]

No more than between 400 and 450 mosques are open for worship in the whole area of Soviet Islam and the clergy are politically more subservient than the clergy of any of the Christian churches. But the Muslim clergy, few though they are, are well educated and their published sermons can be outspoken in claiming the superiority of Islam over Marxism. Their few publications sometimes reach a high intellectual level. Muslim religious life, however, is not expressed so much in the mosques as in the cult of Holy Places, in the almost universal retention of Muslim customs such as circumcision, religious burial, etc., and above all in the all-pervading, though illegal, Sufi religious brotherhoods. These are described by Alexander Benningsen and Marie Broxup as 'well structured hierarchical organizations, bound by absolute dedication'.[21] According to recent Soviet sources they are 'mass organizations numbering hundreds of thousands of adepts'. Indeed a Soviet sociologist even claims that more than half the total Muslim population of certain tribal areas in the North Caucasus belong to such a brotherhood.[22] When some of these Muslim tribes were exiled from their homelands during and after the war, the result was that they spread the Sufi brotherhoods to areas where they had not previously existed.[23] In parts of the Caucasus the policy of persecuting Islam has not only strengthened faith, but has produced an anti-Russian xenophobia, which has made life for Russians and Armenians so unpleasant that their proportion of the population is declining, sometimes rapidly. These facts would be scarcely credible if they did not come from Soviet official sources, which would have no motive for magnifying the influence of Islam, indeed very much to the contrary. It should be added that, so far as my own observations of Central Asia have gone, while there is only a little contact between believers of the two faiths, the old

Islamic hostility to Christianity seems to have gone.

No doubt there are national and other non-theological factors in the faithfulness of the Muslim population. But the fact remains and has great potential significance for international relations. For some years the Soviet Union has sent a small hand-picked delegation to Mecca every year for the Haj, and Soviet Muslims appear regularly in small numbers at Soviet-inspired religious 'peace' meetings, but the Kremlin has not had great success in its attempt to manipulate Islam for political purposes. Indeed nothing shows more clearly how alienated the Soviet government is from its own people than the result of using Muslim troops in the invasion of Afghanistan, in spite of the fact that the same tribes exist on both sides of a border which marks nothing but the high-water-mark of Tsarist imperial expansion. It was indeed possible for the Kremlin to achieve surprise by using the units that were already in position along the border, but they had to be withdrawn rapidly when they began to fraternize with their co-religionists and fellow tribesmen and to exchange army supplies for copies of the Koran. It will be seen that Alastair McAuley (in Chapter 4) and I take different views of the influence of Islam in Central Asia and the Caucasus. The reader must judge between us.

Religious faith in the Soviet Union is so far as possible hidden from foreign eyes except in a few places and at certain times when it has been paraded as an indication of tolerance, but religion is a growing element in Soviet society. Generally this is hotly denied, but occasionally it is admitted in public, as when the Patriarch of Moscow was shown on television at the lying in state of both Brezhnev and Andropov, and at the beginning of April 1983, when the Soviet press published the Patriarch's letter to President Reagan on the subject of peace as officially understood by Soviet policy-makers. Nothing of this has led to the reduction of pressure on believers. But its domestic experience of the strength of religious belief has induced the Soviet government to take into account, though not to respect, the religious susceptibilities of the rest of the world.

Pressure on the churches was increased at the end of Brezhnev's reign and throughout Andropov's short period. It is too early at the moment of writing (April 1984) to say whether the advent of Chernenko will make any difference. He is on record (at the Central Committee Plenum in June 1983) as acknowledging that 'no small part' of the Soviet people remain under the influence of religion, and there is reason to believe that this includes some in his own family.[24] At the same time he blamed 'ideological centres of imperialism' for trying 'not only to support but also to implant religiosity and to give it an anti-Soviet nationalist direction', whatever that means. He added that communists, though convinced atheists, 'do not try to force their *Weltanschauung* on anyone'[25] but would deal firmly with breaches of Soviet law. This was, no doubt, a 'collective' statement and it will be seen that it is open to more than one interpretation. (As of July 1984, there is no reason to expect the present hard line against religion to be modified in the near future.)

It may perhaps be conjectured that the Soviet authorities are nonplussed by the phenomena of religion and that their policy is a hand-to-mouth one. The religious communities on the other hand look further ahead and view the future with confidence.

Notes

1 See for instance leading article in *Pravda* for 14 December 1983, quoted in Keston News Service of 12 January 1984 (obtainable from Keston College, Heathfield Road, Keston, Kent). The disturbed tone of this article indicates the concern of the Soviet authorities over the continued strength of religious belief, which appears to justify the quiet confidence of the believers.

2 Pierre Pascal, *The Religion of the Russian People* (Mowbray, 1976).

3 For a detailed account of this see Wassilij Alexeev and Theofanis G. Stavrou, *The Great Revival: the Russian Church under German Occupation* (Minneapolis, Minnesota, Burgess Publishing Co., 1976). This book draws much of its material from German intelligence reports of the period.

4 See Nikita Struve, *Christians in Contemporary Russia* (Harvil, 1967). I myself was in Russia for most of this time and witnessed some of what is here recorded.

5 Seuil, 1980.

6 See *Religion in Communist Lands*, Vol. 10, no. 1, pp. 96–100.

7 This has been described by some of the contributors to *From Under the Rubble* (Collins Harvil, 1975), and in more detail in a new *samizdat* text *Prikhodyashchiye v Tserkov*, by Vladimir Zelinsky, published in Russian in France (La Presse Libre, 1982).

8 *Religion in Communist Lands*, Vol. 4, no. 4, 1976, p. 46.

9 *Religion in Communist Lands*, Vol. 7, no. 1, 1979, p. 449.

10 See article by John Dunlop in *Religion in Communist Lands*, Vol. 11, no, 2, 1983, pp. 146–60.

11 This incident is also described in an unsigned *samizdat* appeal by several Christians of different denominations received at Keston College in June 1983.

12 Personal observation confirmed by *samizdat* documents published in Keston News Service for 11 August 1983. For further confirmatory information about Abbot Gavriil, see *Documents of Christian Committee for Defence of Believers' Rights in the USSR*, Vol. 11, which can be consulted at Keston College.

13 Private information.

14 *Religion in Communist Lands*, Vol. 10, no. 3, pp. 337–8.

15 I have heard Baptists sing the great Easter hymn of the Orthodox *Khristos*

voskrese iz myertvykh, and I have heard them discuss the Eucharist in much the same way as the Orthodox.

16 Private information given by the late Alexander Karev, a leader of the Russian Baptists.

17 RFE/RL Report No. 261/84, *The Role of the Russian Orthodox Church on Mount Athos.*

18 According to the best information available there appear to be in the Soviet Union about four-and-a-half million Roman Catholics and four-and-a-half million Catholics of the Eastern Rite, but it should be emphasized that there is considerable uncertainty about these figures.

19 See material collected in *Religion in Communist Lands*, Vol. 11, no. 3, Winter 1983.

20 Alexandre Bennigsen and Chantal Lemercier Quelquejay, *Les Musulmans Oubliés* (Maspéro, 1981), pp. 252–3.

21 Alexander Bennigsen and Marie Broxup, *The Islamic Threat to the Soviet State* (Croom Helm, 1983).

22 V.G. Pirovarov, 'Sotsialogicheskie issledovaniia problem byta natsional'nyk traditsii i verovanii v Checheno-Ingushskoi ASSR', *Voprosy Nauchnogo Ateizma*, Vol. 17, 1975, p. 316.

23 Ibid.

24 Private information.

25 Keston News Service for 23 February 1984.

PART TWO THE SOVIET ECONOMY

6 Soviet Industry in Its International Context

David Dyker

Industry, we are told, is the sinews of war, and there can be no doubt that it is above all the development of Soviet industry since around 1930 which has conditioned the emergence of the USSR as a superpower. Yet fifty years on from the start of the industrialization drive, the Soviet leadership must feel uneasy about a number of key industrial problems which, it seems, will simply not go away, namely:

(1) Industrial and industrial labour productivity growth rates have been slackening since the early 1950s, and there is no sign of levelling-out, never mind a reversal of this trend (see Table 6.1). This means that the 'historically inevitable' process of catching-up with the industrialized West has got stuck, even in the context of recession in the West, at a point where the industrial labour productivity gap between the Soviet Union and the West is still very large, but where intensifying labour shortage has made overall growth increasingly dependent on just that variable. We should perhaps not, however, overstress the specifically *labour* productivity problem. Capital productivity has arguably been at least as problematic, and has indeed shown a consistently negative growth rate since around 1960.[1] Growth in total productivity accounted for only about one-quarter of total industrial output growth 1976–80, as compared to about one-half 1971–5.[2] Consideration of general productivity problems leads us on to some rather more specific areas of difficulty, namely:

(2) Industrial labour often appears poorly organized and indisciplined.

(3) The process of adding to industrial capital stock is often painfully slow. Soviet lead-times are still generally from two to three times as long as they are in the West.[3] Long gestation periods in capital construction damages capital productivity directly, but it also intensifies the independent problem of slowness in the development and assimilation of new technologies.[4]

(4) Soviet industrial products are often of poor quality. This point does not need labouring in relation to consumer goods, but it does

affect priority producer goods as well. Soviet machines, in particular bulldozers, lorries, presses, boring plant and equipment for the food industry, still tend to be too heavy, for the simple reason that machinery prices still tend to be based on tonnages.[5] This in a nutshell is the famous 'success-indicator problem'.

Table 6.1 *Average annual rates of growth of Soviet industrial production and industrial labour productivity*

<table>
<tr><th></th><th>Industrial production (official Soviet)</th><th>Industrial production (CIA recalculation)</th><th>Ind. lab. prod. (official Soviet)</th></tr>
<tr><td>1951–55</td><td>13.1</td><td>10.2</td><td rowspan="2">7.4</td></tr>
<tr><td>1956–60</td><td>10.4</td><td>8.3</td></tr>
<tr><td>1961–65</td><td>8.6</td><td>6.6</td><td>4.5</td></tr>
<tr><td>1966–70</td><td>8.5</td><td>6.3</td><td>5.5</td></tr>
<tr><td>1971–75</td><td>7.4</td><td>5.9</td><td>5.9</td></tr>
<tr><td>1976–80</td><td>4.5</td><td>3.4</td><td>2.8</td></tr>
</table>

Sources: Various editions of UN, *Economic Survey of Europe*, *Narodnoe Khozyaistvo SSSR*; R. Converse, 'An index of industrial production in the USSR', in US Congress, JEC, *USSR: Measures of Economic Growth and Development, 1950–80* (US GPO, 1982), p. 195.

We can list the ways in which these various perennial problems impinge on the Soviet Union's relations with the outside world as follows.

First, steadily falling growth rates in industry, coupled with stagnation in agriculture, have ensured that the overall macroeconomic balance is becoming tighter and tighter. However you calculate it, the Soviet ratio of fixed investment to National Income has been steadily nearly 30 per cent for some time now.[6] As Edwina Moreton reports in Chapter 9, US intelligence puts Soviet defence expenditures as a proportion of GNP at anywhere between 12 and 16 per cent in 1981. For our purposes, however, that margin of error is not of great importance. On any set of plausible figures not very much more than half of Soviet National Income has been left to satisfy communal and private consumption needs: defence and investment activity taken together, then, have imposed a heavy burden on the economy, especially on industry. Investment goods are largely industrial in origin, and the same is presumably true of defence goods. Thus faltering industrial production growth, combined with inflexible defence priorities and investment programmes, has exerted intense pressure on consumption trends. Consumption of goods has continued to grow, but at a much reduced rate – 2.1 per cent per annum 1976–80, compared to 5.4 per cent per annum 1966–70 according to the CIA.[7] Certainly that overall figure is pulled down by a very low figure for food – the figure for *consumer durables* for 1976–80 is 5.3 per cent, though it was as high as 9.1 per cent 1966–70. It seems in any case incontrovertible that steady improvement in living standards is a key element in the legitimization and stability of the Soviet regime, and the simple arithmetic of falling industrial growth rates equals falling rates of growth of consumption must be very disturbing for the leadership. On that basis we may speculate that they perceive the *domestic* political value of any international agreement which permitted them to cut their defence ratio. More certainly, we can confirm from dozens of articles in Soviet newspapers and scholarly journals that they would dearly love to find a way of increasing the effectiveness of industrial investment so that they could in principle obtain the same ultimate return from a smaller proportion of National Income devoted to investment. Most of all, of course, they would like to find a way of reversing the downward trend in industrial rates of growth, which would enable them to have more guns *and* more butter.

Secondly, quality and specification problems have meant that the Soviet Union has in general made little headway with the export of the more sophisticated types of manufactures, despite notable exceptions, e.g. with the Lada car and with exports of arms to the third world. As Alan Smith shows in Chapter 8 (Tables 8.1 and 8.2), Soviet machinery exports to the industrialized countries were almost insignificant in 1982, and had grown little since the mid 1970s. Exports of machinery other than arms to the third world were not much more impressive, although they did double between 1976 and 1982. By contrast, Soviet imports of machinery and steel products from the West represented about 40 per cent of total West-East commodity flows in 1982, and this emphasizes the extent of continued Soviet dependence on the outside world for high-technology goods. Bearing in mind in particular the very heavy burden of food imports in recent years, anything that could increase the export potential of Soviet industry, or reduce its dependence on imported technology, or both, would be of great value in moderating the balance of payments constraint on growth. Reduced dependence on foreign technology would also diminish the degree of vulnerability of the Soviet economy to foreign economic pressure. An increase in the importance of Soviet exports of ranges of goods much more highly substitutable than the currently predominant oil and gas would, of course, *ceteris paribus*, intensify that vulnerability.

On the basis of these considerations we are interested in the following aspects of Soviet economic policy:

(1) Policies aimed at generally improving industrial productivity and efficiency, and hence, *ceteris paribus*, growth rates;
(2) Policies aimed more specifically at improving efficiency in the investment sphere;
(3) Policies aimed more specifically at improving the quality of Soviet industrial goods;
(4) Policies aimed more specifically at raising the effectiveness of Soviet R & D;

Let us consider these in turn.

General industrial productivity and efficiency

There can be no doubt that Soviet workers have in the post-Stalin period often 'got away with murder'. Academician Aganbegyan reports that some Soviet factories have had to organize special detachments to stop drunk workers getting to machines and causing themselves or others serious injury,[8] and it is common for workers to do effectively no more than four or five hours of real work in a day.[9] Soviet managers have not traditionally enjoyed any absolute right to fire unsatisfactory workers, and full employment has meant that the threat of the sack has in any case not been very menacing. Under the rubric of his 'labour discipline' campaign, Andropov set out to make sacking easier, and also to tighten up on the regulations whereby a loafer's 'bad record' is entered into his labour book. On a more sophisticated plane, a number of recent articles have stressed that better labour discipline can be achieved only if *planning* discipline is improved. Supply breakdowns mean periods of enforced idleness, which damage morale, quite apart from direct production losses. Yet Soviet specialists have tended to perceive the problem of supply uncertainty in the Soviet economy as primarily the result of a degree of over-centralization which even in the age of computers means that the planners simply cannot do all the sums to a high degree of accuracy. So if we are to take these ideas about better planning discipline seriously, we must look at the implications for the general level of centralization of current trends in industrial policy.

In April 1983 a paper on the problems of the Soviet planning system was read to a closed seminar in Moscow by Tatyana Zaslavskaya of the Siberian Section of the Academy of Sciences of the USSR.[10] Subsequently leaked to the Western press, the paper appears to have been received with some displeasure at Politburo level. Yet its essence must come close to the committee-room view of the majority of Soviet economists and industrial administrators. Zaslavskaya argued that the centralized, command economy had a good deal to recommend it during the period of the 'Great Leap Forward', but it could not cope with the size and technological complexity of the contemporary Soviet economy. In particular, it could not solve the labour productivity problem. More specifically, planning difficulties were blamed on an over-mighty and overweight intermediate planning establishment, which stands accused of obstructing and distorting communication between Gosplan and actual producing units.

Sure enough, a decree was published in July 1983[11] to set up an experimental system to be run in a number of heavy and light industrial ministries from 1 January 1984, which seems to aim, *inter alia*, to follow up this idea. Under the system the role of production associations and enterprises in the drafting of plans is to increase at the expense of the ministries, while the traditional right of the latter to chop and change plans in the course of implementation is also to be limited. Associations and enterprises are to have much more autonomous control over the disposition of gross profits, particularly in relation to incentive payments. In addition, they are to regain a substantial measure of independence in the disposition of decentralized investment funds, financed mainly from the production development fund, and ultimately from gross profits. They will also have more freedom to finance 'technical re-equipment' investments from amortization allowances and credit.

Would this system, if extended to the whole of industry, represent a substantial measure of decentralization? In some ways the downgrading of the ministries may be a little misleading in this respect. Plan *construction* has always been very heavily concentrated in the central planning organs in the Soviet Union, and the ministries have only handled some hundreds of product balances out of 15,000–20,000. It is plan *implementation* which has traditionally been largely the preserve of the ministries, and which is now to be entrusted more to the lower rungs in the hierarchy. This may permit a slimming-down of the planning apparatus, but it does not by itself reduce the number of equations to be solved by the central planners by so much as one. In addition, ministerial chopping and changing of plans has often been very functional in terms of filling the gaps in the official plan. Will the smaller associations be able to do this as effectively? I would have thought not. In sum, then, Andropov's industrial planning experiment seems hardly to touch on the general issue of decentralization, and it could actually worsen supply problems flowing from over-centralization. Greater independence for associations and enterprises in the forming and disposition of 'own' funds should in principle make it easier to ensure that incentives pull in the right direction, and incentive payments go to the right people, two areas which presented serious problems in the late Brezhnev era. But the success-indicator system under the experiment remains highly complex, involving sales/deliveries, new technology, quality, growth of labour productivity, and cost reduction or increase in profits (the 1965 reform placed the emphasis equally on just sales and profit). However desirable all these things may be in themselves, they add up to a nightmare for whoever has to decide on actual pay-outs. In addition, the old Stalinist rule that no bonuses should be paid to managerial workers unless sales/delivery plans are met in full, which had been driven underground in the 1970s, is formally reinstated. It is not difficult to see the reasoning behind this move. With growth rates going down and down, the planners want to maintain some elements of tautness in the system. But in practice this kind of bonus rule tends to make managers play safe, conceal capacity, and to set up a clear opposition of interests between central planners and producers – precisely the thing which the experiment in its more general dispositions is trying to minimize.

The renewed emphasis on decentralized investment effectively under the control of production units is another element in the industrial planning experiment reminiscent of the Brezhnev/Kosygin planning reform. Once again it seems at first sight to be a jolly good idea, but one wonders whether the present Soviet leadership can remember why the original decentralized investment experiment was abandoned so emphatically in the early 1970s. The problem with this kind of partial approach to planning reform is that it decentralizes limited categories of investment and procurement decisions, without, of course, decentralizing the corresponding production and supply decisions. The result, as the Soviet planners found in the late 1960s and early 1970s, is that would-be decentralized investors either cannot obtain the physical supplies they need, or else obtain them by using 'pushers' to filch them away from the centralized investment plan, as happened in a particularly dramatic way in 1971.[12] The general conclusion, then, is inescapably that *radical decentralization of particular sectors or sub-sectors can only work if it is backed up by some generalized decentralization of production/supply planning*.

Thus the 1983 experimental industrial planning decree seems to promise little in relation to this crucial dimension of the balance of centralization at the level of the general or the particular: it consequently fails to provide a substantial basis for the post-Brezhnev leadership's ideal combination of labour discipline and planning discipline. But the supply problems inherent in over-centralization also affect the productivity issue in an indirect, but no less insidious way, as was highlighted in an article by G. Kulagin, published in *Pravda* in late

1982.[13] Why, Kulagin asked, is productivity in Soviet engineering so much lower than in Western engineering plants, even though Soviet plants are on average some six times as large in terms of workforce? The major part of the answer is that a substantial proportion of the 'extra' personnel in the typical Soviet enterprise are low-productivity auxiliaries. In Soviet machine-building, the categories of repair, instrument and transport/warehouse work account for 38 per cent of the total workforce, compared with just 11 per cent in the USA. In the West the size, in terms of workforce, of the average engineering plant has fallen quite sharply over recent decades, with the development of 'micro-specialization'. The Soviet Union has quite simply missed out on the micro-specialization revolution, and the principal reason for this lies in one of the ways that engineering enterprises seek to cope with supply problems. By building up 'dwarf-workshop' capacity to produce vital components they can simplify their supply links with the economy at large to a considerable extent – Soviet engineering plants do, in fact, manufacture most of their own nuts and bolts, screws, tools, instruments and castings themselves.[14] The cost, needless to say, is very high, the return on the resources invested – capital and labour – very low. But this is one of the principal ways in which the top-heavy Soviet planning system is *made to work*.

Kulagin's suggested solution for the problem is interesting. He proposes the creation of a specialized Ministry of Inter-Sectoral Production which would centralize production of all 'bits and pieces'. Such a ministry, he argues, could be allowed to build up its own network of optimal plants without any forcible closing-down of existing dwarf-workshop capacity – in time other ministries would happily close them down themselves and switch their orders to the cheaper and better lines produced by the new specialist ministry, thus paving the way for a productivity revolution in the engineering industry. This idea has two obvious attractions. First, it aims to solve the success-indicator problem that has always militated against production of 'fiddly little things' by creating a *powerful* organization which by definition produces nothing else. Secondly, it implies a fairly radical 'marketization' of a crucial area of the Soviet economy, for it argues that the new ministry should prosper through the forces of competition. But that second point indicates the major weakness of the proposal, the same weakness that we pin-pointed in relation to the provisions for decentralized investment in the experimental industrial planning decree. If the new ministry is to operate on a market basis, how is it going to go about procuring capital, material and manpower resources? Would those resource flows be in the central plan, and if so how on earth would the central planners plan them? Alternatively, if the ministry were left to obtain the resources the best way it could, how would you guarantee that the investment fiasco of 1971 would not be repeated? We should emphasize that this is all strictly hypothetical. Kulagin's article was a discussion article, and his idea seems in fact to have been discussed and discarded.[15] But the discussion strikingly confirms the difficulty of combining specific bits of decentralization with maintenance of the traditionally high overall level of centralization. In addition, the Kulagin material highlights the extent to which wasteful use of factors of production is an *inherent* characteristic of Soviet-style planning.

We can underline this latter point by reference to the *Shchekino system*. Sacking workers for breaches of discipline is one thing, but the issue of redundancy has if anything been handled even more gingerly in the Soviet Union. Under the Shchekino experiment, first introduced in 1967, managers were given the right to lay men off, although they are supposed to find them alternative work with the help of the ministry and the local government, and use some of the money thus saved to pay increased bonuses to those remaining.[16] The experiment has shown good results in terms of productivity, but as of 1980 it is unlikely that much more than around 10 per cent of the Soviet industrial labour force was working under full Shchekino conditions, though the system has been widely introduced in the chemicals industry.[17] The reasons for this limited extension seem to be threefold. Firstly, there were fears about the political dangers of the possibility that an unemployment problem might emerge. While 'labour placement bureaux' have been developed on a regional basis since 1965, the general level of Soviet labour allocation planning remains low. Generalized Shchekino could put an unbearable strain on the system and create large-scale frictional and structural unemployment. Secondly, the bureaucrats are reluctant to allow association and enterprise managements genuine freedom of action in relation to the balance of wage-fund, incentive funds and labour force. Thirdly, and perhaps most important, Soviet managers who keep a certain amount of surplus labour on the books 'just in case' may perceive no substantial self-interest in the introduction of the Shchekino system. In fast-expanding production-line sectors like chemicals Shchekino has helped management to maximize output. By contrast, it is precisely in the engineering sectors, with their tradition of dwarf-workshops etc., that the experiment has been implemented with least success.[18] It is clear that the present leadership is well disposed towards Shchekino and the provisions of the 1983 experimental planning decree may make it easier for associations and enterprises to resist bureaucratic interference from above in this, as in other connections. Once again, however, we have to conclude that interesting little experiments can only get so far in a planning system where the traditional stress on centralization seems almost sacrosanct. There is, in fact, nothing from the area of general planning considerations which point to the possibility of any substantial degree of 'intensification' of the economy in the Soviet Union after Brezhnev. On this basis we can expect no relaxation in the pressure of steadily falling growth rates.

Efficiency in the investment sphere

Attempts to extend the principles of the 1965 planning reform into design and construction failed. In a context where the final product is too massive and often too unique for sales as such to be a meaningful indicator, the Soviet planners spent the 1970s searching with little success for some basis for getting design workers and builders away from the Stalinist world of simply maximizing the number of drawings drawn, the number of bricks laid, etc. But an experiment started in the Belorussian republic showed some success in attacking the problem through placing the main emphasis in the success-indicator system on actual completions, or rather operationalizations. The difficulty here is that you need some kind of quantitative measure of progress, if only so that requisite financial flows can be calculated, especially in an economy where projects often take 7–8 years to complete. It was for this reason that under the Belorussian system operationalization was supplemented in the success-indicator system by marketable output (*tovarnaya produktsiya*). But because marketable output implies saleability, but not necessarily sale, it could very easily turn into something operationally not very much different from the traditional gross volume of construction work, as the Belorussians discovered. Logically enough, then, a 1980 ruling stipulated that construction output could only be counted as marketable output once the capacities involved were actually in operation.[19] This should effectively have turned the marketable output indicator into an alternative (quantitative) expression of the (qualitative) operationalization indicator. But a contemporary source indicates that the problem remains unsolved, with marketable output being counted on the basis of State Operationalization Commission certificates as made out rather than as actually confirmed. This can mean a divergence of up to one year's work between reported marketable output and operationalization as such.[20] Here is a fundamental problem, and it helps us to understand why the universalization of the Belorussian system envisaged by the 1979 planning decree has not happened.

It would be quite wrong to place all the blame for excessive Soviet lead-times on design and construction organizations. The ministries notoriously *overbid* for investment resources – not surprisingly given that they represent an essentially free resource to the ministries – and that is perhaps the major reason why there are always far more projects on the go at any given point in time than the design and construction sectors, with the best will and the best success-indicator system in the world, could possibly cope with. But articles from the post-Brezhnev era have been very frank in admitting that the 'cult of the gross' still rules in the investment sphere.[21] No concrete proposals, however, apart from the rather marginal ones on decentralized investment in the 1983 experimental industrial planning decree, have yet emerged. This is particularly important because the problem of excessive lead-times seems to affect imported turnkey projects as much as purely domestic projects.[22] We have to conclude, then, that there is no immediate prospect of the Soviet Union significantly improving the operational efficiency of the investment process in such a way as to permit either an increase in the consumption ratio, or an increase in the rate of growth of National Income, or a bit of both. This in turn limits the potential for improving performance through technology transfer.

The quality of industrial goods

The philosophy of the 1965 industrial planning decree was that the way to improve the quality of goods was to establish profit as a key success-indicator. The ploy did not work very well, simply because profit, if not backed up by some degree of price and/or contract flexibility, tends to have the same failings as any other success-indicator. The 1979 planning decree was coloured by a renewed confidence in the ability of planners to measure quality directly, and as we saw quality is included as an explicit success-indicator in the 1983 experimental industrial planning decree. But the agonizing details of a *casus* recently reported in the Soviet press illustrate just how deep-seated in the Soviet economic system the quality/specification problem is.[23] For thirty years the Chelyabinsk Tubular Steel Plant, subordinate to the Ministry for Ferrous Metallurgy, has been making iron bedsteads. Over a period of years their main customer for beds – the Chelyabinsk Roskhoztorg wholesale base – tried to get them to start making some wooden beds, but the Tubular Steel Plant just said that they could not possibly, because they had no allocation certificates for timber. The wholesale base then went to the State Arbitration Service, which specified that for the period 1976–80 the Tubular Steel Plant must start to deliver a small, but growing number of wooden bedsteads. This had no effect, and when the Arbitration Service repeated the instruction for the period 1981–5 the Tubular Steel Plant simply reiterated that they could not obtain the materials and equipment, and anyway iron bedsteads were perfectly satisfactory. In fact, wholesale organizations have found it increasingly difficult to sell the iron bedsteads, and have been refusing to accept more than half the planned deliveries of same. Finally the Tubular Steel Plant is being sued by the Arbitration Service for 37,000 roubles.

We can pick out a number of key elements in this sorry tale. Firstly, departmentalist narrowness no doubt does make it extremely difficult for an enterprise of the Ministry for Ferrous Metallurgy to obtain timber supplies. Secondly, sales/deliveries is as insensitive an indicator as gross output to quality/specification considerations if planned levels thereof bear no relationship to demand. Thirdly, the State Arbitration Service is a very weak reed. There is nothing in the 1983 experimental industrial planning decree that would have changed any of those elements.

The effectiveness of R & D

We would expect Research and Development to be a particular problem in a Soviet-type economy, since technological change is even more difficult to reduce to purely quantitative terms than is investment. Again, however, the late 1970s witnessed a growth in optimism about the possibility of measuring technical change on the basis of, for example, the rate of introduction, or rate of acceleration of introduction, of new products. At the same time the development of the mixed scientific-production association gave an organizational form to the notion of a closer link between production and Research and Development. Contemporary case material suggests, however, that one or two problems remain to be solved. When the Inter'er association commissioned the Design and Technological Institute for Furniture to design a new office chair, they came up with a monstrosity containing 40 or 50 pounds of metal. Inter'er did not mind because heavier means more expensive, and the heavy metal aspect may even have helped the thing to be awarded the State Quality Mark.[24] Meanwhile the Soviet economy is suffering from an acute shortage of steel. But when we think of what is happening to steel industries in the West we can only conclude that the whole materials orientation of the Soviet economy is still hopelessly Victorian. A cartoon in a recent issue of *Ekonomicheskaya Gazeta* depicted an excited engineer brandishing a huge contraption and shouting 'We've made the biggest micro-calculator in the world!' On this basis it may be some time before the Soviet Union revolutionizes world export markets.

The situation is more complex for specifically military R & D. The conventional wisdom, backed up by substantial scholarly research,[25] is that there is no systematic technological gap between Soviet and Western military hardware. On the other hand, the Korean airliner tragedy suggests that Soviet communications technology is not all that it might be, and this ties in with what we know about the backwardness of the Soviet computer industry.[26] That in turn may be why Andropov, in one of his last official pronouncements on these matters, seemed to express a genuine fear that the USA might open up a substantial technological lead over the Soviet Union in any future round of the arms race.[27] But there are problems of interpretation here: Andropov may simply have been trying to impress Soviet and world public opinion with the aggressiveness of US intentions. For the time being at least it would be unwise to assume that Soviet weaponry is qualitatively anything else but a match for Western.

Possible alternative institutional scenarios

Speculative economic reasoning could provide any number of these, so it is best to stick to actually operating models. While Soviet leaders have been impressed by the Hungarian market socialist approach to agricultural planning, it is the East German and Bulgarian New Economic Models, which aim to modify, even transform, the traditional Soviet-style approach rather than replace it, which have captured Soviet attention in industrial planning. These are, of course, the two countries of Eastern Europe which have stood up best in terms of growth trends to the difficult circumstances of the late 1970s and early 1980s. Bulgaria's reported growth rates of National Income are still in the 4–5 per cent per annum range, while the GDR has reported growth rates of around 4 per cent since 1979, after a sticky period in the mid-late 1970s.[28]

A theme common to the planning changes introduced in these countries in 1979, and very much echoed in the Soviet experimental industrial planning decree, is that of cutting the ministries down to size. In the Bulgarian NEM the traditional role of the ministries in plan implementation has been largely transferred to the association, combine or enterprise, leaving the ministry as a budget-financed organization mainly concerned with medium-term matters, in particular investment and technical progress. Production organizations make no payments to ministries at all.[29] In East Germany the new system is based on the combine, a conglomerate of related enterprises operating on a commercial rather than an administrative basis. While the ministries retain substantial directive powers and a major role in basic production planning, combine managements are conceded decision-taking pre-eminence in a number of areas which have classically been the prerogative of the ministry. In particular, the combine director can make decisions on shifting equipment around, opening up new departments, and hiring and firing junior management.[30]

Much more important is what has happened in the East German and

Bulgarian models to the position of the enterprise/association/combine *vis-à-vis* the central planners. In Bulgaria the new principle is that production organizations should be wholly self-financing. The Soviet experimental industrial planning decree also predicates, as we saw, an increase in enterprise funds and in management's rights to their autonomous disposition. But while under the Soviet decree that simply means more decentralized investment, under the Bulgarian NEM it means that except for major new capacities or technologies *all* investment is financed from production organization funds. In addition, for the bulk of projects involving lead-times of less than three years, no specific approval from centre or ministry is required, and no specific financial limits are imposed. Production organizations are conceded the right of free contract in relation to association or cooperative agreements with other organizations, and possibly also as regards some categories of supply deal. In the GDR the principle of free contracting within the framework of the plan has been taken a good deal further, and supply contracts are in the first instance negotiated by the combines and other organizations involved, though subsequently subject to approval by ministry and government. Some combines are even allowed to negotiate foreign trade contracts independently.[31] There is some echo of this approach to the problem of earning hard currency in the Bulgarian NEM provision for an enterprise hard-currency own fund, though this does not appear to be backed up by any formalized degree of autonomy on export contracts.[32]

Most importantly, what happens under these new arrangements to the output target? In the GDR the principle seems to be to maintain a substantial dimension of central directive in relation to output planning, irrespective of the degree of flexibility on contracts, but with the combines left to do a good deal of the 'balancing' calculations on which output targets must ultimately be based. In Bulgaria the key innovation in this area is the principle that obligatory output targets should henceforth represent essentially minimal rather than maximal figures. Beyond that Bulgarian enterprises are now to be allowed to formulate 'counterpart' plans on a voluntary basis, in accordance with contracts signed for deliveries of above-plan production. Shortfalls on basic plan assignments for a given year are merely added in to the counterpart plan for the following year.[33] I believe that this represents the first attempt fully to formalize the principle of 'slack' planning in a Soviet-type system. To that extent the Bulgarian approach is clearly at odds with one aspect of the 1983 Soviet experimental industrial planning decree.

There are, of course, obstacles to the export of East German or Bulgarian approaches to the USSR, even if the Soviet leadership resolved that that was what they really wanted. Because the GDR was an industrial country from its creation, because Bulgaria has not encountered a serious slowdown in growth rates, those countries simply do not face the key Soviet dilemma over whether disappointing short-term growth rates can be allowed to fall even further in the hope of medium-term improvement. The Bulgarians are, in fact, currently *planning* for a lower overall growth rate. Again, it may be all right for a culturally and industrially homogeneous state like the GDR to allow enterprises some freedom to shop around for supplies and contracts, but one suspects that free contracting might leave quite a lot of Soviet enterprises, particularly on the periphery, without *any* contracts at all. That brings us right back to the whole issue of industrial restructuring, and its possibly very painful employment implications. Finally, we must remember that the GDR and Bulgaria are very small shows, so that a little decentralization goes much further towards cutting the central planners' task down to size than it could possibly in an economy the size of the Soviet. The planners in East Berlin plan 300–400 commodity groups. Their counterparts in Moscow are trying to grapple with more than 15,000. At the strictly technical level, then, there is an argument that the half-way house of the new East German and Bulgarian planning arrangements may not be enough for the Soviet Union.

Conclusions

(1) The main characteristics of the Soviet industrial sector are likely to inhibit Soviet freedom of action in the international field in the medium-term future. More specifically:

(2) It does not appear the Soviet economy is going to become much more heavily integrated into the world economy in the immediate future. The balance of payments constraint may impinge fairly sharply, especially if agricultural difficulties persist, and even if the upward trend in arms sales to the third world continues. This will make the purchase of foreign technology on a large scale difficult. Given the substantially less than maximum returns the Soviets obtain from technology transfer because of organizational problems, that may not be of dramatic importance, but coupled with domestic R & D problems it must mean that the civilian Soviet economy will remain significantly technically backward.

(3) Under given institutional arrangements, the defence component may be, from the *economic* point of view, the least inflexible component in National Income. We must presume that the Soviets have an economic interest in some kind of arms control.

(4) The new Soviet leadership might be prepared to take a much more

decisive approach to industrial planning reform, by which we mean something going rather further than the East German and Bulgarian models. If so, there would be a definite prospect of performance picking up in the medium term. Adjustments, both organizational and structural, might be so painful, however, as to involve an extended transition period when indicators would almost certainly get worse.

Notes

1 M.L. Weitzman, 'Industrial production', in A. Bergson and H.S. Levine (eds.), *The Soviet Economy: Towards the Year 2000* (London, George Allen and Unwin, 1983), p. 183.
2 United Nations, *Economic Survey of Europe in 1981* (New York, 1982), p. 223.
3 D.A. Dyker, *The Process of Investment in the Soviet Union* (Cambridge University Press, 1983), pp. 35–6.
4 R. Amann *et al.*, *The Technological Level of Soviet Industry* (New Haven, Connecticut, Yale University Press, 1977).
5 A. Tselikov, 'Metall i mashiny', *Pravda*, 6 March 1980, p. 2.
6 Dyker, *The Process of Investment*, pp. 185–8.
7 G.E. Schroeder and M.E. Denton, 'An index of consumption in the USSR', in US Congress, JEC, *USSR: Measures of Economic Growth and Development, 1950–80* (US GPO, 1982), p. 326.
8 A. Aganbegyan, 'Sdelai vse, chto mozhesh' ', *Trud*, 17 October 1981, p. 2.
9 D.A. Dyker, 'Planning and the worker', in L. Schapiro and J. Godson (eds.), *The Soviet Worker* (London, Macmillan, 1981), pp. 55–6.
10 T. Zaslavskaya, 'Doklad o neobkhodimosti bolee uglublennogo izucheniya v SSSR sotsial'nogo mekhanizma razvitiya ekonomiki', paper presented at a seminar in Moscow, April, 1983, published by Radio Liberty, *Materialy Samizdata*, Vypusk no. 35/83, 26 August 1983.
11 'V Tsentral'nom Komitete KPSS i Sovete Ministrov SSSR', *Ekonomicheskaya Gazeta*, no. 31, 1983, p. 5.
12 D.A. Dyker, 'Decentralization and the command principle – some lessons from Soviet experience', *Journal of Comparative Economics*, Vol. 5, no. 2, 1981.
13 G. Kulagin, 'Trudno byt' universalom', *Pravda*, 8 December 1983, p. 2.
14 Dyker, *The Process of Investment*, pp. 38–9.
15 I. Manyushis, 'Sochetanie otraslevogo i territorial'nogo upravleniya', *Voprosy Ekonomiki*, no. 7, 1983.
16 P. Rutland, 'The Shchekino method and the struggle to raise labour productivity in Soviet industry', *Soviet Studies*, forthcoming.
17 V. Fil'ev, 'Shchekinskiy metod i perspektivy ego dal'neishego razvitiya', *Voprosy Ekonomiki*, no. 2 (1983), pp. 58–9.
18 Ibid., p. 61.
19 P. Podshivalenko and V.D. Yevstigneev, 'Puti sovershenstvovaniya stroitel'nogo proizvodstva', *Ekonomika Stroitel'stva*, no. 5, 1980.
20 P. Podshivalenko, 'Organizatsionnyy formy stroitel'stva i upravleniya im', *Voprosy Ekonomiki*, no. 7, 1983, p. 91.

21 E.A. Kudashov, 'Most mezhdu starym i novym', *Ekonomika Stroitel'stva*, no. 9, 1983.

22 P. Hanson and M.R. Hill, 'Soviet assimilation of western technology; a survey of UK exporters' experience', in US Congress, JEC, *Soviet Economy in a Time of Change*, Vol. 2, (US GPO, 1979).

23 V. Chaika, 'Bez ucheta nuzhd poklupatelei', *Ekonomicheskaya Gazeta*, no. 41, 1983, p. 7.

24 V. Virkunen, 'Zheleznyy inter'er', *Ekonomicheskaya Gazeta*, no. 41, 1983, p. 24.

25 See R.W. Campbell, 'Management spillovers from Soviet space and military programmes', in *Soviet Studies*, Vol. XXIII, no. 4. 1972: M. Checinski, *The Military-Industrial Complex in the USSR*, no. AZ 2303, Stiftung Wissenschaft und Politik, Ebenhausen, September 1981.

26 See M. Cave, *Computers and Economic Planning: the Soviet Experience* (Cambridge University Press, 1980).

27 BBC SWB SU/7452/A1, 30 September 1983.

28 United Nations, *Economic Survey of Europe in 1982* (New York, 1983), p. 104.

29 Kh. Kirov, 'O novom ekonomicheskom mekhanizme v NRB', *Voprosy Ekonomiki*, no. 5, 1983, p. 120.

30 M. Melzer, 'Combine formation in the GDR', *Soviet Studies*, Vol. XXXIII, no. 1, 1981; P. Boot, 'Continuity and change in the planning system of the German Democratic Republic', *Soviet Studies*, Vol. XXXV, no. 3, 1983.

31 Boot, 'Continuity and change', p. 332.

32 Kirov, 'O novom', p. 125.

33 Ibid. p. 122.

7 Soviet Agriculture: Problems and Prospects

Alec Nove

The object of this paper is to examine the present situation on the 'agricultural front', to analyse the measures being taken to correct the many defects and distortions from which agriculture has been suffering, and to come to some tentative conclusions as to possible outcomes, looking forward to the end of the 1980s. It must be stressed that the defects and distortions which will be mentioned in the pages that follow have been repeatedly mentioned in Soviet publications. That they all have some negative effects would be agreed by every serious specialist in the Soviet Union itself. More difficult is to give them relative weights. This is important if, as is possible, some of the defects are remedied and others are not. Furthermore, some are interrelated. Thus, as we shall see, an improved system of labour incentives can be frustrated by the non-arrival of the needed material supplies.

It would be wrong not to recognize that there has been some progress. The gross value of Soviet agricultural output compares reasonably well with that of twenty years ago. It can be argued that its relative stagnation after the record year 1978 was due to four consecutive years of poor or very poor weather. Conversely, the fact that the grain harvest in 1982 was better than 1981, and 1983 seems better than 1982, is not yet evidence of any upward *trend*, since it is wholly explicable by the weather being less bad. (The actual grain harvest figures for all three years are, so far, a state secret.)

However, the increase has been achieved at immense cost. Agriculture has, directly and indirectly, been absorbing up to a third of total investment. Productivity (of land, labour, animals) remains low by international standards. The effort to modernize and mechanize has saved relatively little labour. Because labour is now much better paid, while the investments have too often been wasteful and misdirected (for reasons to be examined), the effect on costs of production can be characterized as startling, as the following figures show (in roubles per ton):

	Kolkhozy		*Sovhozy*	
	1970	*1980*	*1970*	*1980*
Grain (excl. maize)	50	76	53	84
Cotton	404	478	362	508
Sugarbeet	22	31	29	42
Potatoes	62	120	76	139
Beef (live weight)	1166	2177	1277	2344
Pork (live weight)	1194	2018	1111	1726
Milk	177	287	189	308
Eggs (thousand)*	73	87	64	64

* Eggs have 'benefited' from the spread of broilerhouses.

Source: *Nar.khoz.*, 1970 and 1980. The handbook published in 1982 gives no data for 1981.

The 1981 statistical handbook does not give the costs figures for that year, but only 1976–80 averages, which imply a still further rise in costs. Except for eggs and pork, *sovkhoz* costs are notably higher and have tended to increase faster.

Statistics on the labour force are of questionable precision and comparability, but for what it is worth we have the following:

	1965	*1975*	*1982*
Kolkhoz members*	18.6	15.2	12.8
Sovkhov workers	8.2	10.3	11.8

* 'Engaged in collective production'.

At all dates the above include some non-agricultural work.

Source: *SSSR v tsifrakh*, 1982, pp. 132, 135.

One must add an unknown figure for extra work on private plots. The decline in numbers is slow by international standards, and meanwhile pay of *kolkhoz* members has more than doubled (from 2.68 roubles per day to 5.84 roubles). As for prices of material inputs, these are supposedly stable, if official price indices are to be believed, in which case the huge increase in costs could be attributed partly to wages rising faster than labour productivity, and partly to inefficiency. Though there is certainly plenty of inefficiency, an important contributory reason is that new agricultural equipment and construction have become *much* more costly, as we shall see.

The following are the principal causes of inefficiency and malfunctioning.

(1) *Labour*. State and collective farms are large and impersonal, and it has proved very difficult to motivate the peasants and to relate effort to result. Many sources refer to the deleterious effects of piecework pay on the quality of the work performed. For example, tractor-drivers engaged in ploughing will tend to plough as shallow as possible, for this is the easiest way to fulfil a work-assignment measured in hectares while economizing on fuel. Frequently it proves impossible to persuade peasants to make extra efforts at harvest-time (some actually go to town to sell vegetables instead), and so a large and increasing number of people have to be mobilized annually to help with harvesting: students, soldiers, workers. According to E. Manevich, the numbers so mobilized more than doubled in the 1970s and reached the huge number of 15 million persons.[1] This is a notable burden for the rest of the economy. In addition, there are problems, by no means peculiar to the Soviet Union, caused by the migration of skilled young people out of the villages, which complicates the task of mechanization. Migration is attributed in part to lack of amenities of life in rural areas.

(2) *Infrastructure*. Soviet sources have referred repeatedly to the high cost of *bezdorozhye* ('roadlessness'), the damage caused to motor vehicles and to communications within the farms and between them and urban centres. There is equally notorious shortage of storage space – for grain and other farm products, for fertilizer, for machines. Lack of packaging materials is another recurrent theme. Very heavy losses of vegetables and fruit arise both from this cause and from the inability and reluctance of the procurement and trade organs to handle them, as well as to transport bottlenecks.

(3) *Capital equipment and material inputs*. Great and costly efforts have been made in the last 15–20 years to mechanize agriculture. In recent years as much as 27% of total investment has gone to agriculture, 33% if one includes the whole 'agro-industrial complex'. Yet many processes remain unmechanized because of what Soviet critics repeatedly refer to as *nekompleksnost'*, i.e. partial and lopsided mechanization. Farms are supplied with equipment by *Goskomsel'khoztekhnika*, about whose operations complaints abound. Thus it is repeatedly accused of making poor-quality and expensive repairs, while refusing to supply *sovkhozy* and *kolkhozy* with needed spare parts. However, this organization in turn suffers from the unresponsiveness of the agricultural machinery industry. Instead of producing the assortment of equipment that is actually needed, industry aimed at fulfilling aggregate plans in roubles. Because what is called *malaya mekhanizatsiya* ('small mechanization', such as loading equipment, grass-mowers, etc.) counts for little in plan fulfilment, orders for their production are not met. Further, there is

much evidence to show that new machinery, and also rural construction, became much more costly, contributing significantly to the escalation of agricultural costs, while quality of the equipment left much to be desired. It is not only in this sector that the influence of the customer over the producer is too weak, but this has had particularly unfortunate results in the context of the big and costly effort to mechanize agriculture.

(4) *Planning and coordination*. There was, firstly, the long-notorious tendency to interfere with everyday operations of farm management. Published complaints on this score could fill many pages. Despite the nominal autonomy of the farms, they receive orders as to what and when to sow, when to start harvesting, which crop rotations to adopt, even how to combat rats and mice; a quite recent article pointed out that before slaughtering one cow it is necessary to obtain seven authorization signatures in the *raion* and the *oblast'*.[2]

Agriculture also suffers from lack of coordination of *industrial* planning: thus fertilizer output greatly increased, but much of it never reaches its destination for lack of bags, storage space, equipment required to spread it. According to *Voprosy ekonomiki*, no less than 20 per cent of mineral fertilizer is lost in transit.[3] In addition land that needed phosphates would receive potash and vice versa.

Last but not least, the 1970s saw an increase in 'service' organizations, so-called 'partners' of *kolkhozy* and *sovkhozy*. Some organs (e.g. *Sel'khozkhimiya*, for 'chemicalization') were new, some (notably *Goskomsel'khoztekhnika*, mentioned above) had additional functions placed upon them, including the provision of many transport services. The effect was well described by I. Suslov:

> In the 1970s the conditions of economic operation (*khozraschyotnoi deyatel'nosti*) of *kolkhozy* altered greatly. . . . The effectiveness of *khozraschyot* methods gradually diminished, becoming largely formal. . . . The major part of means of production was supplied from outside (the farms) and this predetermined both the final results of the activities of the farms and the costs per unit of output. . . . The partners of kolkhozy in the agro-industrial complex are in a dominant position, their economic results depend little on the functioning of the agricultural enterprises. The latter are in a position of dependence on their partners in respect of all technical-production and economic-financial interrelationships. Narrow sectional interests of the sectors supplying means of production to agriculture took priority over the *khozraschyot* interests of *kolkhozy*, as a result of which their revenues ceased in large measure to relate to their real contribution to the final output. This was one of the most significant causes of the worsening of the financial-economic situation of most of the enterprises in the 1970s. . . . In this situation, a large part of enterprise expenditures was financed by state credits.'[4]

(We will see how rapidly these have grown.)

(5) *Private plots*. These still supply roughly a quarter of total Soviet agricultural output, despite the great difficulty in obtaining simple tools and supplies of fodder. For several years now the official line has been favourable to private-plot production. However, progress in this direction has been slow, partly because of chronic fodder shortage in years of poor harvests, partly because the younger peasants are not attracted to private livestock-raising, preferring leisure.

The party leadership expressed concern about the slow progress of agriculture, and gave high priority to the search for solutions. The May 1982 plenum, still under Brezhnev, took the following decisions of importance.

(1) *Organizational*. The long-discussed 'agro-industrial complex' was given a hierarchical structure, all the way from Moscow through the republics and *oblasti* to the localities. Represented at all levels are the large number of ministries and other organizations involved in the complex: agriculture, a relatively new ministry of Fruit and Vegetables, those involved in agricultural machinery production, *Sel'khoztekhnika*, *Sel'khozkhimiya*, the irrigation organization *Sel'khozpoliv*, Procurements, Trade, Rural Construction, and Food Industry. They should no longer work at cross-purposes, fulfilling quantitative plans. They should all be judged in relation to the final result, i.e. agricultural production and its delivery to its customers.

(2) Substantial increase in *investments in infrastructure*, including roads, means of transport, storage, and also rural amenities (housing, schools, water-supply, etc.), intended to persuade young and skilled people to stay in the villages.

(3) Substantial *rise in prices* for a wide range of farm products. This is rendered necessary by the very large increase in costs referred to above. Many farms are heavily in debt, and much of this debt is to be written off. The state of *kolkhoz* finances may be seen in the following figures:

	1965	*1981*
Net revenue	17.9	20.1
Of which, Paid to members	11.5	19.1

Source: *SSSR v tsifrakh*, 1982, p. 132.

'Net' revenue is the total value of output (excluding capital investment and capital repairs), less seeds, fodder, fertilizer, fuel, etc., used in current production. Obviously, this has meant that virtually all investment and capital repairs have been financed by credits, and these have increased very rapidly.

The figures for credits outstanding are truly extraordinary, and are worth citing in detail:

	1965	*1970*	*1975*	*1980*	*1981*
Short-term					
Agriculture, total	4.5	8.7	25.2	57.6	71.4
Of which: *kolkhozy*	0.4	2.45	10.1	25.7	31.6
Long-term					
Sovkhozy	—	0.46	5.1	8.4	8.2
Kolkhozy	3.9	10.3	17.8	34.0	38.3

Source: *Nar.khoz.*, 1922–82, p. 568.

So the rise in price is indeed necessary. However, since it is not apparently to be accompanied by any increase in retail prices, the already very high 'deficiency payment' or subsidy will become even higher. A sum of 50 billion roubles is one estimate.[5]

(4) *New and better labour incentives* include a commitment to expand the so-called *kollektivnyi podryad*, or group contract work. The May 1982 decree did not mention the much-discussed *beznaryadnoye zveno* by name, preferring the word *brigada*, but the principle is the same: a relatively small group of peasants (examples range from five to thirty) signs a contract with the state or collective farm, undertaking to produce a given item or items (wheat, flax, onions, milk, or whatever), or a complete crop rotation for five or more years on the same land, and to deliver these to the farm at an agreed reward related to the amount actually produced, while the farm undertakes to supply the needed material inputs. The essential points are that the group (brigade or *zveno*) organizes its own work, that it undertakes the entire sequence of necessary activities, and that it is paid by results. This is supposed to overcome both the alienation due to the impersonally large size of farms (often with a workforce of 500, scattered over several villages) *and* the lack of interest of peasants in the quality of their work, this being illustrated by the above-cited case of the tractor-brigade charged with ploughing and paid on a piecework basis, and which finds it 'economical' to plough shallow. Obviously, a member of a small group would be much more directly interested in doing an efficient job of ploughing, since his or her income would depend much more directly on the final product, and not on hectares of ploughing. It should be stressed that this approach has been under active discussion, on and off, for at least fifteen years. Some might recall even earlier arguments about the *zveno*,

dating back to the late 1940s and involving Andreyev, but the essential point of the present reform is not the existence as such of the *zveno* or small brigade, but its operational autonomy, expressed in the words *beznaryadnyi* ('without work-assignment') and *podryadnyi* ('contract'). However, official party backing was lacking, and some early experiments and experimenters came to grief; one recalls the sad fate of Khudenko. So the decision could be described as belated.

(5) *Private plots*. The May 1982 decisions had relatively little to say about them, but a number of earlier party resolutions stressed the desirability of encouraging them, in particular aiming to increase livestock production, by making it easier and cheaper to acquire animals and to feed them. Brezhnev in his speech in May 1982 argued that collective pay should once again have a sizeable 'in-kind' element, and clearly this was intended to include fodder for private livestock. Farms are being urged to sign contracts with peasant families for livestock-raising. Also state enterprises of all kinds are urged to set up *auxiliary farms*, to help supply their own employees.

This package of measures has been followed, in March 1983, by a more specific and more urgent commitment to the *kollektivnyi podryad*, this time with the brigade *and* the *zveno* specifically mentioned. The key documents are, firstly, the policy speech delivered at a conference in Belgorod by Gorbachev, the Politburo member in charge of agriculture, and, secondly, a series of sample contracts printed in *Ekonomicheskaya gazeta*.[6]

Gorbachev listed a number of characteristics of the group which are now being actively encouraged (see his speech reported in *Pravda*, 20 March 1983).

(1) The members join voluntarily, run their own affairs, and decide for themselves the system of payment for work done.
(2) They elect their own leader and decide on recruiting other members of the group.
(3) Fields and/or animals are assigned to the group 'for a long period', along with the needed tractors and other equipment, aiming to ensure work over the whole year.
(4) Each group is to have production tasks (*zadaniya*), together with norms regulating the supply of inputs, and the contract is to specify the level of payment and of bonuses for extra output, lower costs, etc.
(5) In years of very unfavourable weather, members of the group would be entitled to the pay which they would have had at piecework rates for the volume of work accomplished.

Gorbachev himself pointed to obstacles to success along this road. Thus in some areas the voluntary principle was disregarded, 'frequently they did not take into account the views of the workers concerning the forms of payment and of bonuses. Not seldom the management of *kolkhozy* and *sovkhozy* do not carry out their contractual obligations, and divert members of the group to other tasks.'

It must be recognized that there are a whole number of difficulties in implementing what seems to be a correct and much overdue decision, additional to those mentioned by Gorbachev. Imagine a typical multi-product *sovkhoz* and *kolkhoz*. Not all its tasks are readily divisible into small groups, and nor are all its tractors and other machinery. There could be substantial income-differentials between groups, and the groups and those still working for *sovkhozy* and *kolkhozy* on the old basis, which could be causes of considerable tension and discontent. There are also uneven peaks and troughs in demand for labour, and unforeseen emergencies of many kinds, which would also tend to introduce strain into the relationship between farm management and the small groups. The more so as they are accustomed to issue *commands* to their workforce, and must now learn to negotiate and observe *contracts* with them, and the task of negotiating a fair and mutually acceptable contract will surely be genuinely difficult.

But, in my view, even more serious is the problem of *material supply*. In books and articles a truly vast number of Soviet writers have deplored the distortions engendered by the supply system on the one hand and the links with industry on the other. Industry's primary task is still essentially one of fulfilling global plans, in roubles of gross or net value, or in units, tons. Transport undertakings have plans in ton-kilometres, irrigation plans are expressed in tons of water, fertilizer plans are in tons of nutrient. The product mix is adapted to these measures. Thus completed machines 'score' better for plan fulfilment than spare parts, large and dear machines more than small and cheap ones. The prevailing shortages make of the customer what one author called 'a supplicant', victim of a take-it-or-leave-it attitude on the part both of industry and of intermediate 'service' organizations such as *Sel'khoztekhnika*. Judging from published criticism its behaviour has not improved since the May 1982 decisions. Prices for services rendered have sharply increased (*vsvincheny*); work which would cost 5 roubles in the *kolkhoz* workshop cannot be done because *Sel'khoztekhnika* refuses to sell spares, and charges 200 roubles for doing the work that might have cost 5. It has increased the charge for delivery of machinery to the farms, yet the farms still often have to fetch them themselves and then assemble them.[7] Similar problems are reported a year later.[8] Long-planned and long-promised equipment for the mechanization of auxiliary tasks, and other kinds of small-scale equipment and attachments, do not enter production. Complaints are published about *nekompleksnost'*, lack of 'complementary' equipment, which causes labour bottlenecks.

Clearly, such deficiencies in industrial planning and material supply gravely handicap agriculture, and, unless they are corrected, the new labour-incentive system cannot operate effectively. Yet can they be corrected without a radical restructuring of the industrial planning system, and without scrapping the impossibly clumsy materials supply arrangements and substituting – at long last – wholesale trade in means of production for administrative allocation? Can one envisage such a reform, either in general or confined to inputs for agriculture?

A decree was published in *Pravda* on 22 July 1983 'on the perfecting of economic relations of agriculture with other sectors of the economy'. This laid down that the performance of organizations serving agriculture (e.g. *Sel 'khoztekhnika, Sel' khozkhimiya*, etc.) will be evaluated in relation to increases achieved in agricultural production on the farms they serve (and about time too, one might add!), as well as carrying out their contractual obligations, with costs and charges limited to the average of the previous three years. The importance of these service organizations, whose number proliferated in the 1970s, has already been stressed. These measures must be seen as an attempt to overcome the absurd situation, described for instance by Ipatenko, when 'partners' (in this case it must be *Sel 'khoztekhnika*) which ought to provide transport services refuse to send much-needed lorries because for them it is 'not advantageous' (*nevygodno*), i.e. it does not help them to fulfil *their* plan. But there is not a word in that decree on the agricultural machinery or chemicals industry, and they too have been gravely at fault.[9]

This brings one to the *agro-industrial complex*. This was and is supposed to cause all concerned to pull together. Yet will this be the case? It looks like yet another restriction on the already very limited rights of farm management. True, these organs are supposed to ensure coordination, but what powers will they have in practice? The enterprises making mowers, harrows, tractor-attachments, bags for fertilizer, milking machines, etc. will still be under the authority of 'their' ministries and not of the agroindustrial association. One has visions of crossed wires, administrative confusion, of coordinators of coordinators, especially at provincial and district level, where the powers to give orders to anyone except the farms is far from clear. Naturally, we must suspend judgement, but scepticism would not be altogether unreasonable, especially given past experience.

The above paragraph had already been written when proof arrived that this anticipation had been correct, though apparently there are considerable local variations. One *kolkhoz* chairman, from the Kursk province, writes: 'No, everything remains as before. Our partners think mainly of their own concerns. So they do not do what *kolkhozy* and *sovkhozy* most urgently need, but follow their own interest. Thus the agrochemical organization transports organic fertilizer to the fields, clocking up ton-kilometres for their plan, and leaves it to us to spread it. But here is our difficulty: we do not have the needed machinery, since hardly any has been delivered to *kolkhozy* since the creation of the *raisel 'khozkhimiya*. Why is the regional agroindustrial association (RAPO) powerless?' True, in the same issue of *Pravda*[10] the chairman of a RAPO from Tula asserts that it has some powers, but he too speaks of a multitude of unsettled problems, one of which was well defined by another *kolkhoz* chairman, this time from North Ossetia: 'the partners, as is known, are under dual subordination' and in many instances are forbidden by their superiors to agree to RAPO proposals. It must be appreciated that their superiors (i.e. for instance the republican or all-union *Sel'khozkhimiya*) have plans to fulfil in value or quantitative terms, and exercise pressure on their subordinates accordingly. This, of course, conflicts with the declared aim that RAPO should exercise control and that reward should relate to the 'final result', i.e. agricultural production. This administrative confusion may be a temporary 'growing-pain', but it will not be easy to find an effective solution, given the nature of the hierarchically-structured planning system.[11]

The other measures taken, and referred to above, should be of some value. Higher prices will improve the financial situation of farms, the expenditures on infrastructure will do something to correct many years of neglect. Some other long-tolerated abuses are to cease, such as for instance the transport at high cost of grain to the state elevators or collection-points followed by transport of some of this grain back to the farm from which it came. We are yet again told that the practice of constant interference with farm management is to cease, but not only is this likely to get worse as a result of the creation of agroindustrial complexes, the habit persists of the party leadership issuing decrees demanding that party and state organs ensure the carrying out of various policy measures concerning agriculture, which logically necessitates interference; the latest example noted is the decree reported on 20 August 1983 on 'additional measures for the ensuring of timely harvesting, procurements and processing of sugarbeet in 1983'. The decree is issued by the central committee and the Council of Ministers of the USSR. Half of the column is occupied by a list of party and state organs (the republican party and government organs, all-union ministries, local party committees and – last on the list – agroindustrial associations) to take a long list of measures, most of which clearly necessitate giving orders to any farm that grows sugarbeet.

Worse: according to yet other critical articles, a recent division of the Ministry of Agriculture into two parts (the other being the ministry of Fruit and Vegetables) has sown confusion.[12] The new ministry is supposed, 'within the agroindustrial complex', to ensure production and distribution of these items. Results: firstly, trade organs are more than ever determined not to handle fruit and vegetables, leaving this to the ministry's network. Secondly, state farms and *kolkhozy* that grow fruit and vegetables are described as being 'under dual subordination', with part of their activities, plans and finances under this ministry and part under the Ministry of Agriculture, in respect of their other crops and their livestock. Orders (*sic*) to grow more vegetables can and do conflict with established crop rotations. The two ministries are in dispute as to whose scarce allocated inputs (*fondy*) are supposed to be sent to which farms for which purposes.

Surely the only sound way out is to grant decision-making powers to *farm management*, and to make the 'service' organs act as subcontractors. This seems still far away.

Also it is essential to prevent what has clearly been highly wasteful use of capital investments. The 1970s saw a big effort to modernize (especially) the livestock sector, and one unintended result was the huge increase in costs shown above. The huge increase was a result not only of the sharp rise in costs of machines and of construction. Evidently the investments were frequently imposed on farms regardless of local circumstances. Thus some reports speak of big expensive and mechanized piggeries and cowsheds, which could not be properly utilized because around them was a sea of mud, and the required fodder supplies were not forthcoming. It is inherently absurd to design an expensive tractor which is supposed to operate with thirty or so attachments, and then supply only five of the attachments. Several sources point out that many tractors, combines, lorries, have a very short life, because of bad roads, poor maintenance, lack of spares, and that consequently the net increase in the supply of these items has been quite small. One must mention again the issue of *nekompleksnost'*: the economic value of one stage of mechanization is nullified because the next stage is still unmechanized. Simple and cheap investments, such as shelters or barns to keep machinery, fertilizer or grain out of the rain or the snow, continue to be neglected, since the farms either do not have the resources or cannot obtain the materials, which does not prevent very large sums being devoted to what have been called 'pig hotels'. One *Krokodil* cartoon showed a pile of fertilizer under the rain on a farm. A visitor said to the farm manager: 'This is disgraceful! What would an inspector say?' To which the manager replied: 'An inspector would come here on *these* roads?' Another satirist suggested that if the piles of fertilizer lying at railway sidings were left there long enough, they would solidify, and could then perhaps be used as building materials – to build storage space for fertilizer.

But enough of catalogues of past errors and omissions. Every effort is being made, under the energetic leadership of Gorbachev and the support of Chernenko, to put things right. We cannot assume that the measures will have no result. Lessons have been learned. Reports which include much (if not indeed much more) of the critical material here reproduced have been on the desks of party leaders. Their will to act is beyond doubt. The only question is the likely degree of malfunctioning of the system, its resistance to change, its inertia, as well as the potential responsiveness of the peasantry to a new approach. It would be absurd to suggest that any of this can be precisely quantified.

Yet we would all wish an answer to the question: what are the prospects of Soviet agricultural production in the rest of this decade? No model can tell us this: the authors of the *Sovmod* projection – in the very interesting *The Soviet Economy to the Year 2000* (edited by Bergson and Levine) would be the first to admit that their projection of agricultural output and of the grain harvest is rather problematic. It is a matter of judgement: how effective will be the measures being taken (allowing for weather variations)? What, on various assumptions, would be the effects on Soviet foreign trade and the world's markets for grain and meat? Given the USSR's declared policy objective of diminishing their import dependence, will it in fact diminish?

Let us list some key variables.

(1) *Grain harvest.* This has been adversely affected by four consecutive years of below-average weather (outstandingly bad in 1981, not so bad in 1982, better in 1983, but all below the claimed average for 1976–80, which was 205 million tons). The plan for 1981–5 envisaged 235 millions. Harvest figures have become a state secret, but the first three years of the quinquennium are likely to average at around 182–5, according to foreign observers. Even if 1984 and 1985 prove well above average in terms of weather, even if the harvest in both years equals the all-time record (which was reached in 1978), the five-year average would not exceed the 205 which was the average for the previous quinquennium. Purchases from abroad could decline from the very high levels necessitated by the four relatively poor harvests (1980–3), but it would still average at least 15 million tons a year – *unless* the new measures would make possible the surpassing of past records, which (in favourable weather) is not excluded. Even in 1978, grain yields in the

USSR were modest by international standards: 18.5 centners (1.8 tons) per hectare. Long-term plans could be reached, import dependence decisively lessened, if 20 centners could be achieved and maintained, for that would bring the USSR close to the objective of a ton of grain per head, and would sustain a notably higher livestock population. But 18.5 centners was only reached under conditions of very favourable weather, and plans must be based on the expectation of average conditions. By the end of the decade, 18 centners *may* become the average which, allowing for the slight decline in area sown to grain, would give a harvest of 225 million tons.

(2) *Policy with regard to livestock and livestock products.* The effect of such a grain harvest on import requirements depends decisively on what it is intended to feed to how many animals. This in turn depends on price policy, in this case the policy for *retail* prices. The big unsatisfied demand for meat and dairy produce is above all the consequence of low subsidized prices, unchanged since 1962 (while money incomes have doubled). To satisfy this demand at existing prices would require so large a build-up of livestock herds as to necessitate substantial imports even if grain harvests in and after 1984 reach 225 million tons on average. True, the diet of Soviet animals is unbalanced, grain requirements could be reduced by increasing the supply of other fodder: hay, root crops, also chemical additives. This is unlikely to make much difference in the short run. There are other policy alternatives. One is a very sharp (and much overdue) increase in retail prices, which could reduce demand for meat and dairy produce. Another is a decision to ration them. Still another is deliberately to go on tolerating shortages, as they are doing today, while placating working-class discontent by selling meat at factory canteens. It must be stressed that there is no fixed coefficient or hard-and-fast rule, which compels policy-makers to act in some definite way. At a given level of grain output, the size of livestock herds and the extent of import dependence are to some degree policy variables.

(3) *Foreign trade policy and the international situation.* Another variable is the degree to which priority will be given to lessening import dependence for grain, and this in turn can affect the level of imports whatever the state of the harvest, if the international situation seems so tense that it can provide an alibi for shortages. Policy can also affect the sources of Soviet purchases. They might wish to 'punish' America for its endless talk of sanctions and 'centre of evil' by buying elsewhere – or on the contrary continue to buy from America in the hope that this might cause pressure on the President to be less disagreeable in his policies. Purchases from Europe (at subsidized prices) may be favoured

not only because prices are low, but also because of Soviet political interests in Europe. So this is another unpredictable variable.

In this connection, it is interesting to note the sharp rise in Soviet imports of grain from Argentina, as a response to the US embargo. Thus in the agricultural years 1980/1 and 1981/2 imports from Argentina averaged around 12 million tons. It was far-sighted of the Soviets never to utter public criticism of the Argentinian military, while they were denouncing the Pinochet regime in Chile (but Chile had no grain surplus!). A reasonable forecast is that the USSR will continue to spread its grain purchases around, seeking to avoid excessive dependence on any one supplier, deriving some satisfaction from not buying as much from the United States as the United States now wishes to sell, while pursuing the clearly-enunciated aim of reducing import dependence. Just as some American economic-warfare specialists used to speak of using 'the grain weapon', so the USSR's policy planners will doubtless try to use the Soviet position as a big grain importer to win friends and influence people – as well as getting the grain as cheaply as possible. Be it noted that the volume of Soviet purchases of machinery and equipment from the West has been falling, no doubt also due in some part to a desire to reduce dependence and vulnerability, even while the Soviet balance of payments position is relatively healthy. Thus the 1983 figures, January–September, are reported to be as follows, in milliards of roubles:

Capitalist developed countries	*Exports*	14.13
	Imports	14.45
Underdeveloped countries	*Exports*	7.60
	Imports	5.65

Source: *Vneshnaya torgovlya*, no. 12, 1983.

Much more serious is the position of most of the USSR's allies, both in Europe and overseas. Few have food surpluses, most have food deficits, *and* acute balance of payments problems too. The USSR's evident inability to supply them is therefore a source of embarrassment. It may in fact be necessary to solve the problem by granting them hard-currency credits to buy in the West. But that is another story.

May I end by forecasting (without too solid a basis) an average grain harvest of 210–20 million tons for the years 1984–8, permitting a 10–15 per cent increase in production of meat and milk, and a reduction of some 30–40 per cent in the high levels of agricultural (especially grain) imports of the most recent years – which, in the absence of a substantial increase in retail prices, will mean continued shortages.

Appendix Output of principal agricultural products

(annual averages)

	1971–5	1976–80	1980	1981	1982	1983
Grain	181.6	205	189	(150)	(180)	(190)
Cotton	7.67	8.93	9.96	9.6	9.3	9.2
Sunflower seed	5.97	5.32	4.65	4.6	5.3	n.a.
Sugar beet	76.0	88.4	79.6	60.6	71.3	82
Potatoes	89.8	82.6	67.0	72	78	83
Meat	14.0	14.8	15.1	15.2	15.2	16.0
Milk	87.4	92.7	90.9	88.5	90.1	96.4

Source: *Nar.khoz.*, 1980, and *SSSR v tsifrakh 1982* and *Pravda*, 29 January 1984. The figures in brackets are rough estimates.

Total livestock numbers (1 January)

(million head)

	1971	1976	1983
Cattle	99.2	111.0	117.1
Of which			
Cows	39.8	41.9	43.7
Pigs	67.5	57.9	76.5
Sheep	138.0	141.4	142.1
Of which private livestock			
Cows	15.5	13.7	13.4
Pigs	16.6	12.2	15.8
Sheep	28.9	25.0	26.9

Source: *SSSR v tsifrakh*, 1982.

Notes

1 *Voprosy ekonomiki*.
2 *Pravda*, 17 December 1983.
3 No. 2, 1982.
4 *Voprosy ekonomiki*, no. 12, 1982, pp. 26–7.
5 Belkin and Ivanter, *Planovaya sbalansirovanost'*, M., 1983.
6 E.g. nos. 15, 27, 31, 36, of 1983, among others.
7 *Pravda*, 3 January 1983.
8 *Pravda*, 17 December 1983, 5 January 1984.
9 *Pravda*, 3 January 1983.
10 17 December 1983.
11 *Pravda*, 5 January 1984.
12 *Pravda*, 25 and 26 May 1983.

8 International Trade and Resources*

Alan H. Smith

This chapter will examine the influence of international trade considerations on Soviet foreign policy. The principal domestic factors are considered to be the nature of the Soviet economic system itself and the domestic resource base of labour and raw materials. An additional domestic factor will be the internal evaluation of economic problems and the sources of advice available to the Soviet leadership. The principal questions are whether these factors cause the USSR to be dependent on imports and whether this requires the USSR to make accommodations in its foreign policy. The trade implications of Soviet relations with Eastern Europe and the third world will be examined to determine whether they represent an item of cost to the USSR or whether they offer an alternative to trade links with the West.

The nature of the economic system and the resource base

A high rate of industrial growth was achieved in the 1930s and the immediate post-war period by maintaining a high rate of growth of industrial inputs of labour, capital and raw materials (concentrating these resources towards priority sectors such as capital goods and defence) and by utilizing foreign technical processes. As reserves of domestic resources are fully employed bottlenecks start to occur which will have to be covered by imports or will require a change in domestic priorities. This pattern of 'extensive growth' has implications for foreign trade and raises critical questions for the leadership.

1. The emphasis on gross output and energy intensive production increases the demand for raw materials. The USSR is favourably endowed with basic materials, but the growth in demand has exceeded the capacity of the more accessible deposits. The development of deposits in the less hospitable terrains of Siberia and the Arctic requires additional capital outlays for the prospecting, extraction and transportation of these resources and in turn leads to bottlenecks in the

* I am grateful to other members of the study group and to Philip Hanson for comments on earlier drafts of this chapter.

construction and transportation sectors. The question of whether it is more profitable to develop domestic resources or to rely on imports has been aggravated by the extension of the growth model to the resource-poor countries of Eastern Europe.

2. As the possibility of increasing the industrial labour force by the transfer of labour from agriculture and by increased female participation has decelerated, the demand for labour-saving technology has increased and enterprises have responded to labour shortage by increasing wage-earnings faster than the growth of output of consumer goods and foodstuffs. Retail prices have not risen to absorb this demand and money balances have accumulated in the hands of the population (estimated by Birman to be almost equivalent to the annual turnover in state retail stores in 1978[1]). The Soviet leadership has to decide whether to meet this demand by imports, by re-allocating domestic resources, by confiscatory financial or fiscal measures, or simply by allowing imbalances to continue.

3. Western research suggests that the hierarchical planning system results in a low incentive to innovate at the enterprise level and in slow diffusion of new processes and poor development of new products.[2] The Soviet leadership has to decide whether to place greater emphasis on improving domestic innovation or on importing Western processes.

4. The Soviet economy is essentially constrained by supply rather than demand. The value of exports lies largely in the resources they permit planners to obtain. The problems analysed by David Dyker in Chapter 6 raise the question of what to export if bottlenecks are to be alleviated by imports.

The importance of trade to the Soviet economy

The net trade balances shown in Table 8.1 indicate the difference between domestic production patterns and resources available to Soviet planners as a result of foreign trade. The USSR has remained a net importer of machinery and industrial consumer goods since the War, while net imports of foodstuffs have become important since the early 1960s. Fuel and energy are the major net exports, while exports of unprocessed metals and raw materials have been offset in the last decade by imports of specialized steel products. Approximately 15–18 per cent of Soviet exports and 4–8 per cent of imports are not identified by commodity.

The importance of trade to the Soviet economy cannot be measured adequately by foreign trade prices, as different price systems are used in the domestic economy, in intra-CMEA trade and in trade with the West. When imports are re-evaluated at domestic prices they are substantially higher in relation to GNP than when measured at external

Table 8.1 Soviet visible trade balances

(million transferable roubles)

	1950	1960	1970	1975	1982
Machinery and equipment	−91	−483	−1272	−4547	−11 257
Fuels and energy	−92	+599	+1586	+6506	+30 440
Ores, concentrates, metals[a]	−14	+171	+1244	+343	−910
Foodstuffs	+103	+43	−701	−4981	−12 359
Industrial consumer goods	−18	−726	−1622	−2696	−5964
Other specified[b]	+100	+112	+213	+428	+632
Unspecified	+310	+227	+1511	+2309	+6171
Balance	+305	−58	+962	−2637	+6754

[a] including steel and metal products.
[b] Chemicals, fertilizers, rubber, textiles, wood and cellulose, raw materials of agricultural origin.
Source: *Vneshnyaya Torgovlya*, various years.

prices. Bogomolov estimates that imported consumer goods accounted for 10 per cent of Soviet retail trade turnover at internal prices in 1978.[3] Treml estimates that Soviet imports measured at domestic prices have been steadily increasing in importance and could now reach 15 per cent of GNP.[4]

Principal features of Soviet trade with non-socialist countries

The principal features of Soviet trade with non-socialist countries are shown in Tables 8.2 and 8.3, in which unspecified trade has, where possible, been allocated by comparison with trade partners' data and other official sources. Unspecified exports to industrialized countries have been largely identified as diamonds, non-ferrous metals and other precious metals, while a significant volume of exports to developing countries cannot be identified and probably comprises arms.

Two Western studies of Soviet trade relations with non-socialist countries indicate a shift in the post-Khrushchev era from traditionalist assumptions of Soviet economic and technical superiority towards a more realistic appraisal of the relative strengths and weaknesses of socialist and capitalist economic systems.[5]

Parrott argues that the more pessimistic prognoses were used by conservative factions as grounds for increased expenditure on defence and domestic research, while non-traditionalists used the same analysis to promote reduced arms expenditure and increased contacts with the West, which would enable the USSR to acquire Western technology.[6] Although Kosygin viewed limited domestic reform and technology

Table 8.2 Soviet exports to non-socialist countries

(million transferable roubles)

	1972	1975	1977	1981	1982
To industrialized nations					
Machinery and equipment	90	262	247	355	327
Fuel and energy	800	3400	5535	13 400	15 100
Precious metals/ diamonds[a]	760	1000	1330	1600	1650
Other	791	1478	1705	1892	1772
Total	2441	6140	8817	17 247	18 849
To developing countries					
Machinery and equipment	670	819	1058	1605	1847
Fuel and energy	79	338	446	1450	1584
Precious metals[a]	100	111	67	62	64
Other specified	212	526	556	623	759
Unspecified	947	1512	3210	4929	5926
Total	2008	3306	5337	8669	10 180

[a] excluding gold.

Source: *Vneshnyaya Torgovlya*, various years cross-referenced to partners' data.

Table 8.3 Soviet imports from non-socialist countries

(million transferable roubles)

	1972	1976	1979	1980	1981	1982
Machinery	1138	4388	4575	4714	4438	6031
of which USA	48	621	342	311	201	169
Metals and steel	537	2091	3041	3360	3525	3767
Foodstuffs of which	1322	3173	4307	6361	9819	7567
(i) USA	320	1283	1880	816	1143	1536
(ii) other American continent	335	832	679	2054	3917	2557
Industrial consumer goods	440	735	695	1194	1815	1648
Total[a]	4719	6425	16 437	20 813	25 889	25 595

[a] including other goods.

Source: *Vneshnyaya Torgovlya*, various years.

imports as complementary, the full move to détente did not materialize until Brezhnev took a midway position and allayed conservative opposition by arguing that technology imports were a necessary substitute for deeper domestic reform.

Until the Brezhnev-Nixon summit of 1972 Soviet imports from the West consisted largely of machinery and equipment and steel products obtained from Western Europe and Japan, and grain from Canada, Argentina and to a lesser extent Australia. Soviet-US trade (with the exception of grain imports in 1964) was neglible. The increase in Soviet imports from 1972 to 1978 was largely concentrated on capital goods, particularly machinery and metal products, and although the absolute growth of US exports of these items was small, the political significance was considerable, while in addition substantial amounts of US grain were imported following the bad Soviet harvests of 1974 and 1975.

In the period up till 1977 borrowing from the West (much of which was government backed) played a significant role in financing Soviet imports. The wisdom of giving official credit support to the USSR was questioned in the USA, and the Jackson–Vanik and Stevenson amendments to the 1974 Trade Act sought to give greater Congressional control over lending to the USSR by limiting official credit support to 40 million dollars on energy projects and by linking increases in US lending to freer emigration policies. This effectively ruled out US cooperation in Soviet proposals to develop natural gas resources in eastern and western Siberia, the sheer scale of which required substantial inputs of financial and physical capital. The USSR cancelled its trade agreement with the USA and concentrated on the development of natural gas deposits in northwest Siberia, with European and Japanese cooperation to supply East and West Europe by pipeline.

These factors are reflected in the structure of Soviet trade. Over 93 per cent of Soviet imports of machinery and equipment from non-socialist countries come from Western Europe and Japan together with 98 per cent of imports of metal products, including material for pipeline construction. Oil and gas predominate in exports to Western Europe (reaching 82 per cent in 1982) while precious metals account for a further 9 per cent. Wood and lumber still predominate in Soviet exports to Japan but the development of BAM (the Baikal Amur Railway) will facilitate exports of east-Siberian coking coal.

A change in policy occurred after 1978. Imports of machinery declined and the value of imported foodstuffs doubled between 1979 and 1981. Although this coincides with bad harvests the volume of food imports was sufficient to allow a small (2–3 per cent) annual increase in per capita foodstuff consumption, according to official statistics. The initial increase in grain imports was centred on the USA, but following the partial US grain embargo in 1980, import growth was concentrated on Argentina and Canada. The level of net indebtedness to the West was also reduced during this period and imports were largely financed through the increase in value of oil exports and gold sales. Finally a shift

Table 8.4 Western estimates of Soviet hard-currency sources

(million dollars)

	1972	1975	1977	1979	1980	1981
Net borrowing from West	555	7451	11 230	10 400	9400	10 800
Arms deliveries to 3rd World	1215	2040	4705	6615	—	—
For hard currency	122	793	1500	—	—	—
Gold sales	380	725	1618	1490	1780	2700
Dollars per rouble	1.21	1.39	1.36	1.52	1.55	1.38

Sources: Net borrowing 1972–79, military deliveries for hard currency 1972–79: Ericson and Miller, 'Soviet Foreign Economic Behaviour: A Balance of Payments Perspective', in Soviet Economy in a Time of Change, Joint Economic Committee US Congress.

Gold sales, arms deliveries: CIA estimates. Net borrowing 1980–81: J. Vanous, Convertible currency indebtedness CMEA countries, NATO Colliquium, 1983.

back towards imports of capital goods in 1982 was again covered by oil revenues, while imports of consumer items were cut back marginally (see Table 8.3).

The analysis of Soviet trade with the third world is complicated by the fact that nearly 60 per cent of Soviet exports are unspecified by commodity and approximately 50 per cent by country of destination. The unspecified commodity trade in the 1970s broadly corresponds with CIA estimates of Soviet arms deliveries to the third world (see Tables 8.2 and 8.4) although some observers consider this to be an underestimate.[7] Machinery and equipment (which includes vehicles suitable for military purposes) accounts for a further 18 per cent of exports. The USSR has restricted its sales of energy and precious metals to developing countries, the major recipient being India.

Valkenier shows that Soviet policy-makers had emphasized the potential economic benefits to the USSR from exporting machinery to developing countries in exchange for raw materials as early as 1952.[8] Khrushchev's implementation of this policy was overtly political and links were developed with non-aligned countries, and particularly from 1959 to 1964 to newly independent, former colonies.

As the latter were not rich in industrial raw materials, trade and aid were closely related with the USSR supplying capital for prestige projects with repayment in traditional exports or local currency over long periods at low interest rates.

A more realistic commercial policy followed the downfall of Khrushchev. The quality of Soviet civilian engineering products frequently makes them uncompetitive on these markets. The armaments industry, as a high priority sector, attracts the best labour and inputs and its products are more readily saleable. The increasing commercialization of this trade in the 1970s is reflected in both the recipients and the method of payment. Middle-Eastern and North-African nations (principally Libya, Iraq, Syria and Algeria) have been the major importers, and it is estimated that between 40 and 65 per cent of arms deliveries in the 1970s were paid for in hard currency, earning 16–21 billion dollars.[9]

An economic motive for deliveries to poorer states in sub-Saharan Africa is less obvious. Here, the USSR appears to be accumulating trade surpluses with countries with no apparent hard-currency balances, although it is possible that subsequent repayment will be made in the form of raw materials.

This type of compensation trade (and its hazards) can be illustrated by the small but growing volume of energy imports from the Middle East which reached 1.5 billion roubles in 1982. This trade largely comprises crude oil liftings from Libya, Syria and until the Gulf war, Iraq, which are immediately re-exported to Europe. Natural gas was also imported from Iran and Afghanistan to supply southern Soviet republics, freeing other supplies for delivery to Europe where prices are much higher. Both sources were curtailed in 1979, but imports from Afghanistan are now running at higher levels than previously, while Iran is demanding higher prices for resumed deliveries.

Finally it is noticeable that Soviet exports to non-socialist countries are heavily concentrated on countries either immediately proximate to Soviet borders or close to European Russia and Black Sea ports. This may be explained by the concentration of Soviet enterprises manufacturing for export in the Baltic region, the areas around Moscow and Leningrad and the Ukraine.[10]

Economic relations with Eastern Europe

The Stalinist economic system was effectively transferred to Eastern Europe in the period 1948–53. Following the outbreak of the Korean war, Stalin placed additional emphasis on the construction of a heavy industrial base in each individual CMEA nation, but as the latter were less favourably endowed with basic raw materials they depended on Soviet supplies of fuel and raw materials to meet industrial output targets. Consequently each separate country developed parallel industrial structures, replicating each other's output patterns, and the radial trade pattern emerged whereby the East European countries concentrated their trade on the USSR and tended to undertrade with one another.

The industrial pattern also resulted in the overproduction of heavy industrial goods and engineering products that were relatively difficult to sell on western markets (soft goods) and excess demand for more readily saleable commodities (hard goods) such as raw materials and more recently foodstuffs and higher quality consumer goods.

By the end of the 1950s the majority of CMEA governments were agreed on the need for greater consultation and integration to overcome these problems, but the methods to be used were the subject of dispute.[11] Two alternative methods of integration are possible in theory. The first involves increased decentralization entailing direct links between enterprises on the basis of price and profit criteria reaching as far as spontaneous trade relations between enterprises in different countries, and the second involves a greater degree of plan coordination so that the bloc implications of domestic investment decisions are examined before national plans are formulated.

In practice most integration proposals combine plan and money levers, but Soviet proposals have consistently implied that the latter should be subservient to the former. During 1962 Khrushchev proposed to establish a CMEA investment bank which would raise capital for joint ventures in the extraction and transportation of energy for bloc use and made proposals to limit the location of material intensive industries to the area of extraction, and in November 1962 proposed to establish a common planning organ to implement these policies. The strengthening of the socialist bloc as a whole was an essential component of Khrushchev's concept of peaceful competition between socialism and capitalism. The supranational implications of Khrushchev's proposals were resisted by Romania, and following Khrushchev's overthrow, Soviet leaders shifted their attention from the problems of integration to the costs involved in supplying energy and raw materials to Eastern Europe. It was argued that the long-run marginal cost of developing energy was higher than the world market price and that if East European nations could obtain supplies more economically from outside the bloc, they should do so. Alternatively CMEA nations should participate in joint ventures to develop Soviet supplies.[12]

Following the Warsaw Pact invasion of Czechoslovakia and the enunciation of the Brezhnev doctrine, Kosygin returned to the theme of joint planning in a speech to a special session of CMEA, held in April 1969, in which he made a number of proposals remarkably similar to those of Khrushchev, but carefully avoided the implications of supranationality by proposing that decisions should be first agreed by joint meetings of representatives of national planning agencies who would then be responsible for their domestic implementation, and that countries need not participate in projects in which they had no interest.[13]

The OPEC price increases of 1974, which made the development of Soviet energy supplies profitable provided a major stimulus to the establishment of joint ventures in the energy sector. In the mid 1970s two apparently significant innovations were the Agreed Plan of Multilateral Integration Measures (1976–80), a series of joint investments in the energy sector, chiefly situated in the USSR, whereby participants' capital costs are repaid in the form of products, and the Long Term Target Programmes, which involve investment coordination over a long-term perspective in five sectors of the economy, but which in practice have been limited to the energy and food supply sectors.

A critical question concerns the distribution of costs and benefits between CMEA members and changes in the system of intra-CMEA pricing have brought world market prices to bear more rapidly on CMEA prices. In 1975 the price for agreed quota deliveries was altered to reflect an average of the preceding three years' world market prices, and from 1976 onwards prices have changed annually to reflect an average of the preceding five years' world market prices. Deliveries not established in quotas are subject to bilateral negotiations, but the general formula for the delivery of hard goods (including over-quota oil) is that they are paid for in hard currency at current world market prices.

The effect of the changed price formula has been to change the terms of trade within CMEA in favour of the USSR by approximately the amount resulting from changes in oil prices (i.e. other price changes have effectively cancelled each other out). In the period 1975–77 approximately two-thirds of this gain to the USSR was reflected in Soviet balance of trade surpluses, while only one-third was paid for by increased imports. In 1978 the value of Soviet imports of machinery from Eastern Europe increased from 6.6 to 9.2. billion roubles, all but eliminating the trade surplus.[14] Table 8.5 indicates that this process has been repeated following the second round of OPEC price increases in 1979. The physical volume of Soviet exports to CMEA in 1982 was slightly below the level for 1979 (row 7). Rows 14 and 15 are crude estimates of the value of Soviet trade with Eastern Europe at 'comparable prices', after allowing for trade with the less developed CMEA members. They indicate a small growth in the real volume of Soviet imports and exports to Eastern Europe in the period from 1979 to 1981, while the increase in the money value of Soviet exports (row 1) can be largely attributed to oil price increases, by comparing rows 3 and 12. Thus the greater part of Soviet oil price gains from 1979 to 1981 were again reflected in a balance of trade surplus (row 6). In 1982 Soviet imports from Eastern Europe again increased substantially in real

Table 8.5 Soviet trade with Eastern Europe

(billion transferable roubles)

	1975	1979	1980	1981	1982
Basic value data					
Soviet exports	11.9	18.5	20.9	24.3	26.3
Of which					
Energy	3.2	7.0	8.5	11.1	13.2
Oil	2.1	5.0	5.9	7.7	9.1
Soviet imports	11.3	17.5	19.1	21.2	24.3
Of which					
Machinery	4.0	9.3	9.8	10.8	12.5
Trade surplus	0.6	1.0	1.8	3.1	2.0
Physical volume of intra-CMEA trade					
Soviet exports	100	122	126	126	121
Soviet imports	100	131	132	135	154
Re-estimates					
Implicit price index in intra-CMEA trade					
Exports	100	132	143	168	190
Imports	100	118	125	135	138
CMEA oil prices[a]	100	185	202	263	334
Value of Soviet oil at					
(i) 1975 CMEA prices	2.1	2.7	2.9	2.9	2.7
(ii) World market prices	3.7	6.2	11.4	13.4	13.4
Soviet trade with East Europe at comparable (1975) prices					
Exports	11.9	14.1	14.6	14.4	13.8
Imports	11.3	15.0	15.3	15.7	17.6

[a] Marie Lavigne, 'The Soviet Union inside Comecon', *Soviet Studies*, April 1983, p. 138.

Sources: Sections A and B directly from *Vneshnyaya Torgovlya SSSR*, various years, Section C – own estimates from (a) and Sections A and B.

terms (rows 8 and 15) which can again by explained by machinery imports (row 5).

The question of whether Eastern Europe is an economic cost or benefit to the USSR depends critically on the assumptions one makes about the alternative trade possibilities available to the USSR. Row 13 indicates the amount Soviet oil deliveries to Eastern Europe would have obtained at world market prices. Comparison with row 3 indicates that oil price preferences reached 4.3 billion roubles in 1982 (recent changes in world oil prices will have substantially eroded and possibly even reversed this preference by 1984). In addition the USSR must discount trade surpluses that are not substantially paid for in hard currency, while the quality of imported East European machinery is often below world market specifications. Thus if the USSR could sell all its available energy and raw materials on world markets at prevailing world prices, and use the revenue to obtain whatever food and technology it wanted, Eastern Europe would be a substantial cost to the USSR, reaching according to one estimate 17.5 billion dollars in 1980.[15]

If, however, the domestic cost of Soviet energy production is compared with the value to the USSR of items obtained from Eastern Europe, a different picture may emerge. Wiles estimates that the marginal cost of Soviet oil production in 1980 was only 13.5 domestic roubles a ton and that additional exploration costs could drive this figure up to 62.5 domestic roubles by 1985.[16] These estimates convert to about 19 and 75 transferable roubles a ton respectively, including the cost of transportation. Compared with a CMEA price of around 72–6 transferable roubles in 1980, which could double by 1985, Soviet oil exports could enable the USSR to obtain food products and machinery and equipment from Eastern Europe that could only be produced domestically at a high cost, if at all. Currently therefore, Eastern Europe becomes a cost to the USSR when meeting its needs diverts Soviet trade from potentially more profitable areas, although further increases in exploration costs could make Eastern Europe an absolute cost to the USSR later this decade.

Soviet attitudes in the 1980s

Does the USSR wish to turn away from the West and strengthen CMEA, and if so, how far can this process go? Western observers detected a declining Soviet interest in imports of Western machinery towards the end of the 1970s and recent articles in Soviet economic journals have emphasized the failings of capitalism, criticized western analyses of the process of innovation in the USSR and have reaffirmed their confidence in the ability of the Soviet system to stimulate innovation and have proposed increased CMEA cooperation in R&D.[17]

More integrationist policies have been pursued following the replacement of Kosygin by Tikhonov as Chairman of the Council of Ministers and as the person responsible for CMEA affairs in 1981. A month before Brezhnev's death Tikhonov published a highly integrationist article in Pravda stressing the need for 'technical-economic independence of the CMEA countries from the West' and for reduced energy consumption and proposed 'a closer moving together of the systems of planning and direction of the national economies' and 'a balanced plan for the coordination of national outlays' which set the tone for a number of integrationist articles in Soviet journals in the Andropov era, indicating a long-run continuity of strategy in which change is reflected by the degree of vigour with which certain policies are pursued.[18]

In May 1983 Bogomolov argued that CMEA nations imported too many commodities from the West that could be produced within CMEA with improved coordination, specifically mentioning machinery, metal products and foodstuffs. Bogomolov emphasized the need for closer plan and investment coordination, joint cooperation in R&D, and the need for economies in energy consumption throughout CMEA.[19] Shiryaev advocates a 'single concerted scientific and technical policy' involving joint planning of the process 'science-technology-production-marketing'.[20]

A more critical indication of Soviet trade policy is provided by the energy sector. Bogomolov argues that price preferences in CMEA are one-sided,[21] and Voloshin and Nefedov argue that preferential prices in CMEA provide insufficient incentive to importing countries to utilize energy economically and to diversify sources of supply.[22] They propose the establishment of a 'single CMEA energy policy' which would reduce the growth of East European dependence on primary energy imports from the USSR by locating energy intensive industries close to Soviet supplies and encourage the substitution of oil in electricity generation by other sources, and in particular a greater use of East European domestic resources in electricity generation, including low quality coals and lignite and nuclear and hydroelectric power.

Soviet estimates of East European energy requirements have been substantially reduced recently (see table 8.6). In 1977 Kozlov and Yakushin expected non-Soviet energy consumption in CMEA to reach 780 million tons of standard fuel equivalent (mtsfe) by 1980 and to reach 1000 mtsfe by 1990, half of which would be imported which would severely strain Soviet capacity.[23] In 1981 Zubkov argued that if East European energy consumption grew only 0.7 times as fast as National Income, which was expected to grow at 4 per cent per annum, demand would reach only 800 mtsfe by 1990.[24] In August 1983, Voloshin and Nefedov proposed even lower elasticities of the growth of energy consumption to the growth of national income (0.62 in the 1980s and 0.55 in the 1990s). On this basis East European demand would be limited to 900 mtsfe in the year 2000, if national income growth were 3 per cent in the 1980s and 4 per cent in the 1990s, or to 1000 mtsfe if national income grew 1 per cent per annum faster.[25] Rows 2–4 provide extrapolations of East European demand for other years based on these parameters. Provided demand is constrained, Western estimates indicate that the USSR would be capable of meeting a constant proportion

Table 8.6 East European energy balances

(million tons of standard fuel equivalent)

Soviet estimates of East European Consumption	*1975*	*1978*	*1980*	*1985*	*1990*	*2000*
Kozlov (1977)[a]	580		780		1000	
Zubkov (1981)[b]		560–80	600	700	800	
Voloshin (1983)[c]						
Minimum			600	661	725	900
Maximum			600	674	762	1000
Western estimates		*1970*	*1975*	*1978*	*1980*	*1985*
East European						
Consumption		417	511	558	636	673
Production	368	414	440	493		522
Gross imports	98	160	200	222		243
Gross exports	50	63	82	77		92
Imports from USSR	75	117	141	174		193

Notes and Sources: Estimates based on data in

(a) I.D. Kozlov and A.A. Yakushin (See end note 23).

(b) A. Zubkov (See end note 24).

(c) V. Voloshin and V. Nefedov (See end note 24).

Western estimates: 1970, 1975, 1978 from J. Bethkenhagen, cited by J.P. Stern, *East European Energy and East–West Trade in Energy*, RIIA, p. 23.

1980, 1985 – Daniel L. Bond (See end note 35).

Conversions at 1 million barrels a day oil equivalent = 71.5 mtsfe per annum.

of East European requirements. There must however be considerable doubt whether such low elasticities of energy consumption can be reached, although the problem may be partially mitigated by lower national income growth.

This analysis may help to explain Soviet-East European trade patterns in 1982. In 1979 Kosygin agreed that Soviet quota energy exports to CMEA in 1981–5 would be 20 per cent higher than the planned level for 1976–80 of 800 mtsfe and that crude oil deliveries would stabilize at the 1980 level of 80 million tons per annum. In 1980 East European energy consumption was 630 mtsfe (30 mtsfe above apparent Soviet estimates), while Soviet exports were 20 mtsfe above plan. As a result total Soviet energy deliveries to Eastern Europe in 1980 and 1981 were marginally higher than the agreed level for average annual deliveries for 1981–5. It appears that in 1982 the USSR attempted to limit supplies to Eastern Europe, to substitute crude oil by other energy sources and to pass on development costs indirectly by increasing imports of other items.

Western economic sanctions

In attempting to assess whether economic leverage can be utilized to influence Soviet economic policy, political scientists distinguish between positive and negative economic linkage.[26] Negative linkage is the attempt to influence policy by trade denial, either by creating obstacles to the implementation of a specific policy (e.g. withholding items of military or strategic value), by withholding trade until specific policy concessions are made (e.g. freer emigration) or to signal disapproval of a specific policy (e.g. the Korean airliner incident). Positive linkage is the use of trade to create a favourable climate which may facilitate political agreements or possibly to use trade concessions to signal approval of specific policies.

Hanson argues that it is essential to distinguish between military-oriented and policy-oriented measures of trade denial.[27] It can be argued that any trade that expands Soviet productive capacity increases the resources available for military purposes, but Hanson argues that only items with a clearly identifiable military potential should be embargoed on these grounds, and proposes that the appropriate instrument for implementing these decisions is CoCom, whose membership comprises NATO members, excluding Iceland plus Japan. If however the intention is to bring pressure to bear on policy-makers by affecting the domestic economy how vulnerable would the Soviet economy be? As the economy is supply constrained, restrictions on exports to the following areas are most commonly mentioned:

1. *Machinery embodying new technology*. Although Soviet development in the long term has benefited significantly from non-indigenous technology, most of this has not been acquired through imports of machinery. Western econometric estimates indicate that technology embodied in imports of western machinery led to an increase of between only 0.5 and 1.2 per cent of industrial output per annum during the 1970s.[28] Hanson's studies indicate that Western technology has significantly increased output in certain sectors (e.g. mineral fertilizers) but that the unreformed Soviet economy is poor at assimilating Western technology and diffusing it throughout the economy.[29] Hanson estimates that the proportion of Western equipment in Soviet machinery investment peaked at 6.1 per cent in 1975 and declined thereafter. This reduction cannot be attributed to hard currency pressures as energy earnings rose sharply relative to food imports during this period and net indebtedness was reduced without any pressure from the West. Hanson proposes that traditionalist factions in the Soviet leadership, opposed to importing Western technology, were strengthened by the deterioration of Soviet-US relations and opposition

to those who favoured giving greater priority to domestic R&D was weakened by the declining health of Kosygin and the perception that Western technology imports were not yielding substantial economic benefits.[30] The Soviet decision to limit Western borrowing appears in retrospect to be reasonably prudent as the USSR has avoided the political problems associated with indebtedness arising through over optimistic assessments of subsequent export potential and unsustainable consumer expectations experienced in Romania and Poland, respectively.

2. *Foodstuffs.* The increase in imports of foodstuffs and consumer goods which has coincided with the emergence of more traditionalist attitudes towards Western technology in the period 1979–81 indicates that the Soviet leadership must attach considerable importance to the problems of consumption. Soviet economists now refer quite openly to the problems resulting from imbalances between the population's demand for consumer items and the available supply.[31] The need to queue for basic consumer goods results in absenteeism and low productivity, for which increased disciplinary measures can only be a short term cure. In the long run the use of money bonuses to influence labour supply will have little effect if the population already has excess money balances which it is unable to spend.

Soviet imports of consumer goods and foodstuffs (with the major exception of US and Canadian grain) primarily come from CMEA and third world countries. The USSR is highly dependent on imported animal feedstocks and over half its supplies of maize are imported. The USA and Argentina are the world's largest maize exporters and the USSR has turned to Argentina for increased supplies after 1980, while planning to double its domestic output by 1985 and attempting to stimulate CMEA cooperation in this area.

3. *Equipment for use in the energy sector.* The major argument for restricting Western exports for use in the energy sector are that they facilitate exports for hard currency which enables the USSR to purchase commodities that may be of strategic importance, and that in the long run certain West European countries may become excessively dependent on Soviet supplies. Although attempts by US administrations to prevent the export of large diameter pipe for use in pipeline construction in the early 1960s and 1980s have not prevented the completion of the specific projects they were directed towards, the construction of the Orenburg pipeline which was nominally a CMEA joint venture, but in practice used 80 per cent of Western equipment,[32] indicates that Western equipment does help to accelerate development in this area.

A more important question may be to ask how the hard currency earnings are used. It is reasonable to assume that if hard currency earnings were restricted in this way that the Soviet leadership would initially curtail those imports to which it attaches lowest priority. It would therefore appear to be more effective to act directly on exports to the USSR where this is possible.

Conclusion

There are strong indications that the USSR has attempted to reduce its dependence on imports from capitalist nations and has sought alternative sources of supply. Towards the end of the 1970s Soviet disenchantment with the political and economic benefits resulting from imports of Western technology increased, and from 1978 to 1981 Soviet imports of machinery and equipment from the West were reduced and replaced by imports from Eastern Europe. At the same time Soviet imports of foodstuffs and consumer goods increased dramatically, but the major beneficiaries, particularly following the US grain embargo, were developing countries. A hardening of attitudes can be detected following the 26th CPSU Congress (1981). Imports of machinery, particularly from CMEA were increased, while the value of food imports (influenced by good domestic harvests and falling world prices) and consumer goods declined. Criticism of the policy of importing Western technology continued and greater emphasis was placed on CMEA cooperation in the production of foodstuffs and scientific progress.

But how far could such a reliance on non-Western sources go? On the one hand the view of an economy on the verge of collapse, propped up by Western technology, is exaggerated and certainly does not accord with Soviet self-perceptions. The Chernenko leadership may well view the Soviet system of planning as capable of directing domestic resources (labour, fuel and raw materials and scientific progress) towards priority sectors without imposing intolerable strains on the rest of the economy. On the other hand if economic growth were to stabilize at, say, 2 per cent per annum difficult economic decisions would have to be made.

How would these affect or be affected by trade? Much intra-CMEA trade is a positive sum game when only internal bloc factors are considered (i.e. there are gains from intra-CMEA trade). These gains only become losses when they divert resources from potentially more profitable trade outside the bloc. Western restrictions on trade with the USSR would therefore increase the incentive to trade within the bloc. A similar argument may also apply to trade with the third world and may be illustrated by the extreme example of preferential prices paid by the USSR for sugar imported from Cuba. In most years the USSR has paid prices up to two-thirds below those paid to Cuba for additional supplies from world markets. When the Soviet sugarbeet crop failed in 1975 the USSR paid Brazil and Australia prices almost double the preferential price paid to Cuba for additional supplies. Soviet planners must therefore attach a far higher value to sugar than is reflected even in the preferential prices offered to Cuba.

The ability to divert agricultural imports to third world sources was revealed by the US grain embargo, although this also revealed the limits to this process. The diversification of grain imports has only substituted one hard currency supplier by another and has not resulted in better terms of trade, while Soviet officials complain about the low level of Latin-American purchases of Soviet machinery. Soviet export penetration in the third world for hard currency remains largely limited to arms exports to a few Middle-Eastern states.

There are also limits to how far the USSR can turn in towards CMEA. East European (particularly Hungarian) opposition to joint-planning continues and has been the subject of attack in the Soviet press, and there are physical and economic limits to the ability of the East European nations to maintain or increase their contribution to joint ventures. Western studies indicate that Western machinery and components are essential to CMEA ventures. This 'inter-system' dependence is described by Soviet economists as 'antagonistic unity',[33] but there appears to be increased emphasis on limiting long-term dependence on Western inputs by substituting 'one-off' purchases of specific capital items and technical processes for CMEA development. Thus Bogomolov proposes that imports of complete installations from the West should be replaced by licence purchases that would be developed by CMEA cooperation.[34] Proposals to reduce long-term dependence on imported animal feedstocks, by the conversion of natural gas, will, if implemented, involve CMEA cooperation in the development of Western processes.[35] It is unlikely that short-run hard-currency pressures alone will force the Soviet leadership to adopt a decentralist reform. Unlike Eastern Europe, where the need to make export industries more responsive to changing world market conditions is a major stimulus to reform, hard currency exports account for only 3–4 per cent of Soviet GNP and are supplied by a few high priority sectors (large-scale energy projects, armaments manufacture, precious metals extraction and a high priority sector of manufacturing industry) which attract high quality inputs. It appears unlikely that a centralist administration would be willing to weaken its control over successful sectors in the pursuit of uncertain economic benefits, but would seek to extend those successes to other sectors.

There are however limits to the ability of priority sectors, including defence, to grow faster than the economy as a whole over a sustained period, or to obtain inputs from other sectors without critically weakening them. Imports do help to alleviate bottlenecks that may arise in other sectors.

It appears unlikely that policy will change substantially following the death of Andropov. Current policy towards international trade was established at the 26th CPSU Congress, before the death of Brezhnev, and may be expected to continue under Chernenko. The keynote speech on trade policy was made by Tikhonov who retains responsibility for relations with CMEA. Chernenko's initial speeches appear to dampen the prospect for policy change.

Notes

1 Igor Birman, *Ekonomika Nedostach* (New York, Chalidze Publications, 1983), p. 71.
2 Philip Hanson, *Trade and Technology in Soviet-Western Relations* (London, Macmillan, 1981), Chapter 4.
3 O. Bogomolov, *Planovoe Khozyaistvo*, 1980, no. 10, p. 83.
4 V. Treml, 'Soviet dependence on foreign trade'; paper to NATO colloquium 'External economic relations of the CMEA countries', Brussels, 1983.
5 Bruce Parrott, *Politics and Technology in the Soviet Union* (Cambridge, MIT Press, 1983) and Elizabeth Kridl Valkenier, *The Soviet Union and the Third World* (New York, Praeger, 1983).
6 Parrott, *Politics and Technology*, Chapter 5.
7 See for example Moshe Efrat, 'The economics of Soviet arms transfers to the third world – a case study: Egypt', *Soviet Studies* 35 (1983), pp. 437–56.
8 Valkenier, *The Soviet Union and the Third World*, Chapter 1.
9 The higher estimate is from David Holloway, *The Soviet Union and the Arms Race* (New Haven, Yale, 1983), p. 125. A lower figure is indicated in Table 8.4. I am currently preparing a paper indicating that these estimates may both be too high.
10 O. Bogomolov, *Planovoe Khozyaistvo*, 1980, no. 10, p. 85.
11 For a more detailed analysis of these disputes and for original sources see Alan H. Smith, *The Planned Economies of Eastern Europe* (London, Croom Helm, 1983), Chapter 9.
12 I. Dudinskii, *Voprosii Ekonomiki*, 1966, no. 4. L. Ladygin and Yu. Shiryaev, *Voprosii Ekonomikii*, 1966, no. 5; I. Kozlov, *Planovoe Khozyaistvo*, 1971, no. 7.
13 A. Kosygin, *Izbrannie Stati i Rechi* (Politizdat, Moscow, 1974) pp. 430–57.
14 Alan H. Smith, 'Economic factors in Soviet-East European relations in the 1980s', in *Soviet-East European Dilemmas*, K. Dawisha and P. Hanson (eds.) (London, Heinemann for RIIA, 1981).
15 M. Marrese and J. Vanous, 'Soviet policy options in trade relations with Eastern Europe', in *The Soviet Economy in the 1980s* (US Congress, Washington, DC).
16 Peter Wiles, 'A note on the cost of Soviet oil', *CMEA Energy 1980–90* (Brussels, NATO Economics Directorate, 1981), p. 134.

17 For example, N. Alekhin, *Voprosii Ekomomiki*, 1982, no. 10; L. Vasilyeva, R. Volodarskaya and P. Kuligin, *Voprosii Ekonomiki*, 1983, no. 4; L. Abalkin, *Kommunist*, 1983, no. 14; V. Sikora, *Voprosii Ekonomiki*, 1983, no. 10.
18 N. Tikhonov, *Pravda* 15 October 1982.
19 O. Bogomolov, *Kommunist*, 1983, no. 7.
20 Yu. Shiryaev, *World Marxist Review*, 1983, no. 4.
21 Bogomolov, *Kommunist* 1983.
22 V. Voloshin and V. Nefedov, *Voprosii Ekonomiki*, 1983, no. 8.
23 I. Kozlov and A. Yakushin, *Izvestiya Nauk SSSR, Seriya Ekonomicheskaya*, 1977, no. 3, p. 94.
24 A. Zubkov, *Voprosii Ekonomiki*, 1981, no. 10, p. 97.
25 Voloshin and Nefedov, *Voprosii Ekonomiki*, 1983, no. 8, p. 108.
26 Angela Stent, *From Embargo to Ostpolitik* (Cambridge, CUP, 1981), Chapter 1.
27 Philip Hanson, 'Western economic sanctions against the USSR', NATO Colloquium 1983, see footnote 4.
28 Hanson, *Trade and Technology*, Chapter 9.
29 Hanson, *Trade and Technology*, Chapters 9–11.
30 Philip Hanson 'Foreign economic relations', in A. Brown and M. Kaser (eds.), *Soviet Policy for the 1980s* (London, Macmillan, 1982).
31 Bogomolov, *Kommunist* 1983.
32 John Hannigan and Carl McMillan,' Joint investment in resource development', *East European Economic Assessment* (Washington, DC, JEC, 1981).
33 E.P. Pletnev, *Dve Sistemi Mirovogo Khozyaistva: Antagonisticheskoe Edinstvo* (Moscow, 1983).
34 Bogomolov, *Kommunist* 1983.
35 Daniel Bond, 'CMEA growth projections for 1981–5', *The CMEA Five Year Plans in a New Perspective'* (Brussels, NATO Information Directorate, 1982).

9 Comrade Colossus: The Impact of Soviet Military Industry on the Soviet Economy

Edwina Moreton

'As always, defence requirements have been sufficiently taken into account. The Politburo has considered and considers it obligatory, particularly in the current international situation, to provide the army and the navy with everything they need.'[1] Mr Yuri Andropov's statement shortly after coming to power in November 1982 followed closely the words of his predecessor, Leonid Brezhnev, in his address to a gathering of senior military men in the Kremlin on 27 October 1982. Mr Andropov's own successor, Mr Konstantin Chernenko, said the same thing in different words in his speech to the central committee as new party leader in February 1984.[2] The continuity is unremarkable in a country noted above almost all else for the strength of its armed forces. Only one word seemed worthy of closer scrutiny. Giving the armed forces what they need to ensure Soviet defence entails a political decision as to what those needs are. All three leaders stopped short of promising them all they might want. Matching military requests with scarce resources is a problem which faces all governments. In the case of the Soviet government, the 1980s may pose the most difficult problems of all.

The Soviet Union is a military giant but, if a number of eminent Western students of the Soviet economy are to be believed, it is in danger of becoming an economic weakling.[3] Mr Andropov was hoisted to power in November 1982, in part in the expectation that he could retrieve a worsening situation and put some muscle into the ailing economy. He and the men around him at the pinnacle of the Communist party knew that the Soviet Union's influence as a superpower is derived from its military prowess, which in turn depends for support on a strong economic base. But that base shows serious signs of crumbling, in large part because of the weight of the military burden it has to carry. Both Brezhnev and his erstwhile protégé, Konstantin Chernenko, who has now inherited the problem, have in the past talked of the 'burden' the arms race places on the Soviet Union.[4]

Chernenko's biggest domestic problem, like Andropov's before him, is to shore up the economy enough to meet not only the demands of his generals, but also the rising expectations of the Soviet people and the need for new investment to modernize Soviet industry. Unless he finds a way of getting to grips with the problem, the Soviet economy could slide deeper into crisis: not the sudden, explosive sort, but an increasingly debilitating, grumbling crisis that will further sap political confidence and eventually, possibly, military strength. One of the surest ways to halt the Soviet Union's economic decline would be to break the stranglehold that the Soviet military-industrial complex has on the rest of the economy. But the greatest resistance to real change in the way the Soviet economy is managed would come not just from conservative party bureaucrats, but also from defence industrialists and their protectors in uniform, battling to preserve their privileged turf.

Robbing Pyotr to pay Pavel

According to Vasily Garbuzov, USSR minister of finance, also speaking in November 1982, 'Our state does not and will not spend on defence a single rouble more than is absolutely essential for ensuring the security of the Soviet people and of its friends and allies. The 1983 USSR budget allocates for the country's defence R17,050m, which is 4.8 per cent of budget expenditure.'[5] In December 1983, Nikolai Baibakov, head of the state planning agency, Gosplan, hinted that although the formal defence budget allocation had not been increased in the state budget, defence spending might have to rise given the deteriorating international climate.[6] Nobody knows how much the Soviet Union really spends on defence. The Russians claim it is a modest 3 per cent of GNP; Western estimates in recent years have ranged as high as 18 per cent, although estimating the true cost of the Soviet defence effort is notoriously difficult.[7]

There is added confusion due to press reports in March and then again in November 1983 that the American CIA and DIA differed sharply in their estimates of Soviet defence spending and consequently on the burden it places on the Soviet economy. Although it is generally accepted that Soviet GNP growth had fallen below 2 per cent in 1981, CIA reports had suggested that the growth in Soviet defence spending had also dropped from roughly 4 per cent per year in the mid 1970s to around 2 per cent by the early 1980s. The estimate was based on a weapons count which turned out to be lower for the period since 1976 than had been anticipated from earlier trends. Two possible explanations were offered: that the Russians were indeed spending less on defence, especially weapons procurement (an explanation rejected by the DIA), or that they were less efficient than presumed and were finding new sophisticated weapons far more expensive to produce (a problem also encountered in Western economies, where cost overruns on new weapons systems are commonplace).

According to analysis by staff of the joint economic committee of Congress, what the intra-agency dispute boils down to is that the DIA agrees with the CIA's dollar estimate for the Soviet defence effort (or what it would cost to replicate the Soviet defence effort in the American economy), but comes to a different conclusion on the rouble cost, on the basis of its own different method of calculation. The CIA has now concluded that the costs of Soviet defence grew at the rate of about 2 per cent in real terms from 1976 to 1981, compared to 4–5 per cent during the previous ten years. Most of the apparent slowdown took place in procurement, which levelled off in the most recent period. Whatever the explanation for the pronounced slowdown, since Soviet GNP and defence spending grew at approximately the same rate over the past five years, the CIA has concluded that the share of the economy devoted to defence did not change from the 12–14 per cent previously estimated. Using its own rouble price methodology, the DIA reckons there was no slowdown in the growth of Soviet defence spending. On this basis the DIA estimates that the Soviet military burden increased from 13–14 per cent in 1970 to 14–16 per cent in 1981.[8] (A NATO study, reported in February 1984, confirmed the slowdown in the rate of growth of Soviet defence spending. This may have been due to the simultaneous tailing off of several weapons programmes. Research and development does not appear to have suffered. Spending may therefore rise again in the latter part of the 1980s.)[9]

It's not just – or even – a question of cash. Whatever the true figure, the size of the real Soviet defence budget is not just a measure of the relentless growth of Soviet military power – which it is – it is also a measure of the drain on the rest of the economy of the military appetite.

Unable to meet all the competing claims on resources – from the generals, the consumer and the need for new investment – Brezhnev had first tried to use trade openings to the West in the 1970s to buy in goods and technologies to plug some of the growing gaps. Even at the height of détente, East-West trade never lived up to his high expectations. When his grand détente strategy finally failed after Afghanistan and the Polish crisis he opted to allow investment to suffer most. The slump in the growth of investment from over 7 per cent a year in the mid 1970s to an average of barely 2 per cent in the past two years has already had a dampening effect on a declining growth rate.[10] Because of the time lag between new investment and a visible return in the form of greater efficiency or higher output, the effect on Soviet industry of this starvation diet will hit harder as the 1980s wear on. Investment was planned to grow by 4 per cent in 1983 and by even more in 1984. But that does not solve the short-term problem. It only forces the Soviet leadership to cut resources from elsewhere: either out of consumption or, less likely, out of defence spending. Andropov's efficiency drive in industry during the first few months of 1983 did push up output, but by the end of his 15-month tenure in office the rate of increase over 1982 was sliding back again and running, according to Soviet figures, at about 4 per cent. The efficiency drive by itself is unlikely to solve the problem either in the short term or the long term. It remains to be seen whether Chernenko will put any political energy at all into the drive for reform.

Productivity, industrial output and growth have all suffered as the roubles that might have gone into modernizing agriculture (another notorious sink hole) and old industrial plants and improving roads and railways have been pumped into defence. But such aggregate figures tell only part of the story. For example, it has been estimated that in the past forty years productivity in the food industry and light industry – those that help keep the Soviet population fed and relatively contented – has increased by between three-and-a-half and four times; in the machine-building, metallurgy and chemicals industries – all of which devote a large chunk of their output to defence – productivity has risen an estimated 15.5 to 19.5 times.[11] Even if the political decision were taken immediately, it would take years, if not decades, to correct the harmful effects on civilian industry of that sort of imbalance.

In short, the priority given to military and military-related production has dominated and helped exhaust the Soviet civilian economy. Reordering those priorities to push Soviet defence spending off its protected pedestal would be hard for any political leader to accomplish, even if the political will existed.

How the grip was tightened

One of the reasons is that, for a country that invests so much of its national pride in its armed forces and its military hardware, the results have been impressive. Twenty years ago the Soviet Union's strategic rocket forces barely existed; today they are a match – some would argue more than a match – for the best a far richer United States can produce. Improvements in naval, air and land forces have been no less spectacular. The Soviet Union boasts the world's largest submarine force. According to United States government figures, its tank production in recent years has outnumbered NATO's (not just that of the United States itself) by three to one, its fighter bombers by three to two, and its production of surface-to-air missiles by approximately seven to one.[12]

This sort of impressive defence output does not happen in a fit of absentmindedness. The Soviet military-economic-political system forms a set of tightly interlocking institutions and practices that ensure both the quality and the quantity of the product.

The absolute priority to defence

The Soviet system of central planning, set up in the 1930s in part to ensure central political control and a strong defence for the Soviet state, is tailor-made to suit the Soviet military establishment. Raw materials or parts in short supply can be re-directed to priority tasks, and military industry has number one priority. All branches of the economy are obliged to satisfy military demands first; civilian factories have to make do with what is left. In many cases defence manufacturing plants maintain their own autonomous suppliers, precisely in order to channel resources their way more effectively. If supplies run out, factories working on military contracts can simply take what they need from civilian factories. The key to the system is that party officials have instructions to make sure they get what they need.

Feather-bedding

Defence industrialists have been known to stay in the same jobs for twenty years or more. Weapons design teams under such famous names as Korolov, Yangel, Ilyushin and Antonov span more than one generation.[13] Although the secrecy attached to defence-related research work has its disadvantages,[14] with little cross-pollination of ideas and research, there is no shortage of funds and research facilities. For additional help these cosseted research teams can call on the assistance of the battery of research institutes attached to the Soviet academy of sciences.

Brain drain

Not only the best skills go into defence. A talented manager would quite simply be out of place in a non-priority job – say, making refrigerators or washing machines – which probably accounts at least in part for the shoddy quality of the products these sorts of factories turn out. And the best workers follow the best managers. An engineer in a military-related enterprise can earn an estimated 20 to 50 per cent more than his counterpart in a civilian enterprise.[15] There are other benefits, too, awaiting a worker in the defence industries: including easier access to education for children, better housing, better stocked factory shops and better services. In many ways workers in military industries live in a world, and an economy, of their own.

Consumer control

Unlike the ordinary Soviet consumer, who has to put up with whatever goods are available, however deplorable the quality, the Soviet Union's defence industrialists and the generals they serve have what could be called consumer command. They not only tell the design teams and manufacturers what weapons and equipment to build, they also send round their own military inspectors, hard on the heels of the civilian ones, to make sure the military's own high standards of production are being met. Faulty equipment is simply discarded. Cost is of secondary importance.

The military-industrial-political complex

As the saying goes, the Soviet Union does not have a military-industrial complex, it is one.[16] In the United States competing defence manufacturers combine with others in or outside government to put pressure on the government for a share in the defence budget. In the Soviet Union the defence industry lobby is a powerful and more unified voice lodged firmly and institutionally inside the political system at the top and all the way down.

There is little point in simply recapping the excellent and exhaustive descriptions of this military-industrial-political hierarchy.[17] Suffice it to say for our purposes here that at the very top the defence council, chaired officially by Chernenko (and before that by Brezhnev and Chernenko), brings together the most senior party and military men to make the important decisions on defence and, presumably foreign policy and arms control. Further down the hierarchy defence allocations within the economy are handled by a separate department of the state planning agency, Gosplan. A military-industrial commission acts as general trouble-shooter to make sure the generals get what they need. Today nine ministries form the core of the military-industrial complex: the ministry of general machine-building (which despite its vague title is in charge of production of Soviet strategic missiles); the ministry of medium machine-building (nuclear weapons); the ministry of machine-building (ammunition); the ministries for electronics, radio and communications industries (electronics) the defence industry (conventional army material); and the more obvious shipbuilding and aviation ministries. But apart from the nine core ministries every ministry, from chemicals to textiles, contributes at some point to the defence effort.

Defence information monopoloy

The system is made virtually watertight by the monopoly of information which the military has on all defence-related issues. There are no civilian think-tanks, such as Rand or the Brookings Institution in the United States or similar less specialized institutions in Europe, to carry out independent research into national arms control and defence policy. Unconfirmed reports during the Andropov months suggested that he at least had physically moved the defence council staff to new premises and brought in some new faces in what may have been an attempt to break this military monopoly.

This jealous guarding of military secrets has its ludicrous side. At the first strategic arms limitation talks, Salt I, then General, now Marshal Nikolai Ogarkov, the representative of the Soviet general staff, took an American delegate aside and asked that the characteristics of Soviet weapons under discussion should not be mentioned in front of civilian members of the Soviet negotiating team, who were not cleared to know them.

A slow strangling

The system of planning that guarantees the smooth running of the Soviet Union's military economy means periodic chaos for civilian industry, which must cope, not just with the bottlenecks endemic in a too-tightly planned and over-centralized economy, but also with the sudden disappearance of vital equipment, spares and raw materials. The result is that already sluggish economic growth is stunted even further.

Civilian industry is starved not only of skills and resources, but also of initiative. Competing with the defence industries is a mug's game. A manager of, say, a refrigerator factory, offered the choice between an efficient and up-to-date insulating material used in military production and an old-fashioned, inefficient sort, is likely to choose the inefficient one simply because his stocks are less likely to be raided. The real loser all the way down the line is the Soviet consumer. (Not that life is entirely uneventful for defence manufacturers either; once on the list of preferred factories the better machines, raw materials and extra money for investment flows in, but military production can also entail frequent and unexpected changes of plans as priorities change.)

On an economy-wide scale the problem goes much deeper. In the Soviet Union the much-vaunted scientific-technical revolution, which in the 1970s was to have revolutionized Soviet industry, science and technology, has been channelled very narrowly. If anything it has been a military-technical revolution. In the West new ideas first developed for use in military and space programmes – especially in computer science, electronics and materials science – have found applications widely in civilian industry in the development of new products. In the Soviet Union the spin-off has been very limited indeed. Instead of industrial innovation it has tended to result in continued civilian industrial decline and consumer frustration.

Recognizing at least part of the problem, in the 1970s Brezhnev several times called on the defence sector to devote more of its effort to the production of consumer goods. In 1971 he claimed that some 42 per cent of defence production already fed back into the civilian economy.[18] He gave no further details but such goods are said to range from aluminium foil and outboard motors (both luxury items in the Soviet Union) to baby carriages, children's toys and vacuum cleaners.

The Russians do not, of course, go short of real tanks and guns to produce toy ones. (Apart from anything else the high level of Soviet arms sales in the third world is evidence of that.[19]) Consumer goods production in military enterprises uses up spare capacity; it does not represent an investment of new technology in civilian production. All the same, the street-wise Soviet shopper will look for factory codes in an attempt to pick out goods made in military factories. The quality control may not be as high as that for rifles, tanks or aircraft, but at least it could not be lower than it is in civilian factories.

Even efforts to get the army to produce more of its own food have run into snags. The Soviet armed forces have long operated a nationwide network of military farms, food processing plants and food reserves. In order to reduce the drain on scarce domestic supplies, as part of Brezhnev's food programme the army and navy were put under orders in 1982 to increase their own production of such staple foods as meat, milk, eggs, potatoes and vegetables by at least 50 per cent by 1985, the end of the current five-year plan. In May 1983, the man in charge of the programme, General Ivan Isaenko, reported production increases – but ones well below the 15 per cent target set for the first year of the scheme.[20]

Choices and trade-offs

Despite all its problems, the Soviet economy still limps along and the Soviet armed forces look like remaining the last to suffer. But now there are small signs that the economic squeeze which has affected the quality of life for the Soviet consumer may be pinching the defence spenders too. Several senior military men, including Marshal Ogarkov, have over the past eighteen months registered their dismay at the poor record of Soviet industry (while nonetheless maintaining their claim to more money for defence). Before he died, Brezhnev, addressing his assembled senior military commanders in the Kremlin, told them that the Soviet Union's economic resources were not unlimited and that the armed forces would have to make maximum use of the resources already at their disposal. Grain, he pointed out, was also a strategic item. Brezhnev came as close as a Soviet Communist party leader is ever likely to come in the near future to saying that not all the army's demands could be met.

Senior army figures appear to have been part of the coalition for change which put Andropov in power in November 1982, and he was careful not to trample too hard on their interests. But that did not stop him echoing Brezhnev's last words in his first major speech on the subject after becoming party leader. No matter how beholden Andropov was and Chernenko is to military backers, there are some economic facts that neither apparatchiks nor generals can ignore: the growing signs are that the crunch in future is not one of just guns versus butter – military needs taking priority over consumer demand – but of guns versus the sorts of investment in defence industry and plant, as well as civilian industry, that can keep up the pace of Soviet weapons development and production. The new CIA estimates of lower procurement levels, mentioned above, could be a reflection of normal cyclical trends in weapons procurement or the thickening edge of the investment versus guns wedge.

Basically the Soviet leadership has three realistic choices. It can shift economic priorities by slowing down or halting the growth in defence spending and devote the extra resources to the rest of the economy. It can introduce some fairly sharp-edged reforms in the system of planning and industrial management which up to now has allowed defence to choke off civilian industrial growth. Or it can keep tinkering with the existing economic mechanism, trying to squeeze greater efficiency and higher output out of civilian workers and farmers – and leave the defence sector relatively unscathed.

Switching around economic priorities to put more effort into civilian industry has been tried before. That was one motive behind Krushchev's short-lived switch of emphasis in the late 1950s from ground forces to nuclear forces for Soviet defence. As Khrushchev saw it, resources saved from feeding the 'steel eaters' could be switched to fertilizer production and so aid the real food economy. Khrushchev's plan foundered on opposition from the armed forces.

Would such a sleight of hand work today? The idea would be that a properly stoked economy could provide a strong enough engine eventually to pull the defence industries smartly along in its wake. That has been the reasoning behind neighbouring China's economic priorities, which put the armed forces fourth in the list of four modernizations, after agriculture, industry and science. But China's leaders do not have the same worries about preserving their superpower status, nor yet the strong defence industry lobby which confronts any new Soviet leader.

And in the Soviet Union the economic obstacles may be just as intractable as the political ones. According to recent American figures, even if the present 4–5 per cent (or 2 per cent according to latest figures) annual increase in defence spending were halted until the end of the 1980s – itself a fairly far-fetched proposition – the annual rate of growth of the Soviet GNP would probably increase by no more than one-tenth to one-fifth of a percentage point a year.[21] The effect on per capita consumption would be greater – up to one-half of 1 per cent. Over the course of the decade that would free some resources for either investment or consumption but either way it would not make the Soviet consumer's lot a noticeably easier one – it would probably only prevent its getting worse.

Part of the problem is that in the short term resources are not that easily transferred from the defence to the civilian sector. Factory re-tooling costs money. On present performance Soviet civilian industry would not only find it hard to absorb extra capacity, but what it did absorb would most probably be plagued by the same bottlenecks and inefficiencies that have worn down the rest of civilian industry. As the experience of Soviet agriculture has demonstrated over the years, simply throwing more money and resources at the problem will not necessarily make the system work any more efficiently – often the opposite. In other words without the sort of economic reform that would rejuvenate the civilian economy and break the stranglehold that the priority given to defence has put on it, any injection into the system of new resources taken from defence would be in danger of being wasted.

On the evidence so far, however, although Mr Andropov was in favour of modest reform, he was not planning a really radical reform of the central planning mechanism. The last programme of quite far-reaching reform, begun in the mid 1960s under then prime minister Kosygin, quickly ran into opposition from party bureaucrats and their military backers, worried that a devolution of economic powers from the centre would also mean a dilution of political control. And since the generals' privileged position in the economy also depends on strict management from the centre they had a double reason to oppose the reforms, which were abandoned.

What Andropov began, even if it is continued in some form, amounts to tinkering only (see Chapters 6 and 7). He tried to put some stiffening into Brezhnev's rather limp-wristed reform of agriculture – the food programme announced in May 1982 – by speeding up the formation of agro-industrial associations to coordinate food output, and by encouraging the use of 'brigades' of farm workers who get paid by results. He fired some of the most incompetent and corrupt of his ministers and rotated in more competent men, including the former minister of general machine building, for eighteen years, Sergei Afanasyev, to give important civilian industries a shot in the arm. A series of experiments has been introduced into selected Leningrad factories, designed to test the impact of incentives and wider pay differentials on output. And a further 'experiment' began in January 1984, which involved two of the Moscow-based ministries and selected industries in Belorussia, Latvia and the Ukraine. It is designed to give managers more scope and autonomy to take their own production decisions. It remains to be seen how far it goes.

When measured against fifty years of tight central planning, none of this amounts to a reform adventurous enough to make much of an impact in the near future on the performance of the economy. The signs so far are that the Soviet leadership is going for the third option: muddling through. Presumably they are thereby hoping to avoid hard decisions and duck the inevitable clash with his generals. They can probably get away with it – though less comfortably than they did in the 1970s.

If Chernenko does intend to avoid reform, he could try a fourth option – the one that Brezhnev tried in the 1970s. The Soviet Union is still very much in the market for imports that can help target areas of the economy, for example, the energy and food industries. But past experience suggests that imports cannot remove the hard policy choices facing the Soviet leadership. They can even cause their own problems, being grafted onto an inefficient economic base. What is more the Soviet Union will find its ability to buy in the West more severely limited by technology embargoes – and also by its own continuing need to spend considerable amounts of hard currency on basic goods, such as grain.[22] Without radical changes of fortune by one means or another, the Soviet economy will enter the 1990s with the same problems that dog it today – and with even fewer reserves to fall back on. The Soviet Union is not alone in feeling the effects of its recent military buildup. On the other side of the world the United States has begun to encounter public opposition to President Reagan's plans for sharply increasing defence budgets in peacetime. It remains to be seen what foreign policy conclusions both powers draw from the economic constraints on their military activities.

Impact on foreign policy

From the Soviet point of view, whatever damage the priority given to defence industry has done to the domestic economy, there is no doubt that the Soviet Union's military strength has given it clout and prestige as the world's other superpower. Even President Reagan's harsh anti-Soviet rhetoric, uncomfortable and unacceptable though it has been for the Kremlin, is a backhanded compliment to a staggering defence effort. When the United States and the Soviet Union emerged as direct competitors after World War II, American superiority was clear, not just in weapons, but also in its global network of alliances and bases. Talks to limit strategic missiles, which have continued intermittently since 1969, were confirmation that parity of sorts had been reached on the weapons front. The more assertive Soviet foreign policy of the 1970s, using its military capabilities and weapons production lines to extend the Soviet Union's military and diplomatic reach into Asia, Africa, the Middle East and Central America, was often a direct challenge to United States influence and allies.

Without the Soviet Union's huge defence effort of the 1960s and 1970s, little or none of this would have been possible. But it has had its costs. First, the strain on the Soviet domestic economy and the poor performance of the civilian economy will have done little to enhance the attraction of the Soviet model of development among countries of the developing world. Marxism-Leninism has been frequently used as a rationale for seizing power. But there seems otherwise little enthusiasm for emulating the rest of the Soviet experience. In recent years, the Soviet Union has seemed to draw its horns in somewhat as regards economic involvement in parts of the developing world. Some developing countries are now paying back to the Soviet Union more on old loans than they are getting in new aid.[23] Might this be taken as evidence that the burden of defence has directly affected Soviet foreign policy? Obviously, to some extent it has. With more resources at its disposal, and a more successful model of development to peddle, the Soviet Union might be more active and successful in the developing world.

On the other hand, at least part of the apparent Soviet disaffection with the developing world is undoubtedly due to hard lessons learned. Neither economic nor military aid necessarily buys lasting influence. For example, Soviet supplies of modern equipment to Syria have been unable to turn the Syrians into anything but prickly, uncertain and potentially dangerous allies. In Afghanistan too, where the Soviet invasion in 1979 was in many ways the culmination of the process linking Soviet military capabilities to a more assertive Soviet foreign policy, the Soviet Union has learned an old lesson the hard way: that having the power to intervene does not mean having the power to force a military solution against determined, if poorly equipped resistance. With these lessons in mind, not just a shortage of financial resources, the Soviet Union prefers to concentrate the vast bulk of those resources it has on what it considers ideologically reliable allies, such as Cuba, Vietnam, Mongolia and Laos.

Is economic difficulty, exacerbated by the burden of defence, likely to induce caution in Soviet foreign policy? Or will it instead induce a beleaguered leadership to throw caution to the winds? From the evidence so far, Afghanistan appears to have marked a watershed in Soviet foreign policy assertiveness. Economic constraints and hard political lessons learned have resulted in a more cautious Soviet Union so far than many commentators had expected to see in the 1980s. The Soviet Union's military clout has not diminished. The political and economic considerations which govern its use have proved more complex than sometimes anticipated, although that need not rule out a return to foreign policy opportunism, where opportunities arise and political and economic costs can be minimized. The exception in some respects is East-West relations, and particularly the Soviet determination to preserve at any cost what it understands to be rough parity with the United States on the weapons front. To that extent military spending will continue to be driven by American-Soviet relations, which remain the centrepiece and main preoccupation of Soviet foreign policy. Although new weapons technologies, such as 'star wars' research, pose very serious challenges for the Soviet Union, there has been no sign whatsoever that, whatever the economic cost, the Russians will fail to put maximum effort into the technology competition, unless it can be limited by some form of arms control agreement. Indeed, if there is a real battle over resources going on in the Soviet Union, the continued challenge to compete with the United States will, if anything, serve to validate the military shopping list. Defence remains the Soviet Union's highest priority, even if also the greatest economic burden.

Notes

1 Yuri Andropov, addressing the plenum of the CPSU Central Committee, as relayed by Tass, 22 November 1982 (SWB/SU/7191/C1 24 November 1982).

2 Report of Brezhnev's remarks, *The Economist*, 6 November 1982; Chernenko's speech in *Pravda*, 14 February 1984.

3 Among recent books Marshall Goldman's *USSR in Crisis: The Failure of an Economic System* (New York and London, W.W. Norton & Co., 1983) gives the game away by its title and offers an extensive explanation of the root causes.

4 *Soviet Economy in the 1980s: Problems and Prospects*, Vol. 1, published by the Joint Economic Committee of Congress (Washington DC, 1983) (hereafter JEC Vol. 1), p. 333, footnote 2.

5 Addressing the Supreme Soviet in Moscow on 23 November 1982 (SWB/SU/192/C/7 25 November 1982).

6 *Financial Times*, 29 December 1983.

7 Table, collating different Western and other estimates, in David Holloway, 'The Soviet Union', in Nicole Ball and Milton Leitenberg

(eds.), *The Structure of Defence Industry* (London, Croom Helm, 1983), p. 59; also table and explanation in IISS, *The Military Balance 1982–1983* (London, 1982), p. 12; Abraham Becker, *The Burden of Soviet Defence*, RAND R–2752–AF, October 1981; Stan Woods, *Weapons Requisition in the Soviet Union*, ASIDES (Aberdeen Studies in Defence Economies) no. 24, September 1982.

8 *Soviet Defence Trends*; a staff study prepared for the Subcommittee on International Trade, Finance and Security Economics, JEC September 1983.

9 *Observer*, 19 February 1984.

10 For a discussion of the impact of declining investment see Myron Rush, 'Guns over growth in Soviet policy', *International Security*, Vol. 7, no. 3 (Winter 1982/83), pp. 167–79; figures illustrated in 'Central Intelligence Agency briefing on the Soviet economy' before the JEC Subcommittee on International Trade, Finance, and Security Economics, 1 December 1982 (Figure 10).

11 Michael Checinski, 'The military-industrial complex in the USSR; its influence on R & D and industrial planning and on international trade', Stiftung Wissenschaft und Politik, Ebenhausen (West Germany), SWP-AZ 2302, September 1981.

12 *Soviet Military Power*, second edition, March 1983 (US Defense Department, Washington DC, 1983).

13 Robert Berman and John Baker, *Soviet Strategic Forces: Requirements and Responses* (Washington DC, The Brookings Institution, 1982), Appendix A.

14 Mikhail Agursky, 'The Soviet military-industrial complex', Jerusalem Papers on Peace Problems 31, Hebrew University of Jerusalem, 1980, pp. 12–16.

15 For estimates of the numbers of workers in the different industries see Checinski, 'The military-industrial complex in the USSR', p. 43; also Holloway, 'The Soviet Union', p. 57.

16 The point is explored in Becker, *The Burden of Soviet Defence* pp. 42–50 and also at length in Hannes Adomeit and Mikhail Agursky, 'The Soviet military-industrial complex and its internal mechanism', National Security Series No 1/78, Centre for International Relations, Queen's University, Kingston, Ontario.

17 See Holloway, 'The Soviet Union'; by the same author, 'Technology, management and the Soviet military establishment', Adelphi Paper no. 76 (London, IISS, April 1971), and *The Soviet Union and the Arms Race* (New Haven and London, Yale University Press, 1983), especially Chapters 6 and 8; Adomeit and Agursky, 'The Soviet military-industrial complex and its internal mechanism'; Arthur Alexander, 'Decision making in Soviet weapons procurement', Adelphi Papers no. 148 (London, IISS, winter 1978/9); and by the same author, *Soviet Science and Weapons Acquisition* (RAND, R–2942–NAS, August 1982).

18 Holloway, 'The Soviet Union', p. 58, gives the reverse figures for the amount of industrial production, even in non-military industries, that goes to defence.

19 Ibid., pp. 67–72.

20 Peter Kruzhin, 'Army food program encounters difficulties', Radio Liberty Research, RL 244/83, 23 June 1983.

21 JEC, Vol. 1, p. 338; for a similar estimating exercise see Mark Hopkins and Michael Kennedy, *The trade-off between consumption and military expenditures for the Soviet Union during the 1980s* (RAND, R–2927–NA, November 1983).

22 For a full explanation of these points, see Philip Hanson, *Trade and Technology in Soviet-Western Relations* (London, Macmillan, 1981); and Angela Stent, 'Economic strategy', in Edwina Moreton and Gerald Segal (eds.), *Soviet Strategy Toward Western Europe* (London, George Allen and Unwin, 1984).

23 Complete breakdown of figures in report drawn up by the Foreign and Commonwealth Office, 'Soviet, East European and Western development aid 1976–82' (1983).

10 Siberia: Heartland and Framework

Stuart Kirby

Three-quarters of the Soviet Union is in Asia. Russia-in-Asia must accordingly weigh very heavily in any consideration of Soviet policy, internal or external – and it must be noted at once that internal and external policy are fully intertwined.

The word Siberia is loosely used to indicate the whole area east of the Urals. In Russian, it means the northern part of that vast tract, excluding Soviet Central Asia. Though the two are strongly linked – as is the whole Soviet Union – they are two different areas. Siberia is a very 'Russian' land – using Russian in this case to mean particularly Great Russian (i.e. Muscovite). That can be illustrated, *inter alia*, by the fact that Siberia and Russia-in-Europe as far as the borders of the Byelorussian Republic, the Ukraine and the Baltic, are conjoined in one Republic, the RSFSR, by far the largest in the Russian federation, or by the fact that 80 per cent of Siberia's population are 'European' Russians and the rest highly Russianized. Yet Siberia and the Siberians are different; and their importance in Soviet policy, obviously large and special, cannot be relegated to an appendix or to footnotes (as is done in almost all Western discussions; in contrast to the huge mass of material in Russian, which treats Siberia very integrally).[1]

Integral is the word. Not long after its formation, and as soon as it could emerge from vassalage to the Mongols, the Russian state began, just four hundred years ago, the conquest of Siberia. That conquest was by far the largest, and one of the most thorough, in all history; and one of the swiftest, being accomplished in little more than half a century, in advances over huge distances under difficult natural conditions. This has been a conquest not merely in terms of drawing lines farther and farther out on the map, but for integration: 'making it one's own'. In Russian, such is the term literally used for this process: *osvoyenie*, sharing all the shades of meaning of the English words acquisition, appropriation, assimilation, absorption. This ingestion is still going on; and, as so often in history, works both ways. The process is, in Soviet parlance, 'dialectical'.

But there are further misconceptions in non-Russian minds. Siberia is not impossibly cold, empty of people, remote. Siberia really resembles Canada, rather than the North Pole, in belts, south to north, of prairie, forest, tundra and Arctic, with corresponding climatic and other conditions. Also in geology, with a wealth of minerals. Indeed it should be richer than Canada, since it is much larger; and there are Siberians, as well as people in the West, who could ask why such is not the case (but dare not). Siberia's population, approaching thirty millions, is similarly far from negligible. That population is more cohesive than is generally imagined. The average of about one person per square kilometre gives a false image; in fact nearly 75 per cent of Siberians are urban dwellers, exactly the same proportion as in the United States, many in modern cities with housing space per capita about the same as in European Russia, similarly engaged largely in industry and urban services.

The area is garrisoned accordingly with border concentrations, including all arms, land, sea and airborne forces; medium and long-range missiles; and bases for a fleet rivalling, if not excelling, that of the United States. It can be argued that far from Siberia tailing along with Russia's policy, the situation may rather be the opposite: that Siberia's position, resources and potentials are highly formative of Russia's policy.

The supposed remoteness of Siberia is another misconception. To Europeans and to Muscovites, it is remote, but to millions of people on the frontiers, from Japan all round China to Afghanistan, Soviet power in Siberia is oppressively close. This is a 'two fronts' situation for Russia; something the Russians are supposed always to have feared, but now they seem certainly acceptant of it. Lenin, when the Revolution failed to occur in Europe (which Marx postulated was the place for it), turned to the East, but eschewed creating more than one *main* front at a time. Half a century after Lenin's death, the Soviet Union's policy is of major commitment *globally*; and Siberia, greatly strengthened since his time, is an emplacement for this of hardly less importance than Europe. It is a springboard – the Russian word for this is again literally significant, being *platzdarm* (*place d'armes*) – for projections in all directions, Asia, the Pacific, and across the Arctic Circle. The evolution of Siberia from an 'Empty Quarter' to world significance furnishes many useful indications.

History of Siberia

The Republic of Novgorod, with Scandinavian and Hanseatic connections, had traders who penetrated northwestern Siberia in the eleventh to thirteenth centuries, but was then subdued and incorporated by Muscovy, which 'gathered the Russian lands' under its aegis. It is a common misconception that Russia was 'destroyed' by the Mongols. They certainly instilled fear and hatred, lasting to the present day, of the 'savage hordes of Asia'. In fact, however, they did not directly 'occupy' the Russian lands, but reduced them to humiliating tributary and vassal-state conditions; not interfering in their religious or other usages.

There is thus inaccuracy in speaking of the 'Mongol yoke'. The Mongols were terrible, so far as the Russians were directly concerned, primarily as tax-gatherers. Essentially a 'Danegeld' situation rather than a 'Vandal' incursion. Others were more villainous and frightful than the Mongols, in their descents upon the persons and property of the Russians; in Russian one does not speak so much of the Mongols as of Tartars. Which (without the first 'r' in Russian) covers a whole array of 'Turkic' and other peoples wreaking mayhem more directly and personally upon the Russians and on Russianism. And blending more with them than ever the uppish Mongols did; 'scratch a Russian', the old saying runs, 'and you will find' not a Mongol but 'a Tartar'.

All these aspects, and especially the emphases on them, are highly arguable; but one residuum is clear, namely fear and mistrust of the surrounding hordes. Explicitly, 'Yellow Peril' sentiments remain strongly current in Muscovy; but naturally stronger, more cogent and actual in Siberia, that colossal salient that overlays the whole of 'yellow' Asia. The Chinese alone outnumber the Russians, in total, about five to one; on the Siberian frontier the ratio is more like forty to one. But that frontier is far more complex than a calculus of numbers of persons; it is about three times as long as Europe's 'Iron Curtain', far more varied in terrain and physical features and in clashes or complications of systems, of cultures, in all the objective and subjective aspects. Soviet effectives face six or seven nations in Europe, the same number in Asia; but a more mixed and 'tricky' situation in the latter than the former, with more choices and more possibilities of 'things going wrong'.

Siberia fronts also on Islamic Central Asia, of which Soviet Central Asia is an important part; another complex and portentous direction, as well as the Far Eastern one. This aspect, too, must be viewed historically. In AD1380 the Mongol Empire was disintegrating and its grip over Russia relaxed, after the Russian victory at Kulikovo. The Russians took Kazan in 1552 and the Tartar Khanate of Sibir′ (in Western Siberia) in 1581, opening the door to a swift onrush all through Siberia. This was effected by speedy long-distance advances. In 1558 Ivan the Terrible appointed the Stroganov family of merchant adventurers as factors, primarily to collect tribute for him. The Stroganovs commissioned Yermak, a Cossack *ataman*, who traversed Western Siberia – with 800 men, but no horses at first – in 1581–4.

The resistance of the natives was not great; they were not numerous, were scattered in conflicting groups and lacked firearms. The Russians set up log-forts (*ostrogi*) at intervals as garrison, trading and tax-collection posts. The sovereign Republic of Novgorod, never invaded by the Mongols, had also earlier extended its mercantile interests not only in its Scandinavian and Hanseatic League connections but in penetration of northwestern Siberia.

The lure was Siberia's enormous wealth in furs, of the most valuable yet plentiful kinds; exacted mainly as tribute for the Tsar, called *yasak* (a Tartar word) and reckoned in pelts. It must be stressed that this was an extensive, not an intensive industry, in the economist's sense; the trappers, hunters and conveyors of the furs were highly mobile over long distances, the locations and types of activity varied. (Analogy is again with Canada, with its *voyageurs*.[2]) The movement, out of the northwest as well as the Urals, had naturally to be joined by clerical personnel (*diaki* etc.) as well as the trappers and the Cossacks or military (*sluzhilishchie*), for the formidable logistical, provisioning, accounting and administrative problems; and there were missionaries and others. Small in numbers but great in impact, the Russians reached the Yenisei in 1610; by 1640 they were on the Lena, the Yana and the Indigarka, in the Transbaikal.

There they met at last a great and irreducible obstacle: the might and intelligence of the China of the Manchus, which barred that route to the Pacific, and deflected the Russian movement towards the northeast. The intrinsic expansionism of Russia, evident as a prime factor even in this first phase of their national history, was checked only when it met a force stronger and better organized than itself; but only checked, the impetus remaining and being deflected into areas of less, preferably of least, resistance. This point, it is suggested, is the first axiom for understanding Russian policy. The Nerchinsk and Kyakhta treaties of 1689 and 1727 drew the Chinese line firmly along the Amur river, or north of it, though allowing some caravan access to China itself.

The Russians were already at Okhotsk on the Pacific in 1645, at the Bering Strait between 1648 and 1671 and in Kamchatka in 1679. In that period another element was added to the Russian cohorts, as Siberia was made a place of exile for political and 'ordinary' criminals. The Russian impetus then carried on even further, into Alaska; exploring and setting up posts there from 1791 and along the coasts as far as the vicinity of present-day San Francisco (Fort Ross 1812). In that area there was a significant change; the operations in the New World were placed under the direct (but very remote) control of a State Russian-America Company. However, the American venture proved 'a bridge too far'. The Russian response was withdrawal – to concentrate more on

Siberia. Alaska was sold to the United States in 1867. This, it may be suggested, presents a second main axiom or criterion in the study of Russian foreign policy, to add to the previous postulate that Russian expansionism is halted or deflected only by encountering an irreducible obstacle. Namely that the impetus can also overreach itself, in terms of distance or of capacity, of engendering more difficulties and dangers than advantages; whereupon it will go into reverse to some necessary extent, to live to leap another day.

Siberia had meanwhile, in the eighteenth century, been very greatly consolidated, assimilated and developed, by the lights of Imperial Russia. In the first third of the nineteenth century Russia, and with it the now more largely integrated Siberia, underwent its first great convulsion in the modern age: the Napoleonic Wars and their aftermath. Siberia received new types of exiles: Russian Decembrists (aspiring modernisers participating in the unsuccessful revolt of 1825), European prisoners and Russian supporters of Enlightenment. These were no rough persons, but intellectuals or *intelligentsia*, of educated and professional calibre. Poles exiled after the 1830 and subsequent revolts added to this key component, as did scientists and others needed for the development of Siberia.

By the mid-century the towns of Siberia had developed from their ancient primitivism, stagnation and parochialism, and were quite comparable, in social, cultural and commercial life, with towns in Europe and America. Also in political discussion; in which, on both the revolutionary wing and the reactionary one, Siberia was henceforward to be as great a 'seedbed' of thought, organization and action as European Russia (if not, as a land of exile and of new horizons, even more so).

A band of iron was eventually created to link Siberia most solidly to the 'centre' of Russia (as the Moscow-Leningrad region is still termed today in Russia) in the shape of the railway. Earlier, in fact, the telegraph had brought instant communication, the press a full transmission. What the railroad signalled was the spread of the first great industrial revolution in Russia. The tracks joined Moscow and St Petersburg in 1851, but the great Trans-Siberian reached Irkutsk only in 1894 and, beyond the Baikal, Chita was reached in 1900, only just before the war with Japan (of 1904–5) in the 'cockpit' of Manchuria. A most significant but never-referenced utterance by Count Witte, a great advocate at that time of Russian expansion, though through *economic* means, was that 'Manchuria is the hand on the Siberian arm'.[3] There followed a huge movement eastwards of settlers, prospectors, trade, investment – and mental ferment.

This highlights another fundamental perspective: the persistent shift (despite some movements in the opposite direction) of Russia's 'centre of gravity', material and conceptual, in successive epochs, towards the East. This trend had already matured by the time of the Russo-Japanese war; it was enhanced by the Soviet industrialization of Siberia and the part Siberia's resources played in sustaining Russia during World War II, and it continues to operate today.

While the main Russian advance in Asia had thus strongly incorporated Siberia, policy looked also towards Islamic Central Asia; which is not a separate but a conjoint topic (see Chapter 4). The motivation in that direction was less 'integrationist' (for *osvoyenie*), the area not being the 'vacuum' that Siberia had been, but evinced, besides considerations of living-space and resources, more emphasis on world influence, military prowess and religious and political Messianism. Control of that area was only completed 'basically' – with resistance continuing thereafter – in the second half of last century, in what is now Soviet Central Asia. The history of that move is not for this chapter, but it may be noted that whereas Siberia was and is a major area of Russian settlement, the dispositions in Central Asia resembled rather those in British India: *pax (et lex) russica*, military Governor-Generalships, a Russian minority segregated in their cantonments, though not intellectually aloof (especially at higher intellectual levels).

From Central Asia, Russia pushed little, in substantive terms, to the southward and eastward: less than in the East Asian area. Afghanistan today is a significant breach of that posture. In that area, 'classically' the *mise en scène* was that of the 'great Game'; in reality nothing very substantial occurred there, while around Siberia prodigious changes and enormous new opportunities took shape. The cataclysm for East Asia was the decline and dissolution of the Chinese Empire, marked by the seizure of Hong Kong (1841), the Taiping revolt and that of the Boxers, featuring a Russian occupation of Manchuria and Allied forces taking Peking.

These were incidents in a scramble between the Powers to divide out spheres of influence in China, in which Russia strongly participated, via Siberia. The length of that route hampered Russia; but it must be noted that Russia had for three centuries not only been China's large neighbour but had maintained a continuous representation and presence in China, unlike the other Europeans who appeared much more sporadically as raiders from over the sea, in a scattering of interests divided among themselves.

The next cataclysm was to occur in Russia in the aftermath of World War I with the Revolution and Civil War, which raged more widely and longer in Siberia than in European Russia; and Siberians played major roles, heroic and tragic, in those events. In a characteristically allusive

Siberian saying, the Tsar was dethroned in Petrograd but had to be killed in Siberia. The Allied intervention in the Civil War in Siberia was on a scale larger than in European Russia and it was during this period (1920–2) that Siberia east of the Baikal became an independent state, the Far Eastern Republic, with its own government and flag. Certainly this was a counter-revolutionary (*Kolchak*) creation and avowedly a buffer state, but it cannot be curtly dismissed as a 'fascistical' and insignificantly ephemeral creation, because it did produce an interesting constitution, ideas and practices; expressive, at least in part, of longstanding hankerings for an identity and some kind of autonomy or independence for Siberia.

In the following years it was 'not accidental', as the Marxian phrase has it, that the New Economic Policy permitting wide private enterprise, preliminary to the introduction of full planning, flourished especially in Siberia and lasted longer there than in Russia-in-Europe; it still prevailed in the Soviet Far East in 1931, when Stalin's power and his Plan had the rest of Russia well in hand. Collectivization, in the 1930s, was brutally pursued in Siberia as elsewhere,[4] but the stress by Stalin on heavy industry at the expense of light was more marked in Siberia, as a proportion of the total *tableau économique*, than in other parts of the country. Stalin – literally the 'man of steel' – prescribed 'socialism in one country' on the physical basis of iron and steel, most extensively and most innovatorily in Russia beyond the Urals. He set the course firmly and lastingly for autarky – which would have to draw especially on the resources of Siberia.

Character of the Siberians

Any impression that Siberia is a vacuum from the point of view of political thought is as inadequate as the depiction of it, from the geographical standpoint, as an empty part of the Polar Ice Cap. In fact Siberia has played a great part in the ferment of ideas, the soul-searchings, the psychology and the organization of revolution and of movements for reform. A seedbed in the eyes of progressivists, a hotbed of dissidence in those of reactionaries, a place of exile, of refuge or of adventure for persons of all sorts of views, Siberia was and is no mental blank.

Siberians, like peoples in other 'colonial' areas, have for the past two centuries sought most essentially for an identity of their own. Besides protesting against evils or unfairnesses, such peoples demand respect for their qualities, consideration of their special needs and circumstances, reasonable degrees of autonomy according to their growth and progress – or according to norms elsewhere. There is a phenomenon well remarked and noted in Russia – not excluding Soviet studies and documentation – as being significant in Siberia and other main parts of Russia, referred to by the blanket term 'provincialism' (*oblastnichestvo*). This covers a whole spectrum of thought and action. At the 'lowest' or 'darkest' end there is provincialism in the pejorative sense of parochialism or rural idiocy, moving up to positive consciousness of local values and to asserting them. Devolution of functions, demands for various degrees of autonomy complete the scale, right up to claiming complete independence. There is of course no Pan-Siberian nationalism – though nationalism is involved in the cases of two major groups, the Yakuts and the Buryats (but the Buryats are divided between three countries: USSR, Mongolia and China). Others would deserve mention in a fuller treatise, such as the Chukchi, the last group to be in open resistance to the Russians except for some Central Asians, but these are not major factors. What there is is Siberianism, best described as Regionalism: of a calibre deserving the capital 'R'.

This is another matter which must be stressed, because it receives so little attention in the West, compared to the amount of information in Russia, Soviet as well as pre-Soviet. Direct and substantial Western coverages of it are in fact limited to two PhD theses, one American and one German.[5] The record shows the whole of the spectrum mentioned above. A groping for identity is detectable from the earliest days – the 'Cossack' and 'conquistador' images. The eighteenth century saw some such development of a 'civil' society, increasing prosperity and *embourgeoisement*, as occurred in the North American colonies: and something of the same kind of friction with the remote control of the inefficient bureaucracy in the 'mother' country and its ignorance of local conditions and aspirations.

Development brought, thenceforward, a 'Frontier' image and self-conceit – again analogous to that celebrated component of Americanism – of the Siberian as the man of the wide-open spaces, sharpshooter, thruster-forward, hard-rider and pioneer. This has nowadays about the same objective validity as it has in North America; pioneering is the only element which remains largely of the essence today. But all this is (or is believed to be) still imprinted in the ethos and behaviouristic canons of the Siberians. Their patriotism remains a general-Russian patriotism, but regionalism gained strength *pari passu* with consciousness of the natural wealth and special quality of Siberia; and through pride in its great historic achievements. Namely, the original conquest, the provision of so much of the means that made Russia a great power (and a two-hemisphere power), the carrying of the flag (to Cathay and California), the role of joining a New World to Russia (comparable to America for Europe), the great part in Russia's Revolution, industrialization, civil war and defence. (In World War II, when the enemy reached the gates of Moscow, Siberia's capacity, material and human, can be claimed to have saved the nation.) Today Siberia represents a large part of the Soviet Union's power and presence in the world.

Dissidents and eccentrics of all kinds have been deported to Siberia; there is no need to list here the thousands of names, all through from the eighteenth century to the present day, of those sent to what Dostoyevskii described as the *House of the Dead*. In such a fostering, regionalism grew very strong in the nineteenth century; and still haunts the Russian consciousness, though suppressed by the Tsars, and more drastically by the Soviets, whose definition of 'internationalist' is one subservient to the current Moscow line. Specific emanations included growing demands for provincial and national minorities' autonomy, regional independence, actual 'dominion status' for Siberia (the British term was not used, but this went so far as proposals for a bipartite Empire: a Russia and a Siberia, though under the same Crown). And, at the final extreme, to call for actual independence for Siberia as a separate state. Much canvassed, especially in the last two schools of thought, was the example and federalist concept of the United States of America, considered by many as an obvious model and a close economic and political partner for Siberia. This was quite definitely and specifically advocated with considerable publicity, including regionalist newspapers and journals (which naturally had a hard and varied struggle against censorship and suppression).

These trends were, from the 1880s, largely submerged by the great tides of populism and radicalism, in all varieties of the latter from advanced liberalism through socialism to anarchism. Their amplitude and depth were however great; and they must, to some unquantifiable extent, be alive (though certainly not well) in Siberia today. Hypothetically these aspects might acquire key importance if some cataclysmic change occurred in future: say, just for the sake of example, war with China, or the present depression, malfunctioning and crisis in the Soviet economy and society becoming more acute.

The great maker of contemporary revolutions is 'rising expectations'. Siberia today is largely a land of youth: manned largely by Russians of the younger generation, who go there, as a rule for temporary residence and work, drawn by a desire for change, for adventure, but also bluntly for higher wages, the rates being double what they are in European Russia in the more temperate parts of Siberia, and treble in the Arctic and 'hardship' postings. A mobile and opportunist population predominates over the settled 'old-timer' element.

Siberia's resources

Siberia's capacity must be considered as part of the whole Soviet resource base, including the other CMEA countries. The resource-potential of Siberia is at present especially and predominantly in hydrocarbons. Four-fifths of the USSR's potential in the production of energy – coal, oil, natural gas and hydroelectric power – is in Siberia, in terms of what are now classified as 'probable' endowments, and it is the site of experiments in new minor sources of power (geothermal, tidal and wind-power). Diminishing returns broadly apply in the older area, European Russia, but increasing ones in Russia's 'New World' Siberia; so there is some desire to call in the latter to redress the balance of the former, where power and raw material shortages are now acute.

In 1950 the USSR production of energy was two-thirds from coal, less than one-fifth from petroleum, and negligibly (2 per cent) from natural gas. The proportions are now petroleum still nearly one-half, natural gas and coal each a quarter. Much of the natural gas and oil is for export – particularly from West Siberia (northern Tyumen′), which is producing over half the Soviet Union's output. Major foreign policy implications are first that these flow to Russia-in-Europe, the East European bloc (greatly dependent on the USSR for its energy balance) and to West Europe. This creates a considerable new dependence on Siberia by West Germany, France, and Italy in particular; not really a decisive dependence, as Europe has other sources, but real, constituting interdependence, with Europe becoming an important market for the USSR. Second, the pipelines and other installations, onstream and downstream, cause a heavy diversion of Soviet investment (ultimate total about $50bn) to this westward linkage. The Soviet Far East is otherwise geared largely to supplying Japan. Eastern Siberia can be 'pulled' in both those directions but also holds vast resources for Russia's own development.

However, there are many difficulties, either soluble only through advanced engineering and management techniques which have, besides possibly running counter to the assumptions of the Soviet system, largely to be procured from abroad – or more intrinsic to the local conditions. The latter include diminishing returns, poor transport and harsh climate, the need to extend mining far into the Arctic and other remote areas, and the 'infrastructural' needs of housing and social services, all of which are at high and sharply rising cost. In addition, the world energy situation is subject to extreme fluctuations.

In the Stalin era Russia's thrust into its new Iron Age featured large fresh bases in Siberia (Kuzbas etc.). The Soviet Union as a whole has about 30 per cent of the world's entire 'ascertained plus probable' reserves of iron, manganese and vanadium ores; it is in the 20 per cent range for most others, below 10 per cent only in chrome, molybdenum and tungsten. In actual production the Soviet Union furnishes more than 10 per cent of world output in every kind of essential mineral; in manganese, chrome, iron and vanadium over 20 per cent, in some others more than 30 per cent. What is the position of Siberia, actual and potential, in this calculus?

The 'Black Industrial Revolution', in coal and iron, has been passed through; a different spectrum now applies. In iron and steel production Siberia does not have a dominant position. It has the great integrated steel base of the Kuzbas (Kuznetsk basin), farther east two smaller steel centres at Bratsk and Komsomolsk-on-the-Amur, but Siberia's production of steel at 12 million tons a year and processed iron, nine million tons, is less than a tenth of all Soviet output of these. Siberia's own production of iron ore barely suffices for this; it draws moderately on Kazakhstan for it, as does also the Ural region.

Siberia produced 6.8 per cent of the USSR's iron ore in 1975, 6.6 in 1982. Kuzbas itself produces only about half the iron ore it uses. Much is carried from East Siberia; at high cost, but bigger and better developments are in prospect there (the Kansk-Achinsk fields). Though the Kuzbas magnetite-iron deposits are estimated at two-and-a-half billion tons, their utilization is clearly lagging. The *US Minerals Yearbook* reckons the USSR has 111 billion tons of iron-ore reserves (average Fe content 38 per cent), and uses about 10 per cent of them. Most of this is in East Siberia – principally in Angara-Pitsk and in South Yakutia, towards which the BAM Mainline is reaching. West Siberia has enormous potential under this heading, too, but as a leading Soviet expert academician Trofimuk stated in 1982, the terrain is watery, there are four great seams in a stretch of 1500 kilometres from south to north lying at depths of 150–200 metres under a huge overlap of complicated topsoils, so this is developable 'only in the future'.

In ferro-alloys there are more immediate questions. The USSR has nearly 40 per cent of the world's reserve of manganese; of which Siberia has a mere 2 per cent (mainly Krasnoyarsk and Kuznetsk-Alatau) but, with improvements, beginning to be used. The deposits of the Soviet Far East are of low content (23 per cent Mn) but large and usable (as is the brown coal widely found there and in Siberia) and are on the agenda, urgently to diminish the 'monopoly' of the Ukraine in this matter. Vanadium is produced in the USSR mainly as an iron-furnaces by-product in the Ural; more is developable, more directly, in Siberia.

Siberia is much more to the fore in the copper-nickel-cobalt sector. Around Noril'sk, especially, besides nickel are cupro-nickel ores generating 95–8 per cent in cobalt, 10–20 per cent in copper, a large part in silver and gold and the main part in selenium and tellurium.

Two-thirds of the Soviet nickel production – 17 per cent of the world's, in the second place after Canada – is from the Noril'sk Talnach-Oktyabrskii fields in East Siberia north of the Arctic Circle. In 1982 furnace capacity was installed with Finnish assistance at Nadezhda, where most of the Soviet nickel deposits are.

In cobalt the USSR has 7 per cent of the world output. From 80 to 90 per cent of this is from the Noril'sk area, but production is developing also in Tuva at the new Khovu-Aksy combine. In response to United States restrictions, the Soviet Union has set up a joint product with Cuba to get nickel-cobalt concentrates from there. This appears to be an instance of foreign policy ambitions competing with 'domestic roots' which might prefer to look to Siberia.

The production of molybdenum is predominantly in Krasnoyarsk province with main centres also in Kazakhstan and the Caucasus, but East Siberia is moving ahead in this, with the intention of smelting there the ores from Erdenet in Mongolia. The USSR is the world's second producer of wolfram, with 16 per cent; yet that does not suffice its own needs. In both output and reserves the Transbaikal and the Magadan and Maritime provinces in the Far East loom large, though the latter are of moderate quality and high cost.

In connection with BAM, a large new metallurgical base is envisaged in South Yakutia, where there is both coking coal and iron ore; coal production has started and the remainder of the project will certainly be proceeded with, but to what extent is still uncertain, particularly since the Japanese for the most part (though not entirely) backed out of it. There is in the Soviet posture, when foreigners fail to oblige, some adaptation of the classic phrase of the Italian nationalists in the nineteenth century, *l'Italia fara da se*. Russia will 'do its own thing'; and Siberia is very much the big and fresh place to do it.

In reserves of non-ferrous metals the USSR has as a whole – according to foreign experts, the figures being secret in the Soviet Union – less than 10 per cent of the world's antimony, cadmium, copper and bismuth, though more than 20 per cent of the mercury. Here also Siberia's potentials are marked. In copper production the USSR ranks second to the USA, with 12 per cent of the world's resources in 1981; authoritative estimates vary from each other, however, by up to 20 per cent. Siberia is fairly prominent in this, in the actual production at Noril'sk and from the Erdenet ores, but potentially much more, especially because of the huge Udokan deposits; which are very remote, but in the BAM zone. Udokan is supposed to be a 'copper mountain' larger than those in southern-central Africa. It is credited with 700 million tons of copper ore with a content of 1.15 per cent Cu – another field for which Western cooperation has been sought since the end of the 1960s. It is projected to make it a second Territorial Production Complex alongside South Yakutia, but that is still thought unfeasible without foreign participation and it is meanwhile considered preferable to exploit the ores on the spot and process them 'in a big plant farther south in Siberia', as stated by the same Trofimuk in 1983.

Currently Noril'sk (on a by-products basis), Central Asia, the Urals and the Caucasus contribute four-fifths of Soviet copper output, the rest of Siberia (directly as metal) little more than 10 per cent, but this last will be greatly developed. Western estimates concerning lead and zinc vary greatly, but rate the USSR as a main producer, in the order of 15 per cent of world output; and Siberia is credited with 15 to 20 per cent of the Soviet Union's output in terms of ore, but in terms of metal only 10 per cent of the Soviet total in lead and 5 in zinc. Two-thirds of the reserves are deemed to be in Kazakhstan; but intended, again, to be largely processed in Siberia. Siberia's own main deposits of lead and zinc are at Gorev on the lower Angara, which Trofimuk rates as half to one-third cheaper to develop than any others; this has not yet happened, but is in prospect. In tin, domestic production does not cover the USSR's needs, but Yakutia and the Far East have assets which are very promising and are to be developed.

In aluminium Siberia has the commanding advantage of abundant and cheap electric power, around its great power plants of Bratsk, Krasnoyarsk, Irkutsk, Novokuznetsk, Sayansk and others coming on stream. Siberia's own reserves of bauxite are not of the best quality; local alunite and nepheline are processed, notably at Achinski, but better clay is fetched all the way from Nikopol in the Ukraine, at high transport cost, which there is a high motivation to reduce.

Turning to the noble metals, the USSR is the world's biggest producer of platinum and associated metals, exceeding South Africa with 48 per cent of the world's output. It gets three-quarters of its production in Noril'sk, another 15 per cent from the Kola (Archangel-Murmansk) peninsula. In gold, the Soviet Union is second in world production to South Africa. This is a domain of the deepest secrecy, but clearly East Siberia and the Soviet Far East produce some two-thirds of the Union's output, and have corresponding reserves, ubiquitously worked and prospected.

In the immediate postwar period the Soviet Union was short of diamonds, of which the import was impeded by the Cocom embargo. It determined to find its own, and by colossal effort did so in the Siberian Plateau; with signal success, now rivalling southern Africa in this item. This happening – astonishingly little noticed in the world at large – exemplifies another point. Namely, that the USSR is able, and on occasion minded, to mount some colossal 'drive' for a new objective –

not least in its Great Open East, Siberia, a huge, still largely unprospected, 'lucky dip' for resources containing enormous prizes.

Next to minerals, the extensive resource of Siberia is its forest-cover; on such a scale as to be considered the world's largest potential supplier of non-tropical wood. This has however not had corresponding priority or success. The cutting of timber has seriously declined; between 1965 and 1980 by only 5 per cent in quantity, but by 25 per cent in terms of the proportion of it that is of 'commercial' quality. This is ascribed to bad planning, poor central and regional control (the cardinal Soviet sin) and 'gigantism' (over-large administrative units having been created, where several smaller ones would have done much better). And there are environmentalist objections; there is ecological protest, though no 'Green Party' or movement is allowed in the USSR. The emphasis in this industry is on the development of pulp and paper production, which has greatly increased.

L. Dienes pointed out at the International Colloquy on Siberia in Paris in 1983 at the quatercentenary of the Russian entry into Siberia that without oil and gas – but that is a very high exception – Siberian industrial growth has recently lagged noticeably behind the average for the country. Not only did other processing industries perform poorly, but evidently so did other extractive 'branches'. However, in the Soviet dispensation, where the lag is, there the spur is most likely to be applied.

Nevertheless, a large and profitable function for Siberia requires, *inter alia:*

(1) A technically qualified labour supply prepared to live and work in Siberia;

(2) Improvement (modernization and recasting) of the transport system, primarily the railways; Russia is (by modern industrial-country standards) drastically lacking in roadways. Rivers are much used; and air-freight, including helicopters, expensively resorted to in the 'pioneering' outlands.

'Gigantism' remains strong in the Soviet ethos, the primacy of the large-scale, 'complex', heroic and prestigious undertaking, instanced by the Baikal-Amur Railway, to be completed in 1984 after considerable delay. The motivation for this remains however in large part strategic, doubling the Trans-Siberian farther away from the Chinese border. Functionally, BAM was originally boosted as opening up a huge new area for large integrated industrial 'complexes' within its (undefined) 'zone'; but it is no longer publicized as 'the project of the century' and it has become basically for the extraction of primary resources to feed into the national central pool – and partly to supply what has been contracted to Japan. From the 'Siberianist' viewpoint this is a 'colonial' role;

(3) A more generalized industrialization, including the further development of many non-fuel minerals (nickel, platinum, copper and others). Their utilization in turn depends on further development of the engineering industry, which has traditionally been of good quality in Siberia, since that region has always been short of labour, hence obliged to have a higher level of mechanization;

(4) The fourth requirement is further exploitation of Siberia's hydro-electric potential. This potential – three-quarters of the total of the USSR – is little emphasized in practice. Thermal power stations still represent 70 per cent of the Soviet Union's capacity, over three-quarters of that of the part west of the Urals, and over one-half of that of the part east of them. The overall concept is that there will be transmission of electricity – at very high voltages, which are being developed, over huge distances – on a vast grid serving the whole Soviet Union and extending into East Europe, which makes large demands on the USSR for its 'energy balance'.

Given all the shortfalls which have to be made up, the imports that are desired to be replaced by home production, and on the other hand that so much of the resources that could be major foreign exchange earners if exported are in Siberia, the 'pull' and 'specific weight' of Siberia in the calculus of the future of the Soviet Union (and the whole Bloc) is very marked.

This is to take only the economic aspects, vital though they are. There is also the enormous global-strategic position and importance of Siberia. If Paris was worth a mass to the old French king, Siberia may well be worth a heavy investment outlay to the Soviet leadership.

Japan and the development of Siberia

The main pillars of the East Asian construct are China and Japan. The total failure of Soviet Russia to deal with China, under the most favourable political circumstances of alliance, has been sufficiently noticed elsewhere. Japan, as well as China, has attempted a major and purposive link with the Soviet Union, actually involving a substantial Japanese presence in Siberia during the later 1960s through the 1970s, which is still continuing. That experience must be briefly noted here, since it is regarded in Asia and elsewhere as a test-case of the practical possibility of constructive relations with Siberia.

It was however complex. The suggestion that Japan should invest heavily and participate directly in major development projects in Siberia came in 1965 from the Soviet side. An exciting proposal: opening gates in the great autarky of Russia, could this be a breakthrough? Consider first the overall situation from the Asian point of view. The Soviets make much of their being encircled by a hostile world; but East Asians could see the boot being on the other foot, with Russia holding the whole northern half of their continent, Siberia hanging like the sword of Damocles (modernized into the Bomb). And (to mix metaphors still further – as is done more freely in Asian languages than in Western) acting like a growling dog in a large manger. That aspect must not be overlooked; in the following connection.

As has been seen, Siberia is by far the world's largest remaining area of under-utilized basic resources, of the kinds sorely and eagerly needed and desired by industrialized and industrializing countries and peoples, particularly the Asian ones that are Siberia's neighbours, to whose economies and aspirations Siberia's 'frozen assets' are, in all rationality and constructive desirability, directly and massively complementary. And *vice versa*, Asia has so much to offer that is complementary to the needs and best interests of Siberia and Russia. Did this *démarche* herald the end of the old stalemate, a new course of partnership? Committees were formed in each of the two countries, Japan and the USSR, to plan and operate the scheme. The Japanese, prosperous in their economic miracle and avid for new opportunities anywhere in the world, were immediately affected by a 'Siberia fever' and rushed to interest themselves. The Russians remained more orientally inscrutable; there was no such fever there, though official encouragement and competence were shown.

To summarize a complex history, useful investments proposed by the Japanese totalled about five billion dollars; of which just over a quarter have been realized. Successful major projects were in port construction, communications, forestry and mining equipment. Causes of shortfall, and of cancellation of some projects, included financial problems (interest and credit terms, exchange rates); Soviet suspicion of foreigners and their 'demonstration effects', both material (affluence) and psychical (life-style and freedom of thought); and bureaucracy (despite some delegation of responsibility and procedures from Moscow to Dal'torg and other representatives).

Whether or not it was an *a priori* intention on the Soviet side, there were some divisive effects within Japan, as well as gains to it. In the 'Siberia fever' the famous big firms of Japan naturally led (especially iron, steel and heavy machinery interests), but a swarm of small firms were eager to 'get in on' the act, to the extent that it became a scramble or free-for-all (the Japanese press used the term *tatakiai*, like rush-hour on the Tokyo underground, almost a brawl). Rash and weak small enterprises competed wildly and often failed; the gainers were the giant Japanese corporations – and the Soviets, who acted in monolithic unity, beheld the lower echelons of Japanese capitalism being brought down and Finance Capital dominant, in fulfilment of Marxist prophecy.

The process then settled down; activity still continues, most practically in respect of offshore gas and oil in northern Sakhalin, otherwise largely reduced in scope and pace in the later 1970s. Wider considerations intruded, on a world-wide scale: oil crisis, sanctions after the invasion of Afghanistan – in which Japan joined – and the development of gas and oil at the other end of Siberia (Tyumen′) linking to West Europe.

In the deeply and swiftly changing world scene macropolitical and strategic evaluations alter greatly and rapidly. In this case, China entered into positive relations with the United States and the rest of the capitalist world, the United States was displaced by the USSR in Vietnam, the Soviets deployed a large navy in the China Seas and Pacific and Indian Oceans. What occurred was partial (though far from extreme) failure, from Japan's point of view, in the Siberia scheme, but meanwhile much larger, more pleasant prospects arising in China.

The cultural and psychological affinities between the Japanese and the Chinese enable much more *entente*, whereas with the Japanese the 'unjust conquests' (Sakhalin and the Kuriles) by the Soviet Union still rankle. It is also to be noted, on the practical plane, that the Chinese appear to be more open to discussing longer-term prospects, a sequential basis of successive accords looking farther ahead; whereas the Russians, belying their image of being the integral and far-sighted exponents of Planning *par excellence*, insisted in the relations with Japan on proceeding mainly project by project, or with evaluation of each sector mainly in and for itself.

It was China's actual or possible sensitivity regarding the construction of the Baikal-Amur Railway (BAM, the second Trans-Siberian) that was a turning-point in the Japan-Siberia venture. The Japanese were initially interested in participating in this project, but were deterred in some part by the practical and financial difficulties, in some major part by the strategic anxieties of the Chinese regarding the consequent strengthening of the military and general capabilities of the Soviets in the area beyond Lake Baikal.

On the Soviet side the stance was largely from the beginning a preference to carry out the project themselves. However certain lessons ought to be obvious, in all this, to Soviet policy-makers. One is that international exchanges in the present epoch are intensely competitive. Another is that the basis of bargaining has become largely, in business and other relationships, that of the package deal.

China has entered into 'triangular' conjunctions with the other main powers and interests; and 'triangulation' is, though not explicitly so defined, a real basis of Japan's policy, i.e. always to involve third parties, as bilateral undertakings necessarily appear pointed against someone else. The Soviet Union, so long as it adheres to Marxism-Leninism as interpreted by itself, insists on dwelling in a bipolar world, its dialectical world of synthesis coming through clash, while all others are building towards synthesis through multilateral arrangements, in terms of broadening understandings rather than sharpening particular clashes. Such are the real tests facing Soviet policy.

Inferences and conclusions

In brief, Siberia is a large, very important, formative or even decisive part of the corpus and heterogeneous amalgam that is the Soviet Union. It has needs, conditions and aspirations, also perils and possibilities, that are its own. Lack of responsiveness towards Siberia, of *simpatia*, make it impossible for the remote and distinctly non-humanistic bureaucracy and dictatorship of Moscow to respond to the situation of this region. So too does the ossification of the system and the structure, the hardening of the arteries after half a century of hierarchically privileged summit-control at long distance. Lenin's world revolution stalled (until World War II gave new opportunities to advance by force of arms) first in Europe; he then turned to the East. Sixty years later it has stalled in the East. Russia has turned to the alternative of a new global strategy.

In this, Siberia has played and continues to play a causal and formative part. As Russia's colossal projection into Asia, now the largest area of fundamental and portentous change in the world, and a main physical base for the new-style (ballistic and other) global Soviet capacity, Siberia looms large, not as an appendage to Russia but as a major component. It must continue to do so, or to weigh still more heavily in future, because it is the Soviet Union's main reservoir of all natural resources, while such are being depleted elsewhere or obtainable only under diminishing returns. The difficulties in Siberia are however great, as well as the possibilities. Investment has steadily increased in Siberia as a proportion of total Soviet investment, but the system is intrinsically unsuccessful there as in other regions of the country. Most relevatory to the economist are the conclusions of recent Soviet analyses, at a high academic and planning-office level, of the experience and problems of Siberia; which conclude bluntly that the era of extensive development in Siberia is over and the future must lie in intensive, and more efficient, development there.[6] Russia's 'centre of gravity' continues to move, as it has for three centuries past, gradually eastward. In Siberia lies a great part of the evolution of Russia from being a Great Power into being a Superpower.

Notes

1 The Russian literature specifically on Siberia would fill a large modern library, the non-Russian at most a few shelves. Translations of key Russian works would be most valuable, in two categories: general surveys and close geographical and practical descriptions. For example, in the former A.P. Okladnikov's monumental history of Siberia (*Istoriya Sibiri*) in five volumes and the Siberian Encyclopedia (*Entsiklopediya Sibiri*) embarked on in the late 1920s, when the Siberianist caucus (*sibiriaki*) was influential in government and planning-office circles; publication was begun, but the work was suppressed by Stalin before it had proceeded very far, and copies are now scarce. In the latter category V.V. Pokshishevskii's guide to the Trans-Siberian Railway, *Moskva-Vladivostok* (Mysl', Moscow, 1968) may be cited for the Russian bibliography and E. Stuart Kirby, *The Soviet Far East* (Macmillan, London, 1971) for the English.

2 E. Stuart Kirby, 'The trail of the sable: new evidence on the fur-hunters of Siberia in the seventeenth century', in *Slavic Studies*, Hokkaido University, 1981, No. 27.

3 Personal evidence of contemporaries, quoted by direct hearers, though not to hand in print. Count S.Y. Witte, 1849–1915, Minister of Finance 1892–1903, headed the Russian delegation for the Portsmouth peace treaty; and proposed constitutional reforms in 1905. Only fragments of his extraordinarily frank memoirs are available in English. The remark quoted was of course made in French: the Russian word, *ruka*, does not distinguish between 'hand' and 'arm'.

4 E. Stuart Kirby, 'Communism in Yakutia – the first phase', in *Slavic Studies*, Hokkaido University, 1980, No. 25.

5 Stephen D. Watrous, *Russia's 'Land of the Future': Regionalism and the Awakening of Siberia*, PhD thesis, University of Washington, 1970, published only in photocopy by University Microfilms (Ann Arbor and London, 1981) and Wolfgang Faust, *Russlands Goldener Boden*, doctoral dissertation, Cologne, 1979, published by Böhlau Verlag (Cologne and Vienna, 1980). A more general treatment, on the background of 'populist' movements, is D. von Mohrenschildt, *Toward a United States of Russia*, Associated University Presses, 1981.

6 *Razvitiye narodnovo khozyaistva sibiri* (Novosibirsk, Adacemy of Sciences 1982). For a full study of Siberia's natural wealth – in 700 double-column pages – see R.G. Jensen, T. Shabad and A.W. Wright (eds.), *Soviet Natural Resources in the World Economy* (Chicago, University of Chicago Press, 1983). Stuart Kirby, Special Report on *Siberia*, Economist Intelligence Unit, to be published in summer 1984, presents this writer's further view of the subject.

PART THREE: FOREIGN POLICY MAKERS

11 The CPSU Local Apparat

Peter Frank

Two elements make up the governmental process in the USSR: *rukovodstvo* and *upravlenie*. One element, *rukovodstvo*, is superior to the other. *Rukovodstvo* means 'leadership', 'direction', and it is the function that is invariably identified with the Communist Party of the Soviet Union (CPSU). *Upravlenie*, on the other hand (which means administration, or policy implementation), is carried on variously by the soviets, trade unions, and public organizations generally.

This strict separation of policy-making and policy-implementation is quite different from the pattern that prevails in, for example, Britain, where the two elements of government overlap and intertwine (as is exemplified in the doctrine of individual ministerial responsibility).

It is, therefore, in the sense of its having a monopoly over *rukovodstvo* that the CPSU can be said to rule, and its Politburo equated with 'the Government'. But having arrogated to itself the right to govern, and having adjusted Marxism-Leninism in such ways as to justify its monopoly, how does the Party ensure compliance? What are the mechanisms of control by which it not only maintains the separation of *rukovodstvo* and *upravlenie*, but also makes certain that society observes the boundaries of these two roles?

In substantial part, the answer lies in CPSU membership. At the beginning of 1983 there were 18,117,903 members of the Communist Party,[1] some 9 per cent, or one in eleven, of the adult population of the USSR. These are, in the Party's terms, the most conscious and politically active members of society: the 'best of the best', as they are sometimes called.

Party members are enjoined by the Statutes of the CPSU to give their undivided loyalty and allegiance to the Party. Each member, too, must belong to a primary party organization (ppo) which is situated, not in the area of residence, but in the place of work. Thus, there are currently 425,897 ppos functioning in factories, schools, military units, farms, hospitals, ministries – anywhere, indeed, where three or more communists work together. So, at one extreme, there are simple-cell ppos consisting of only a handful of members; while at the other there are primary organizations embracing several thousand communists in a labour force numbering tens of thousands. Such large units are, in their structure and organization, microcosms of the total CPSU.

As industrial enterprises have become larger and more complex in their division of labour and production process, so have ppos adopted a more complex infrastructure. Now there are sub-units of the ppo in the various workshops of a factory; and even different shifts of workers are organized into discrete Party groups. In sum, therefore, there are today 480,256 workshop Party organizations and 659,955 Party groups subordinated to the 425,000 ppos. As each one of these units and sub-units has at its core some person with executive authority (be it a lowly *partgruporg* or the secretary of the Party committee of a major industrial combine, such as the Gor'kii Autoworks), this means that over one-and-a-half million communists, about one in twelve of the total Party membership, are at any one time holding Party office. This is a very effective way of both extending Party influence into the non-Party workforce and reinforcing individual commitment to Party goals and policies.

Moreover, ppos have certain rights of *kontrol'* (the Russian usage has the connotation of 'supervision', but this often shades into outright 'control' in the English sense of the word) over the administration of enterprises and this, again, is an important mechanism to ensure compliance with Party policy. But the most important means are the doctrine of Democratic Centralism, which not only helps to sustain the Party's claim to *rukovodit*, it also has the effect of funnelling authority upwards to the centre *within* the Party itself, and the ban on intra-Party fractionalism, dating from the Tenth Congress in 1921 as enshrined in the resolution 'On Party Unity'. And finally, less obtrusive now but still present as, as it has been described, 'the inertia of fear', there are the agencies of the Party-state which have the physical capacity to force compliance: the police and the military.

It would be a mistake, however, to visualize Soviet society, or indeed the mass Party membership, as being a grey, regimented, nondescript aggregate of individuals. As educational levels rise and as life becomes more variegated, Soviet citizens, including members of the Party, exhibit a greater awareness of the outside, non-socialist world and a much greater curiosity about it. Sometimes this is only on the level of a desire to know about, and perhaps to acquire, articles of personal consumption of Western origin; but even this may lead to a curiosity about foreign affairs in a broader sense. Consequently, the Party is careful to maintain its monopoly of *rukovodstvo* in this realm; it takes pains to ensure that the interpretation of foreign policy is the Party's and considerable effort is expended to make certain that the 'correct' interpretation is provided.

Interpretation takes the form, most obviously, of media presentation (over which the Party has monopoly control), but also of various kinds of meeting. Here a different approach is used. A 'peace' meeting or a 'Hands off Grenada!' rally would be open to the entire labour force of an enterprise, Party and non-Party, and the ppo would make sure that everyone turned up, that speakers were ready and that their speeches took the correct line, and that the appropriate resolutions had been formulated in anticipation of their unanimous approval. But a closed Party meeting on, say, the situation in Poland held in, say, a scientific research institute would be a somewhat different matter. The gathering would be arranged in more or less the same way, but the amount of information divulged and the range of discussion permitted would be markedly different. This is what is known in Soviet political parlance as the 'differentiated approach'.

The main point, however, is that there is a predominantly downward flow of instruction, especially in matters of foreign policy; while the decision-making goes on exclusively at the apex of the political structure. I do not regard that statement as being in conflict with Seweryn Bialer's view that:

> During the Brezhnev era the number and variety of those involved in the foreign policy-making process have expanded. Many groups now participate and their influence has increased. Those involved include individuals at the apex of the various bureaucratic hierarchies – political, military, economic and academic – and experts attached to those hierarchies.[2]

After all, it is the Politburo, the 'directing core', which has eventually to sift and balance the often contradictory inputs before taking the *political* decision. As Bialer wisely says:

> In a Soviet-type regime, the ambitious bureaucrat tries to tailor his selection of data, explanations, and advice to the perceived needs and preferences of political superiors. One has to remember also that the opinions of experts are quite heterogeneous and that the political leaders may quickly select those views that suit them best.[3]

It will have been noted that Bialer refers to 'individuals at the *apex* of the various bureaucratic hierarchies'. These are dealt with in a different section of this study. In the present section, I shall deal with the relationship of regional and local Party functionaries to the foreign policy-making process. As has been mentioned already, the base of the Party pyramid is the recipient of policy decisions from above, and in foreign policy matters probably makes very little input into the decision-making process, even in a purely informational sense. However, above the level of the ppo, the Party *apparat* proper begins, and it might be reasonable to suppose that hereafter the degree of input and participation, at least by professional Party functionaries, will increase. At the regional (*oblast'* and *krai*) level in particular, where many of the Party *obkom* first secretaries are members of the all-Union Central Committee, it might be expected that the *apparat* would be fairly closely involved in policy formulation.

That *obkom* first secretaries, more especially those who are members of the Central Committee, are uncommonly well-informed on foreign-policy matters there can be little doubt. However, my *a priori* hypothesis is that the regional *apparat*, including the first secretaries, is largely, perhaps entirely, excluded from the foreign policy-making process.

Such a hypothesis will seem intrinsically odd in view of the fact that out of the twenty-two men who at the beginning of 1984 made up the CPSU Central Committee Secretariat and Politburo no fewer than fourteen had served previously (or currently) as first secretaries in the local Party *apparat*, six of them as *obkom* first secretaries. Yet there is scant evidence to suggest that any of them had access to the policy-making process prior to their arrival at the centre. However, in an attempt to illuminate and perhaps substantiate the hypothesis, I will examine three aspects of the regional *apparat* in detail. These are: (i) the occupational and educational backgrounds of *obkom* first secretaries, with a view to inferring the degree of interest in and attitudes towards foreign-policy issues; (ii) the phenomenon of removing *obkom* first secretaries from the Party apparatus and placing them in ambassadorial posts; and (c) the involvement of representatives of the regional *apparat* in the work of the USSR Supreme Soviet's two standing commissions on foreign affairs.

The entire Soviet educational system is closely supervised by the Party. At all levels, there is a substantial 'ideological' component in the curriculum. However, despite this surveillance, social-science and humanities subjects do seem to encourage some independence of mind and a broadening of intellectual horizons that appear to foster curiosity about the world beyond the USSR, and, possibly, an inquisitiveness about and understanding of foreign affairs. The same is true – perhaps even more so – in the realm of the pure sciences. On the other hand, an education in one of the production disciplines seems to have less impact. It is, of course, notoriously difficult to ascertain attitudes in Soviet society; yet observation plus impressions gained from literature and the mass media tend to suggest that education received in technical institutions, whatever its strictly professional merits, does not produce graduates with a questing turn of mind. There is evidence, too, to show that students recruited into the production disciplines are not drawn from the intellectual cream of the school population.[4]

Now, it is from the production disciplines that the professional, full-time, Party *apparat* is drawn. No doubt the content and level of instruction of, say, a course in mechanical engineering has improved markedly since the early 1930s, when the Soviet Union embarked upon its great industrialization drive. But the same is true of other disciplines and the discrepancy in standards has been at least maintained.

Analysis of the educational backgrounds of Party functionaries reveals two salient characteristics: (i) that the *apparat*, down to the ppo level (and increasingly there, too) is now staffed entirely by higher-educated personnel; and (ii) the *type* of educational background of the *apparat* (as distinct from level of attainment) is overwhelmingly from amongst the production disciplines.

If, for instance, we consider the educational backgrounds of the fifty-five *obkom* first secretaries staffing the Russian *oblast'* Party organizations in the RSFSR, then it turns out that all but one of them had received a higher education.[5] However, only two were educated at university; the rest had attended mainly a technical institution of one kind or another (please see Table 11.1).

Three further points need to be made in connection with the education of the *apparat*. Firstly, the first secretaries received their education in the 1930s, 1940s and early 1950s, a time when not only were technical levels lower than they are now, but also a period when Stalinist dogma was at its most stultifying. Secondly, many gained their diplomas by evening study or correspondence course, and, although praiseworthy

Table 11.1 Educational backgrounds of CPSU obkom *first secretaries serving in 'Russian' oblasts of the RSFSR, 1979*

Industrial subjects (including eight secretaries who received additional training at a Higher Party School)	23	(41.8 per cent)
Agricultural subjects (including four who attended Higher Party School)	20	(36.4 per cent)
Higher Party School only	4	
Pedagogical institute	3	
State university	2	
Other higher educational institute	2	
Secondary specialized education only	1	
Total	55	

Source: Compiled from data abstracted from *Deputaty Verkhovnogo Soveta SSSR* (Moscow, 1979) and *Ezhegodnik Bol'shoi Sovetskoi Entsiklopedii 1981*.

in itself, this was unlikely to have encouraged a broad intellectual curiosity. And, thirdly, most of the secretaries had attended provincial educational institutions where, if anything, pedagogical levels were likely to have been lower than in Moscow, Leningrad or one of the republic capitals.

If we take into consideration, too, the fact that many Party functionaries acquired or supplemented their education by attending *Party* higher educational institutions, then it becomes even less likely that they will be independently minded on foreign-policy issues. On the contrary, the exigencies of their professional Party careers and the forces of political socialization to which they are subjected might be expected to encourage an orthodox or conservative attitude.

Are there, then, any aspects of the local *apparat's* work that are likely to encourage innovative attitudes towards foreign-policy making?

Some republic and *obkom* first secretaries travel abroad occasionally as leaders or members of official delegations. It is, however, striking that such visits are almost always to a fraternal socialist state or to a friendly third-world country (visits to capitalist states are undertaken mainly by professional diplomats and foreign-ministry staff); there is thus little likelihood of a local official's being exposed to, much less influenced by, unconventional views.

Another possibility is that Party officials serving on the periphery are more interested in foreign-policy issues, if only to the extent that their own territories might be affected by them. But, quite apart from the fact that posts on the periphery are very often less prestigious[6] and hence their incumbents potentially less influential, it is also probable that this circumstance reinforces traditional, dogmatic foreign-policy preferences. For example, if a preoccupation of, say, the first secretary of a Baltic republic Party organization is combating nationalism and alien bourgeois influences, it is hardly likely that détente, with its cessation of jamming of broadcasts, more foreign visitors and tourists, and so on, is going to make his job any easier.

Similarly, to the extent that Party secretaries in border areas are members of regional military councils, it might be expected that they would be better informed about, and more anxious to contribute to, the formulation of foreign policy. Yet that, too, seems improbable: the Soviet military is careful not to transgress the boundaries of political decision-making, and it is unlikely that much opportunity to do this would arise at the local level anyway.

In short, in so far as the local *apparat* is interested in foreign policy at all, it seems certain that it will incline towards orthodox, traditional positions such as maintaining a *cordon sanitaire* of socialist states around the USSR at all costs, and keeping at bay alien, corrupting bourgeois influences. In other words, to the extent that it exerts pressure upon the centre at all, it is likely to be conservative.

Anyone who has studied the Party *obkom* first secretaries will have noticed that from time to time an individual is removed from Party office and posted as ambassador to a foreign embassy. Given that the regional first secretaries' main concerns are to maintain social control and maximize material production within the territorial boundaries of their area of competence, such transfers seem to be intrinsically inappropriate. However, closer examination of the phenomenon reveals that this is rational political behaviour.

Transfers of this kind are always out of the CPSU regional *apparat* and into a posting in a fraternal socialist capital. To take a concrete example, A.N. Aksenov, a Belorussian, was born in 1924. In 1941 he completed his formal education and became, briefly, a *kolkhoznik* before being called up into the army for a short period in 1942–3. The next fifteen years were spent as an official of the Komsomol in Belorussia, culminating in his appointment as first secretary of the republic organization. In the meantime, in 1945, he had joined the Communist Party, and, later, he had taken a correspondence course with the all-Union Central Committee Party Higher School, graduating, and thus receiving the designation 'higher educated', in 1957. Following a brief spell (1959–60) as deputy chairman of the KGB in Belorussia, he spent five years as Minister of Internal Affairs for the republic. Between 1965 and 1971, Aksenov was first secretary of the Vitebsk Party *obkom*, before being appointed second secretary of the Belorussian republic Party Central Committee. Although chairman of the Council of Ministers of the Belorussian Republic since December 1978, Aksenov was passed over for the post of first secretary when P.M. Masherov was killed in an automobile accident in 1980, and again in 1983 when T. Ya. Kiselev, Masherov's successor, died; he was appointed Soviet ambassador to Poland in July 1983.[7]

Aksenov's appointment to a diplomatic post exemplifies *par excellence* the adage that foreign policy is but an extension of domestic policy. In Warsaw – and in other socialist capitals, particularly those of countries geographically contiguous to the USSR – the ambassador must be vigilant to see that the ideological and organizational rules of a Soviet-type system are being observed, and this, especially following the fiasco of Poland's massive foreign debts, extends into the realm of economic decision-making.

It is true that the Soviet ambassador and the local national leadership do not always see eye to eye with each other on all matters. The tensions that existed between P.A. Abrasimov and the East German leader between 1975 and 1983 are notorious.[8] But on the essential point of the maintenance of the regime in the socialist countries and the preservation of the security of the USSR there is much more common agreement. Soviet ambassadors, therefore, are in these countries more like viceroys than conventional diplomats. Nor do they require prior training in the arts of diplomacy: the transition from local Party *apparat* to ambassadorial posting is immediate. These men are 'politicals', rather than professionals; their entire background, political socialization and Party career experience are wholly consonant with what is now expected of them; and their appointment, therefore, is not inconsistent with the hypothesis that the domestic *apparat* at the local and regional level is excluded from policy formulation in the realm of foreign affairs.

'Political' ambassadors serving in postings in socialist states amount to only a small proportion of the total ambassadorial corps. But as they either retain or acquire full or candidate membership status of the Central Committee they suffer no loss of status or prestige; indeed, their career prospects may be enhanced. It is true that an ambassadorial appointment is occasionally used as a device 'to kick someone upstairs': the former Leningrad Party first secretary, V.S. Tolstikov, is a case in point. Having incurred the displeasure of the top leadership, in 1970 he was posted to Peking. Not only did this effectively remove him from the arena of domestic politics, it also occurred at a time when Sino-Soviet relations were moribund and there was therefore relatively little for him to do.

A similar example of fall from grace is that of D.S. Polyanskii. Ousted from the Politburo, in 1976 he was posted to Japan, and since 1982 he has been Soviet ambassador to Norway, whence in due course he will no doubt be quietly retired. However, there are many examples of 'political' ambassadors' 'looping' back into the domestic *apparat* at the highest level and thus gaining access to policy formulation, *rukovodstvo*.

It may be no more than a peculiar conjunction of circumstance, but it is nonetheless striking that the present Party leadership contains a significant number of members with 'political' ambassadorial experience. Moreover, the USSR's late leader, Yuri Andropov, following service in the regional *apparat* and briefly at the centre, was himself ambassador to Hungary (coincidentally with the Hungarian revolution in 1956). He returned to the Central Committee apparatus in 1957, since when his career is well known. Gromyko's background includes a posting in London (although he, of course, is a professional); while V.I. Vorotnikov, since December 1983 a full member of the Politburo, was transferred from the regional Party *apparat* to the embassy in Cuba, before being brought back once more into domestic politics in 1982. M.V. Zimyanin, currently a Central Committee secretary with responsibilities in the ideological sphere, made his name in the Belorussian Party *apparat*, and was Soviet ambassador to Vietnam in 1956–7 and then to Czechoslovakia from 1960 to 1965. The head of another extremely important Central Committee department (relations with ruling communist parties), K.V. Rusakov, was engaged in diplomatic work in the late 1950s and 1960s, including a short spell as ambassador to Mongolia in 1962–3. N.M. Pegov, a one-time local Party functionary, was ambassador successively to Iran, India and then Algeria before returning to the central apparatus in 1975 to head the Department of Foreign Cadres (to be succeeded in turn in 1983 by S.V. Chervonenko, a former member of the Ukraine Party *apparat* before service as ambassador in China, Czechoslovakia – he helped to coordinate the quelling of the 'Prague Spring' in 1968 – and France). In other words, while it would be too much to suggest that 'political' ambassadorial service is an enhancer of career prospects, it certainly does not appear to be a drawback. Moreover, it may prove to be no more than an interlude before 'looping' back into domestic politics at the highest level of decision-making. But it is the diplomatic service, and *not* the previous local *apparat* career as such that draws the individual into the foreign policy realm.

We turn now to the third test of the hypothesis: the role played by *obkom* first secretaries (and other local Party officials) in the USSR Supreme Soviet's standing commissions on foreign affairs.

Each chamber of the USSR Supreme Soviet (the Council of the Union and the Council of Nationalities) has its own standing commission on foreign affairs. It is assumed that these particular standing commissions, given the intrinsic importance of foreign affairs, have high status and prestige. Support for that assumption may be found in the fact that the chairman of one commission (Council of Nationalities) is B.N. Ponomarev, candidate member of the Politburo and head of the Central Committee's International Department; while the other commission (Council of the Union) was chaired until his death in 1982 by Mikhail Suslov, followed by Konstantin Chernenko.

Analysis of the composition of the two standing commissions reveals that local Party *apparat* representation is very weak indeed. Out of a total joint membership of seventy, there are only fourteen who could in any sense be regarded as representative of the local Party-State elite (and these include four republic Party first secretaries and seven *obkom* first secretaries, the inclusion of at least one of whom, L.B. Shapiro, should be regarded as mainly symbolic). On the other hand, a major segment of the membership is made up of media persons, artists, actresses, heads of cultural organizations, plus a number of 'statutory' dairy maids and factory workers. Included, too, are very important members of the *rukovodstvo* and, as will be shown below, these dominate the proceedings.

To further support the hypothesis that the local Party *apparat* is virtually excluded from foreign policy-making, a topical, recent foreign policy issue is now analysed.

In June 1983 the President of Finland and the Finnish prime minister had discussions in Moscow with the Soviet leadership, culminating in the signing of a protocol on Soviet-Finnish friendship and cooperation. On 4 November 1983 a joint meeting was held of the standing commissions on foreign affairs of both chambers of the USSR Supreme Soviet. The session was chaired by Chernenko, while the protocol was introduced by B.F. Mal'tsev, a deputy minister for foreign affairs (and, incidentally, a former ambassador).

Mal'tsev's speech described the meeting in June and recounted the history of post-war Finnish-Soviet relations. There was nothing in the speech to invite discussion, nor was there any. Speaker after speaker endorsed the decision that had been taken already at the centre. However, it is instructive to note who the participants were:

Zaikov, L.N. First secretary, Leningrad Party *obkom* (recent successor to G.V. Romanov upon his promotion to a Central Committee secretaryship)

Epishev, A.A. Head of the Chief Political Administration of the Soviet armed forces

Zhukov, G.A. Chairman of the Soviet Committee for the Defence of Peace; political observer of *Pravda*

Line, V.M. Actress, State Drama Theatre of Latvia

Shamyakin, I.P. Writer; chief editor of the Belorussian Soviet encyclopaedia

Ponomarev, B.N. Head, International Department of the Central Committee of the CPSU.

As *Pravda* reported, 'All the speakers approved of the protocol and recommended [its] ratification.'[9] Not surprisingly, the decision to recommend approval was unanimous. At the session of the presidium of the USSR Supreme Soviet held on 11 November 1983, the unanimous recommendation was duly made, and in turn was unanimously accepted and approved by the presidium.

The point of this example is not to illustrate the workings of the Soviet legislative process. It is, rather, to demonstrate that even in a matter as uncontroversial as current Soviet-Finnish relations the policy-making goes on in an extremely restricted circle, that the local *apparat* has only limited access to even the formal, ritualized, public policy process, and that, even here, the formalities are conducted exclusively by officials either from within the policy-making elite itself (Chernenko, Ponomarev), or by 'individuals at the apex of the various bureaucratic hierarchies' (Epishev, Zhukov), or by purely symbolic personalities who, in foreign policy terms, are nonentities (the Latvian actress). How much less likely still is it that the forum of real decision-making would be extended were the issue, say, the Geneva disarmament talks!

It is on the face of things paradoxical that the Soviet Union has a foreign policy-making elite which draws heavily upon the regional Party *apparat* for replenishment, yet that local *apparat* is virtually excluded from the policy-making operation. It should be remembered, however, that the Soviet political system does not usually produce sharp, wholesale changes of top leadership personnel. There is time, therefore, for relatively slow, incremental recruitment into the elite, with the consequence that each recruit receives a gradual induction into foreign policy-making under the tutelage of the established membership. The paradox, therefore, is superficial, rather than real.

In the essay cited already, Bialer asserts:

> The overwhelming majority of the political elite, as represented, for example, by the Central Committee of the party, is isolated from foreign policy making. The leaders inform the large group on the policies in the foreign area they have adopted, rather than ask what the foreign policy should be.[10]

I concur with that view, and have attempted to provide empirical evidence in support of it. The findings are positive. That is to say, out of the foregoing case studies emerges an image of a local Party *apparat* which is conservative in its foreign policy outlook, has extremely limited foreign policy horizons in terms of personal career prospects, is virtually excluded from the policy-making process, yet which constitutes the principal recruitment reservoir for replenishing the top elite. There is no place in the system for the backbench MP or the Congressman specializing in international relations in either a critical or even an independent, informed supporting role. *Rukovodstvo* in the foreign policy realm is the preserve of the top leadership group. How that central elite functions is the subject of Chapter 13.

Notes

1 All data on Party membership and structure are taken from 'KPSS v tsifrakh', *Partiinaya zhizn'*, 1983, no. 15, pp. 14–32.

2 Seweryn Bialer, 'The political system', in Robert F. Byrnes (ed.), *After Brezhnev. Sources of Soviet Conduct in the 1980s* (London, Frances Pinter, 1983), p. 6.

3 Bialer, 'The political system', p. 7.

4 See, for example, G. Zabulis (Minister of Higher and Secondary Specialized Education, Lithuanian SSR). 'Otbor i vybor', *Pravda*, 5 January 1980, p. 3.
5 Information on the educational backgrounds of *obkom* first secretaries relates to 1979 and is derived from data abstracted from *Deputaty Verkhovnogo Soveta SSSR* (Moscow, 1979) and *Ezhegodnik Bol'shoi Sovetskoi Entsiklopedii 1981*. The educational backgrounds of first secretaries appointed subsequent to 1979 appear to have changed very little; they are still drawn overwhelmingly from amongst the higher educated in the production disciplines.
6 'The Party worker on the periphery might get a higher salary and a symbolic rise in his status, but the job is looked down upon.' – A. Pravdin (pseud.), 'Inside the CPSU Central Committee', an interview by Mervyn Matthews in *Survey*, Vol. 20, no. 4 (94–104), p. 100.
7 Biographical data are taken from: *Deputaty Verkhovnogo Soveta SSSR* (Moscow, 1979), p. 17; *Ezhegodnik Bol'shoi Sovetskoi Entsiklopedii 1981*, p. 564.
8 See *The Times*, 3 June 1983, p. 9; 9 June 1983, p. 8.
9 *Pravda*, 5 November 1983, p. 2; 12 November 1983, p. 2.
10 Bialer, 'The political system', p. 60.

12 The Military Role in Soviet Decision-Making

Malcolm Mackintosh

Introduction

This chapter concentrates on the role of the Armed Forces of the Soviet Union in influencing or even formulating Soviet foreign policy in the present period of Soviet rule. It also touches briefly on the activity and influence of that other influential institution in the Soviet Union – the KGB – and the links between its domestic role and its involvement in the Soviet decision-making process. We have to recognize that both aspects of the subject are traditionally very secretive matters in the Soviet Union, and much of our material will inevitably be circumstantial and our judgements speculative. In the circumstances it may be helpful to outline some of the Russian as well as Soviet historical evidence on military influence in decision-making in order, perhaps, to understand some of the traditions and background which form the basis for the present situation.

Historical background

Military power and the security needs which accompany it have always played a dominant role in the development of the Russian state. This was mainly because of the open and exposed nature of the territory in the northern part of the Eurasian land mass inhabited by the Russian and other Slav peoples which was without barriers to population movements and, more importantly, without natural defences. But it was also due to the almost instinctive urge of the state to expand as the country grew from a small Grand Duchy around Moscow to an Empire stretching from the Baltic and Black Seas to the coasts of the Pacific. This expansion itself involved military conflict with powerful neighbours: the Tartars and the Mongols of the East, the Ottoman Empire in the South, and the Poles, Swedes and Germans in the West. These were conflicts which consolidated the autocracy of the Russian rulers, but they also underlined their dependence on reliable and efficient military leaders who would serve them loyally and were without ambitions to usurp political power for themselves.[1]

As a result of these protective measures and the watchful security policies of the Tsars, no serious or successful attempt by the Russian military leadership to seize power, carry out a *coup d'état* or even to acquire dominant influence over foreign policy decision-making took place in Russia during the period of the Empire. There was some military involvement in the various Palace revolutions which took place from time to time, but it was marginal and had no effect on the role or the authority of the Generals and Admirals involved. Indeed, it is possible to say that there evolved in Russia a deep-seated tradition of military obedience to the political leadership which is quite different from the experience of other Slav and East European nations: a tradition which is still valid today.

After the Russian Revolution in 1917 and the long drawn-out Civil War which followed, experience and ideology led the Soviet regime under Lenin and Stalin to intensify these traditional efforts to subordinate the Armed Forces – the Red Army – to the political leadership: the Communist Party of the Soviet Union (CPSU). Harking back to the French Revolution, Stalin and his colleagues expressed their fear of 'Bonapartism' by establishing machinery designed to dominate the Army and its role in decision-making by creating the Party-controlled Revolutionary Military Council. They also established Party control throughout the forces by the appointment of Political Commissars at all levels, and extended the network of the Secret Police, then known as the Cheka or OGPU, within the Armed Forces. Even the General Staff, the one military organization of the Imperial Army which had, partially at least, survived the Revolution and retained many of its professional officers, was tightly controlled by the Party in this way.

As Stalin faced the growth of political and military threats to the Soviet Union in the 1930s, especially from Hitler's Germany and Japan, his reliance on the size, strength and competence of the Armed Forces clashed with his fears – however unfounded – of the power and influence and popularity of his military leaders. He also retained a deep jealousy of some of these leaders for their active role in achieving victory in the Civil War, during which Stalin's own contribution was far from distinguished. For these reasons he decided to decimate the Red Army's High Command in 1937–39, including three out of five of the Marshals of the Soviet Union, Tukhachevski, Egorov and Blyukher, and up to 30,000 officers – from Army and Fleet commanders to junior leaders – including a high proportion of the Political Commissars.[2] The fact that this purge deprived the Red Army and the Red Fleet of a competent and experienced leadership at the beginning of the German invasion of the Soviet Union in June 1941 did not seem to have troubled Stalin at that time or later.

The experiences and final victory of the Soviet Armed Forces in

World War II brought the military leadership to the height of its prestige, authority and, indeed, popularity. This might have been the time for a serious challenge by the Forces to Communist Party domination, but Stalin took urgent measures to re-establish the strict Party control which he regarded as essential in the Army-Party relationship. War heroes, such as Marshal Zhukov, Marshal Rokossovski or Marshal Malinovski, were either dismissed in disgrace, dispatched abroad or posted to distant areas of the Soviet Union. Promotions were virtually frozen – no officer was advanced to the rank of Marshal of the Soviet Union between 1946 and 1953, though the Army retained a peacetime strength of 215 divisions, and only four senior officers reached the next most senior position of 4-star General or the equivalent in the Air Force or the Navy. The commands of the Moscow Garrison and Military District were entrusted to NKVD (KGB) Generals, that of the Leningrad Military District was almost eliminated in a purge, and all the senior General Staff and Ministry of Defence posts were held by favourites of Stalin. It is no wonder, according to later accounts in Soviet Military *mémoire* material, that the Army cowered in an atmosphere of suspicion, distrust and fear, not only of Stalin personally but of the Party and Secret Police network which so dominated their lives.

The period of Khrushchev's rule from 1955 to 1964 provided good evidence of the relationship between the Armed Forces and the Party at a time of change in internal affairs, foreign policy and military development in the Soviet Union. By the mid-1950s, for example, the Soviet Union had become an established nuclear power, and Khrushchev formulated his own military doctrine on the role of nuclear weapons in defence planning and war: not necessarily with the full support of his professional military advisers. It was also an interesting period because Khrushchev appointed to the highest military commands officers with whom he had served as a Political Commissar during the war, and to whom he entrusted the development of the Armed Forces in the early phases of the nuclear age – with some readiness to permit a modicum of debate on defence issues to appear in published military journals.[3]

One particular event in this fascinating and turbulent period in recent Soviet politico-military history is directly relevant to our subject. In mid-1957 Khrushchev was faced with opposition to his policies by a majority in the Politburo (then called the Presidium) – the so-called 'Anti-Party Group' led by Molotov, Malenkov, Bulganin and Kaganovich, whose action threatened his survival as Party leader. To defeat his rivals Khrushchev summoned a meeting of the whole Central Committee of the Party – at that time about 630 men – and turned to Marshal Zhukov, his Defence Minister, to order the Air Force to fly the members of the Committee to Moscow.[4] This Zhukov did: by the same evening over 300 members of the Central Committee were in Moscow or on their way to the capital. And in the ensuing Committee meeting the 'Anti-Party Group', outnumbered and cornered, was broken up and its senior members dismissed in disgrace.

On the basis of official Soviet material, it seems certain that Zhukov sought, as a quid pro quo, increased military representation in the highest-level bodies concerned with defence: especially in the Higher Military Council, the senior military advisory council to the Politburo.[5] This council had always consisted of civilian Party and military-industrial leaders. Immediately 'Bonapartism' raised its head again, and Khrushchev, rejecting Zhukov's proposal out of hand, dismissed the Marshal from all his posts in October 1957, and even deprived him of one of his four 'Hero of the Soviet Union' orders.

The significance of this event is that it demonstrated how close to the surface in Army-Party relations is the fear of a growth in military influence in Soviet decision-making in Moscow, and how rapidly the Party leadership can act to counter it. It is particularly dramatic in the case of the 'Anti-Party Group' because Marshal Zhukov had just saved Khrushchev from defeat in the Politburo; and because not one professional Service Chief rallied to the defence of their leader – to whom many of them owed their posts and their promotion. At that time, at least, in the Soviet Armed Forces, the military leaders knew instinctively that they must support the Party in any conflict with an individual serving officer – however senior or prestigious he may be – in the interests of preserving their careers.

Army-Party relations today

Against this historical background, we now look at the machinery and procedures in the Soviet Union through which the Party and the Armed Forces conduct their relations and see how, in practical terms, the Armed Forces might be able, if their leaders so wished, to influence decision-making on defence and foreign policy. Before doing so, however, we should recall the exceptionally deep-rooted element of 'compartmentalization' within the Soviet system – partly for reasons of secrecy and partly because of the naturally restrictive nature of the Soviet bureaucracy.

Not only is the military organization of each branch or element in the Armed Forces tightly closed to those serving on other branches – for example the naval or air force planners are not privy to what is going on in the ground forces, air defence or the strategic rocket forces, even in exercises – but the Ministries, even in their higher reaches, are not informed about the activities and capabilities of the other Ministries: and this is especially true of the Ministry of Defence. There is some evidence that in negotiations with foreign powers involving several Soviet Ministries or organizations, the various elements of the Soviet delegations – Foreign Ministry, Military, Party, or KGB – report directly to their own Ministry without showing their papers to their colleagues from different Ministries or Departments.

This means that the lowest level in the Soviet hierarchy at which decision-makers or advisers see *all* Soviet material on a particular issue is very near the top. On some major and, in security terms, sensitive subjects in the defence and foreign policy field, it could be the Politburo itself, or possibly, on a purely military matter, the Defence Council. In these circumstances we have to assume that military options developed in the General Staff may reach the Politburo without prior consultation with the Ministry of Foreign Affairs, and similarly that foreign policy recommendations formulated within that Ministry are not discussed with the Ministry of Defence before reaching the highest Party authority. It is not even certain that the KGB shares all the secrets of the military planners. Of course, when the plans are debated in the Politburo the members of that body will have all the material available at their disposal and can call on professionals to come to the meeting to support their case. But the system, which is very unlike that in Western countries, does limit the amount of consultation between Ministries, and narrows the channels through which one element in the machine can reach and convince the actual decision-makers on defence and foreign policy. The strong essence of secrecy in the whole process also makes the task of the analyst even more difficult.

But to return to the structure of the Party and the Government organizations involved in Army-Party relations. Here we must distinguish between the exercise of power in the Soviet Union and the degree of influence which any particular body may have over those who take the final decisions on policy: in this case on defence and military and military-industrial matters. At the head of the decision-making apparatus is the Politburo of the Central Committee of the CPSU; it has, at present, twelve full voting members and six candidate members. The Politburo is under the leadership of the General Secretary of the CPSU, who is also Chairman of the Defence Council. The Central Party apparatus under the Politburo consists of 22 Central Committee departments which supervise the government administration over the whole range of internal and external policies including defence and the defence industries. These departments play a major role in the selection of personnel, in the preparation of policy options and in checking the implementation of policy decisions. In the military sphere the most important are the Administrative Organs Department (which supervises the work of the armed forces, the KGB, the Ministry of Internal

Affairs and the Judiciary) and the Defence Industries Department. The whole structure rests on the Central Committee of the Party itself. Its 319 full and 151 candidate members, of whom 20–30 are nominated by the Armed Forces, are appointed by the national and regional Party organizations and approved by the Secretariat and the Central Committee and the Politburo. The Committee meets, on average, in Plenary Session, about three times a year.

With the exception of the Central Committee, these organizations represent the decision-making element of Soviet power. No serving soldier, sailor or airman belongs to the Politburo or the Secretariat of the Central Committee, and only a very few are members of the Central Committee itself, which has, in any case, very little weight in the decision-making process. It is true, of course, that Marshal Ustinov, the Defence Minister, is a full member of the Politburo, but he is a civilian engineer by training and expertise, and appears to regard his position in the Party as more important than his role as an exponent of the professional service viewpoint. For example when Brezhnev, just before he died in November 1982, summoned a meeting of the leaders of the Armed Forces to assure them that, whatever their doubts, the Party was giving them all the resources they needed, Ustinov clearly supported Brezhnev on this issue.

It is here that we move from the power structure in the Soviet Union to the process through which the professionals influence the decision-makers. In the military fields this takes place through the Defence Council which advises and puts military recommendations to the Politburo for final decision-making. The Chairman of the Defence Council has, since 1965, been the General Secretary of the Party, and, according to the Soviet Constitution of 1977, its members are appointed by the Supreme Soviet. Membership of the Defence Council has never been published in the Soviet Union, and we can only speculate on its formal composition. But it appears to be dominated by senior Party officials, some of them members of the Politburo or the Party Secretariat, with very few serving officers: in this sense it is probably a kind of sub-committee of the Politburo for defence questions.

On the limited evidence we have available it seems likely that today the Council includes Marshal Ustinov, Andrei Gromyko, Nikolai Ogarkov, the Chief of the General Staff, and possibly a senior Secretary dealing with the military-industrial complex of the Soviet Union. It may also include the Head of the KGB and the Chairman of the Government's Military-Industrial Commission (VPK). According to historical evidence, it seems likely that the Secretary of the Defence Council is a Deputy Chief of the General Staff.[6] It also seems probable that the responsibilities of the Defence Council include formulating proposals and recommendations to the Politburo, based on professional military advice, on the defence budget, major weapons programmes, military doctrine, major training exercises and force deployments. It may also, in a more executive role, be in charge of monitoring the progress of defence decisions issued by the Politburo.[7] The important point about its composition in a study of Army-Party relations is that its professional military membership is, on present evidence, limited to the Chief of the General Staff, and that therefore Party influence must be all-important in its deliberations and recommendations.

The next military authority in the defence hierarchy is the Ministry of Defence. A component part of the Council of Ministers under Nikolai Tikhonov, the Ministry of Defence is a vast organization comprising the General Staff, the five branches of the Armed Forces, the Strategic Rocket Forces, the Air Defence Command, the Ground Forces, the Navy and the Air Force, a large number of Central and Chief Directorates dealing with administration, personnel, logistics and armaments, military science and technology, and the Chief Political Directorate, now under Army-General A.A. Epishev. The Ministry also houses the headquarters of the Warsaw Pact, most of whose most senior military and political officers are Soviet.

Within the Ministry of Defence the Minister, Marshal Ustinov, chairs a 'Collegium' of the Ministry. All Soviet Ministries have a Collegium, which is a committee of senior officials who advise the Minister, primarily on formal occasions and on issues relating to status, honours and recognition of services to the Armed Forces.[8] It seems to have no role in the decision-making process, though it can report cases of disagreement within the Ministry to the Council of Ministers.[9] There has in the past been evidence of another senior committee in the Ministry of Defence – the Main Military Council; though the most recent references to this body date back to the late 1960s and we are not sure if it exists today.[10] When the Council did exist – and more recent evidence may be lacking for reasons of secrecy – it appeared to be a committee at which the Minister met his senior deputies: his First Deputy for General Questions, the Chief of the General Staff, and the Commander-in-Chief of the Warsaw Pact, together with the Commanders-in-Chief of the five branches of the Armed Forces and other Deputy Ministers and the Head of the Chief Political Directorate of the Armed Forces. Probably the nearest analogy to its role and status is that of the present-day Military Council at the headquarters of the Warsaw Pact and at Military District, Army and Fleet Commands. These seem to include, under the chairmanship of the Commander, the Deputy Commanders and Chiefs of Staff of the formation concerned, the Chief Political officer, and those concerned with training and logistics. If the Main Military Council does exist today, its role is likely to be as a channel of communication between the various headquarters in the Armed Forces and the Defence Council. If so, it could exert some influence on the latter, by providing the fullest and most professional advice for onward transmission to the ultimate decision-makers.

On the purely military side the most influential and professional element of the Armed Forces is the General Staff, once called the 'Brain of the Army' by one of its former chiefs.[11] Modelled on the old Prussian and Austro-Hungarian General Staff, its officers enter it at an early stage in their careers and tend to stay there until they retire: more than one senior officer is known to have served over thirty-five years just in the General Staff.

The General Staff is extremely 'compartmentalized' and subject to rigorous security. Its three main components are the Chief Operations and Intelligence Directorates and Directorates dealing with planning, administration, personnel and logistics of all branches of the Armed Forces, as well as having its own senior Political Staff.[12] No one can doubt its high standard of professionalism, but, in many ways, the most important point is the isolation in which it works – partly for traditional Russian and partly for security reasons – even from the other elements in the Armed Forces and the Ministry. As far as we can tell, General Staff requirements and assessments are often sent upwards through the Chief of the General Staff to the Minister of Defence and the Defence Council, without, apparently, full consultation with all the relevant Staffs and Councils of the Armed Forces. But the General Staff is also under close Party supervision through its Political Directorate, through which the Party monitors and supervises the work of even this very closed section of the Armed Forces.

Of particular importance in Party control of the military is the Chief Political Directorate of the Armed Forces. This Directorate, which, according to the Soviet Military Encyclopedia, has the status of a Department of the Central Committee of the CPSU, controls the huge network of political officers throughout the Armed Forces.[13] Every element of the Ministry of Defence and every headquarters, formation, and unit down to the lowest level has a political department, staff or officer as an integral part of its complement. Each political officer is expected to play an active role in the military or naval programme of his unit or formation; many in the Air Forces, for example, are qualified pilots or air crew.

The primary role of the political officers is political indoctrination, through lectures, publications and meetings; they also play some role as 'welfare officers' in their units, helping national servicemen to contact their families in times of personal difficulty. They have no formal responsibility for the security and the loyalty of their officers and men: that falls to the KGB. But the political officers' status, rights and duties give them an extremely important role in ensuring the control of the Armed Forces by the Party and maintaining the flow of official Party doctrine to the forces at all levels.

These, then, are the main organizations within the Party and the armed forces which participate in the advisory and the decision-making processes. The available evidence suggests that as long as this structure is adhered to, the Party will continue to be the dominating authority in Army-Party relations on foreign and defence policies. While the Minister of Defence is a member of the Defence Council and the Politburo, he has only one officer, the Chief of the General Staff, to support him – if he is putting forward military views or recommendations – in the Defence Council, and no professional ally at the present time in the Politburo. It is, of course, always possible that this balance could change in the Soviet Union under a new leadership, especially if a future Minister of Defence were once again a serving officer – like Marshals Zhukov, Malinovski and Grechko. But with tight Party control, supported, no doubt, by the KGB, it is difficult to envisage a situation in which the armed forces, however important their professional advice and recommendations and their potential influence may be, could in practice come to dominate decision-making in defence and foreign policy or dictate policies to the Party and Government for their own military or national reasons.

Policy issues: the military view?

The title of this section of the study includes a questionmark because when we come to try to identify specific areas in which the Armed Forces may press a view on the Party particularly strongly or in which disagreements might appear or perhaps occur, the available evidence is very limited and sometimes, indeed, obscure. We realize that the current Soviet military leadership is more sophisticated and technologically better trained and prepared, for example for nuclear as well as conventional war, than their World War II predecessors. Some of the latter, however, are still on active service: for example, Marshal Kiril Moskalenko, a Deputy Minister of Defence and Inspector-General of the Armed Forces (who was an Army Commander in 1943–45) who is now 82, and many of the leaders are in their sixties or seventies and are veterans of that campaign.[14]

In these circumstances it is likely that on most defence issues the present military leaders will hold traditionalist Russian views, augmented by their experience in World War II and their conclusions on the role and effect of nuclear weapons in modern warfare. Naval leaders will, in fact, be absorbing new concepts of 'distant area' maritime operations, and the Strategic Rocket Forces have, no doubt, evolved interpretations of the role of their advanced weapons systems of which they have, like their Western opposite numbers, no operational experience. The army and the air force, as well as the Air Defence Forces, will have absorbed their new battlefield weapons, partly through training and exercises in addition to observing and analysing the experience of other countries engaged in contemporary warfare.

There is no doubt that the composition and nature of the Soviet Armed Forces today has changed since the days of the massive forces which emerged victorious in World War II: 588 divisions were mobilized in 1944. The middle-ranking and junior officers of the forces now belong to a new kind of 'officer class' in the Soviet Union, and many officers, as in other armies throughout the world, are drawn from traditional 'military families'. Education, particularly in the military sciences, is better and more advanced among officers and men; and most of the former now come from urban rather than peasant backgrounds as they tended to do in the past.

At the same time, the leaders of the Armed Forces and the political authorities have to recognize that with the growing number of non-European citizens in the Soviet Union reaching military age, and therefore national service or a career in the Armed Forces, the proportion of non-Slavs is bound to increase in the forces. There is already evidence that national servicemen from Central Asian Republics speak inadequate Russian, and that this is already worrying the Army leaders. There is also the problem of the growth of Islamic religious beliefs in the demographically expanding areas of the Soviet Union. This too is bound to cause anxiety among the Russian leadership, but we cannot predict at this juncture how they might attempt to cope with it in the future.

In the difficult area of military influence on policy-making in foreign affairs, the evidence is even more clouded in secrecy. To take, for example, the Polish crisis of 1980–81, when the Soviet Government was faced by the collapse of the 'leading role' of the Communist Party in Poland in those years, the advice of the Armed Forces must have been sought at a very early stage by the Politburo in Moscow, given the military and political importance of Poland's position in the Warsaw Pact as well as its relationship with the Soviet Union. No doubt on military grounds the leaders of the Armed Forces pressed for a solution to the crisis which would not weaken Poland's loyalty and military efficiency, and expressed their readiness to mobilize and use the necessary forces to recover full control over Poland, if necessary, by invasion. Indeed, the evidence suggests that a large force capable of invading Poland was in position in Western Russia and East Germany by November 1980, and remained in position throughout 1981.

At the same time, it is possible that the Soviet military chiefs, aware of traditional Russo-Polish antagonisms and the probability that the Poles would fight if an invasion took place, might have been reluctant to recommend a full-scale invasion, with potentially high casualties. The military may have urged the Soviet Government to consider other means of bringing Poland back into the fold, ranging from 'special measures' by the KGB and Special Forces to action by the Poles themselves, carefully planned in advance and co-ordinated with the appropriate Soviet political and military authorities. This was the option which, as far as we can tell, was chosen, and formed the basis of the Polish decision to proclaim martial law in December 1981, which placed the government of the country under General Wojciech Jaruzelski.

General Jaruzelski already held the positions of General Secretary of the Polish Workers' Party (PZPR), Prime Minister and Minister of Defence. He was, therefore, the logical choice for implementing this decision; and while Jaruzelski appears to have kept the Army as far as possible from direct conflict with the 'Solidarity' workers, it seems likely that he concurred with the plan. It would have the advantage in his thinking that it would avoid a large number of Polish casualties and prevent a full-scale Soviet military occupation of Poland. We may conclude, therefore, that both the Soviet military and the Polish authorities may have supported and recommended this solution to their Government in the critical decision-making process in 1981.

Returning to the main subject of this study, Army-Party relations in the present phase, it seems likely that military recommendations put by the military High Command to the Defence Council and the Politburo will continue to lay strong emphasis on numerical and qualitative 'over-insurance', doubling and trebling the men and resources needed for the Armed Forces on a 'worst-case scenario' basis. There will be powerful support for the vested interests of the Army and the Air Force 'in the mass', for large and mobile land armies operating on traditional lines in, for example, a major campaign in Europe or against China. There may, in very professional and traditional terms, be an element of 'military conservatism', a reluctance to create forces with which to embark on *adventures* in distant areas or in geographical conditions of which the Soviet forces have little or no experience: high mountain warfare in Afghanistan was probably just such a case. While the present fairly elderly leadership of the Armed Forces remains in the highest military positions, it is possible that the military voice on defence policy and military doctrine in the Ministry of Defence, as expressed through the Defence Council, when it reaches the Politburo, will speak along these lines.

Another issue discussed at high level between the Party and the Armed Forces is defence expenditure and weapons procurement. This again is a topic on which we have relatively little detailed information: we are even uncertain on the figure of about 4 per cent annual increase in defence expenditure which is generally ascribed to the Soviet defence budget.[15] What is known is well described in another chapter; but on the point of debate and decision-making it may be worth recalling that in the past when the Party leaders sense, or are fully aware of, military dissatisfaction on resource allocation and procurement policies, they have called the military chiefs together in a major meeting to tell them publicly that they are getting all that they need in resources. It is of particular interest to note that such a meeting was held on 27 October 1982, just before Brezhnev died, at which Brezhnev and Marshal Ustinov conveyed this message to the military leaders. There are, therefore, precedents for this potentially contentious issue to be dealt with, partially at least, and in very general terms, in a public forum which demonstrates the Party's supremacy in the defence allocation field as well.

Soviet military advice to the Government on military action in Afghanistan in 1979 may have been less complex and, as it turned out, possibly inaccurate. It seems unlikely that, although there was a Soviet military advisory presence in Afghanistan after the Revolution of April 1978 and senior Soviet military leaders visited Kabul in 1979, military action was seriously considered by the Soviet Government until the autumn of that year – as the political situation in the country steadily deteriorated. The Soviet military leaders, when asked how long it would take the Soviet Army and Air Force to occupy Afghanistan and restore Soviet political control there, no doubt convinced their political masters that a force of about 80,000–100,000 men with air support could do the job in a matter of weeks – especially if the 'renegade' government of Hafizollah Amin could be removed in advance by the KGB or the Special Forces – which is what seems to have happened. The main defects of this recommendation were lack of proper understanding of traditional Afghan readiness to resist – mainly through insurgency – any military invasion, and little Soviet military experience of high mountain warfare and counter-insurgency tactics. If this is a reasonably accurate picture of Army-Party consultations before the invasion of Afghanistan, and the evidence is extremely speculative, the military leaders' reputation may have suffered in the opinion of the Party chiefs. Military influence on Party decision-making on this kind of international crisis or problem in the future may, in fact, have weakened.

Alongside these issues of military influence and advice on policy-making abroad, there are some areas of Soviet foreign and defence policy on which the military leaders appear, for traditional and professional reasons, to object to the Party's official attitude and policies. Some of these may have been aired in the last few years and, again, in a very speculative way, it may be possible to identify one or two of them – though, we stress, without concrete evidence or firm data.

These possible disagreements may relate to the field of arms control. Both in the strategic arms reduction talks and especially in the recently abandoned negotiations on intermediate-range nuclear forces (INF) in Europe in Geneva, the Soviet Government has made a unilateral declaration of 'no-first-use' of nuclear weapons, has offered to count warheads instead of missiles in calculating force levels, and to destroy those SS-20 missiles withdrawn from Europe rather than re-deploy them in Central Russia or in the Far East. These proposals formed part of a series of Soviet offers designed to persuade NATO to cancel the deployment of Pershing II and cruise missiles in West Germany and cruise missiles in Britain and Italy, including the 'freezing' of existing missile force levels and their reduction to the combined strength of the British and French independent nuclear forces.

On a speculative basis it is possible to argue that the Soviet military leaders objected to these three public offers by the Party and the Government. To the Soviet military, a 'no-first-use' promise, publicly given (valuable as it would be in keeping the conflict at a conventional level for a useful period – given Soviet conventional superiority in Europe), would seriously damage the Armed Forces' capacity to launch a 'pre-emptive' strike in a critical situation, if required, with nuclear weapons. The Soviet chiefs could see such a commitment as limiting their professional options.

Secondly, it is possible that the principle, again publicly announced, of counting warheads rather than launchers could be useful in negotiations, but would be a worrying precedent if it was transferred from the INF (SS-20) area to the strategic weapons field. Given that the Soviet ICBM force relies so heavily on its huge land-based SS-18s and SS-19s, part of whose importance in the strategic weapons balance rests on the large number of warheads each missile can carry, calculations on the numbers of warheads might, in the Soviet military view, degrade their ICBM force in its intercontinental role.

Thirdly, there is the issue of the Government's public undertaking to destroy missiles withdrawn from Europe rather than re-deploy them. Soviet military men do not like destroying any kind of weapon or weapons systems on principle – witness the retention at the end of 1983 of over 200 SS-4 missiles in Western Russia six years after the initial deployment of the SS-20 there: to say nothing of the large stocks of

T-54/55 and even T-34 tanks retained in Soviet arms depots. It is true that under the SALT I and SALT II Treaties the Soviet Union undertook to, and did, dismantle various strategic systems, and made their action available for 'national means of verification' – satellite photography. But there are less pressing reasons for destruction of theatre-level weapons systems than those involved in the superpower strategic missile balance; and it seems unlikely that the Soviet military leaders were at all happy with this public commitment of their Party and Government.

Whatever the truth of these speculative judgements, it is clear that since the Soviet Union continued to offer these and other similar proposals – at least until their delegation walked out of the talks in Geneva in December 1983 – the Party maintained its line and military objections were overruled. The evidence suggests, therefore, that while the professional competence and technical skills of the leaders of the Armed Forces have grown on a continuing basis in the Soviet Union, the Communist Party has not given up any of its well-established pre-eminence in decision-making in defence and foreign policy. While the military chiefs continue to formulate their requirements and make their demands to the Party, it is channelled through the existing machinery; and they know that in the last resort the Party's views prevail.

The influence of the KGB

Finally in this brief survey of the instruments of power in the Soviet Union which may influence policy-making we consider the position and role of the KGB – the Committee of State Security of the Council of Ministers. The KGB which came into being in its present form in March 1954[16] as the successor to Stalin's NKGB, NKVD, OGPU and CHEKA (which was founded during the Civil War) is, along with the Communist Party and the Armed Forces, one of the main centres of power in the present Soviet system.

A detailed and thorough examination of the KGB is outside the scope of this chapter. For our purposes we recall that formally, as a State Committee, it is in the Government rather than the Party hierarchy, though its responsibilities cross all borders, including the Party network, the Armed Forces, the Government Ministries and all elements of Soviet society. The Chairman of the KGB is sometimes a full member of the Politburo, as in the case of Yuri Andropov from 1967 to 1982. The present incumbent, a long-serving KGB officer, Viktor Chebrikov, was elected a Candidate member in December 1983, and has the rank of Army-General. Most of his senior deputies, some of whose identities are public knowledge, also hold military-style ranks.

Officially the KGB – along with the Interior Troops and Militia of the Ministry of the Interior, now also under a KGB General, Vitaly Fedorchuk – is responsible for internal security in the Soviet Union. It is also in charge of the Frontier Guard Force, commanded by Army-General V.A. Matrosov, which has its own ground forces, air force, air defence and, in coastal areas, naval units, grouped in districts modelled on the Soviet Army's military districts. A third Chief Directorate handles what the Russians call 'counter-intelligence', by which they mean the formal appointment of KGB officers and men in any organization and at any level in the Soviet Union and in the allied States in Eastern Europe and Asia. Finally, the KGB is responsible for Soviet espionage and subversion abroad, particularly in non-military subjects; the latter are dealt with by the Chief Intelligence Directorate (GRU) of the Soviet General Staff. There are many indications that relations between these two elements of the Soviet intelligence-gathering machine are often at loggerheads in Western countries and in the Third World.

Of particular interest is the role of the third Chief Directorate within the Armed Forces. They are known as the 'special sections' (*osoby otdely*) and are to be found in all headquarters and offices.[17] Their responsibility is to monitor the political and ideological reliability of all military personnel, including the political officers, and may, in fact, appear anywhere they wish dressed in any uniform and with any rank, according to their current tasks. Not unnaturally they inspire fear and apprehension among the troops, including senior officers. They maintain personal files on all personnel, independent of their normal records, and report back to the KGB Headquarters with no obligation to show them to military or political officers.

While a good deal of valuable material is available on the security, intelligence-gathering and subversive tasks of the KGB,[18] it is difficult because of the secrecy which surrounds the upper echelons of the Committee to assess how influential they are in decision-making on foreign and defence policy. We have little recent evidence on relations between the KGB and the Party or, apart from that noted above, with the Armed Forces. In his 15 years as Chairman of the KGB, Andropov's appearances in public in Moscow were relatively few, and nothing is known of his views or his influence in the Politburo – to which he was promoted in 1973 – even on security matters. There were reports that he opposed the Soviet invasions of both Czechoslovakia in 1968 and Afghanistan in 1979, but their authenticity is suspect, and they could have been put about for 'disinformation' reasons or to create a more favourable image in the West of the man who headed that organization. Indeed this caveat has to be remembered when considering most of the published or reported material on the KGB, whatever aspect of its work is under discussion.

What can be said, however, is that the KGB is very much in the tradition of the Secret Police concept in Russia, and although its excesses and brutality under Stalin, in particular, can and will never be forgotten by the Soviet people, some form of state-run secret supervision of all aspects of life in the country has so far been traditional. In a sense the KGB performs, with varying degrees of unpleasantness, a role to which the peoples of the Soviet Union – and, indeed, of Russia – have become used, and seem to have to live with.

In these circumstances it seems likely that the influence of the KGB on decision-making probably runs on three main lines. First, its leaders presumably have an unchanging requirement issued by the Politburo, to monitor security and loyalty in the Soviet Union, to keep 'human rights' activity under control and to limit or allow emigration as ordered by the Party leadership. It seems likely that the Party would accept, willingly in most cases, requests by the KGB for additional authority to intensify or speed up their general activity in this area. Secondly, the Chief Directorate in charge of the frontier guards has a major claim on the appropriate resources in manpower (some national servicemen do their service in the KGB frontier guards) and in weapons and training requirements. And thirdly, there seems no doubt that the 'counter-intelligence' networks in the Armed Forces and elsewhere receive the resources and authority to carry out their duties, as do those involved in intelligence-gathering and subversion abroad, whether in the West, against China or in the Third World.

Against this background it is possible to speculate that the KGB leadership may, if anything, be inclined to 'caution' in major areas of policy-making. Clearly they are professionals with considerable experience and expertise; their aims are the fulfilment of the tasks with which they have been entrusted to the best of their ability. And in a sense each of the assignments and priorities that they have been given can best be carried out – with the exception of some kinds of subversion, for example in an overseas crisis situation – when the other elements of Soviet society and Soviet powers are in a stable condition. This certainly applies to the internal security role of the KGB, to the Frontier Guards and to 'counter-intelligence' and the 'Special Sections' in the Armed Forces. Even under the heading of 'intelligence-gathering' abroad, especially in the light of Western democratic freedom to publish scientific, technical and military material, the KGB may find it easier to operate at will in a stable society and a stable country.

As a final thought, therefore, and underlining the exception of certain types of subversion, it may be realistic to conclude that the professionals of the KGB may not support or recommend 'adventurous' or 'risky' policies abroad when they give their advice to the Politburo for the reasons described above, in the present phase. In doing so they may see eye to eye with the present generation of military leaders, whose main aims may include policies designed to re-create the atmosphere of the 'SALT period' in Soviet-American relations, to return to the pre-INF balance in Europe with its inbuilt Soviet military superiorities, to retain their superiority over China, and, under these umbrellas, to feel free to exploit opportunities for the expansion of Soviet influence in key areas of the Third World. Perhaps for the time being, the Party, the Armed Forces and the KGB, are able to find some common interests when advocating and carrying out their country's foreign and defence policies.

Notes

1 This, incidentally, was one of the reasons why some Tsars recruited military leaders from abroad in, for example, the seventeenth and eighteenth centuries, placing the Army and Navy under men who were foreign professionals and had no such political motives.

2 One military leader who survived this purge and went on to be Chief of the General Staff, Marshal S.S. Biryuzov, described in his memoirs how in 1938 he was posted as a Captain to the 30th Rifle division to find that he was the senior officer left in the division.

3 Raymond L. Garthoff, *Soviet Strategy in the Nuclear Age* (London: Atlantic Books, 1958).

4 See Carl Linden, *Khrushchev and the Soviet Leadership, 1957–1964* (Baltimore, Johns Hopkins Press, 1966), pp. 40–4.

5 Yu P. Petrov, *The Party Construction in the Soviet Army and Navy, 1918–1961* (Moscow, Military Publishing House, 1964, in Russian). There is some evidence that the Higher Military Council was renamed the Defence Council after Khrushchev's fall.

6 Marshal K.A. Meretskov, *In the Service of the People* (Moscow, 1969, in Russian).

7 See Edward L. Warner III, *The Military in Contemporary Soviet Politics* (New York, Praeger, 1977), pp. 36–47.

8 As an example of the work of the Collegium of the Ministry of Defence see 'Krasnaya Zvezda' (Red Star), Moscow of 8 April 1980, which reported a message of congratulations to the Trans-caucasus Military District for the high standard of its 'military-patriotic work'.

9 General Statute on USSR Ministries, 10 July 1967, para 18.

10 See *The Soviet Military Encyclopaedia* (Moscow, Military Publishing House, 1976, Vol. 2), p. 567, for the background to the Main Military Council (in Russian).

11 Marshal B.M. Shaposhnikov, *The Brain of the Army*, (Moscow, Military Publishing House, 1929).

12 Edward L. Warner III, *The Military in Contemporary Soviet Politics*, pp. 24–6.

13 *Soviet Military Encyclopaedia* (Moscow, Military Publishing House, 1976, Vol. 2;, p. 562 (in Russian).

14 Marshal Ogarkov is 66, Marshal Kulikov 62, Admiral Gorshkov is 73, Marshal Petrov, C-in-C Ground Forces, is 66, Air Marshal Kutakhov, C-in-C Air Force, is 69, and Chief Marshal of Artillery Tolubko, C-in-C Strategic Rocket Forces, is 70. Army General Epishev, the Head of the Chief Political Directorate, is 75.

15 *The Military Balance 1983–84* (London, IISS, 198), p. 13.

16 *Soviet Military Encyclopaedia* (Moscow, 1977, Vol. 4), pp. 265–6.

17 Edward L. Warner III, *The Military in Contemporary Soviet Politics*, pp. 33–4.

18 For example, John Barron, *The KGB: the Secret Work of Soviet Secret Agents* (London, 1974).

13 The Foreign Policy-Making Process

Archie Brown

The weight of different institutional actors in the policy process in the Soviet Union has varied over time. This is no less true of foreign policy than of other areas of policy. Furthermore, in the Soviet Union (as elsewhere) the same individual may wield greater influence at one stage of his career than at others, even while holding what is formally the same office. That is clearly true if one examines the part played in foreign policy-making by the same party General Secretary at different times. It may be equally applicable to a Soviet Minister of Foreign Affairs, not least in the case of Gromyko who took over from Shepilov as long ago as 1957. While Gromyko was never as uninfluential as it was fashionable in some Western Sovietological circles to assume, he undoubtedly carried more weight in the early 1980s than in the early 1960s.

It falls to this chapter to consider some of the major institutions involved in the making of Soviet foreign policy. The Defence Council, the military as a whole, and the KGB are treated elsewhere, and will be touched upon only in passing here. But what remains is such a formidably large and important complex of institutions that some of them of necessity are treated exceedingly briefly, and rougher justice may be done to certain institutions than to others. Nevertheless, within the limits imposed by a single chapter, attention will be paid to the General Secretaryship of the Central Committee of the CPSU, the Politburo, the departments of the Central Committee with foreign policy concerns (most notably, the International Department and the Department for Relations with Communist and Workers' Parties of Socialist Countries), the office of Minister of Foreign Affairs and the role of the Ministry of Foreign Affairs. Brief consideration will be given to the General Secretary's assistants (*pomoshchniki*), to the community of foreign policy influentials and the policy-oriented research institutes.

The General Secretary

During most of the Soviet period, the General Secretary has been the most powerful individual influence on Soviet foreign policy, but there have been times when this was not the case, and the extent to which he has had a relatively free hand has varied enormously. Though Stalin gradually became the most authoritative figure in Soviet foreign policy-making in the course of the 1920s, and though it formed part of the battleground in his successful struggle against Trotsky, it was not until the 1930s that he was truly dominant in Soviet foreign policy-making. When, initially, Stalin became General Secretary in 1922, he was less important in this sphere than the Foreign Affairs Commissar Chicherin, not to speak of Lenin, so long as the latter was alive. In the earliest years of the Soviet era, it was neither a secretary of the Central Committee nor the Commissar of Foreign Affairs, but Lenin, the Chairman of the Council of People's Commissars, who was the dominating influence on this as on other major areas of Soviet policy. Chicherin spoke with Lenin by telephone several times a day, discussing important current diplomatic issues and often receiving detailed recommendations on steps to be taken, 'including the precise terms of diplomatic notes'.[1]

The story of how Stalin defeated his rivals in the 1920s and consolidated his power in the 1930s is well known, but it was the war, the Soviet Union's post-war East European acquisitions and the country's emergence as one of the world's two Great Powers which forced the Soviet top leader (no matter which particular office he nominally held) to devote vastly more time to foreign policy than hitherto. Though Stalin was, of course, during the last twenty years of his life (and for some time earlier) the *de facto* party leader, the title, 'General Secretary', was not used after 1934; during the war and post-war years it was as Chairman of the Council of People's Commissars (Council of Ministers from 1946)[2] that he formally governed, though in reality his powers derived from the fact that through his personal secretariat and the political police, he had subordinated every important bureaucratic hierarchy to his will, even if increasing preoccupation with foreign affairs, together with his declining physical strength, meant that his post-war interventions in a number of areas of domestic policy became more intermittent.

Discussing Stalin's preoccupation with foreign policy and noting that his interest became 'obsessive when the United States began its repeated overflights of the socialist countries', Khrushchev observed in his memoirs:

> The rest of us in the leadership were careful not to poke our noses into these matters unless Stalin himself pushed our noses in that direction. He jealously guarded foreign policy in general and our policy toward other socialist countries in particular as his own special province. He had never gone out of his way to take other people's advice into account, and this was especially true after the war.[3]

On Stalin's death in March 1953, Khrushchev, who was soon to emerge as the leading figure within the Secretariat of the Central Committee and who from September of that year was accorded the title, First Secretary, did not instantly become the dominant foreign policy-maker. The period between 1953 and 1955 was one in which Malenkov, Molotov and Khrushchev all vied for supreme influence in this area. Until mid-1954 Malenkov's name headed the list of members of the Presidium of the Central Committee (as the Politburo was known at that time) and Molotov's voice in foreign policy matters was almost certainly more influential than Khrushchev's in the earliest post-Stalin years. Molotov at first enjoyed high prestige within the leadership and had the great advantage over Khrushchev of years of active involvement in Soviet foreign policy-making and knowledge of the international scene. By 1955 Khrushchev had, however, sufficiently strengthened his position within the leadership to be able to take foreign policy initiatives, though he had not yet reached a position in which he could dictate to his Minister of Foreign Affairs. It was still necessary to build a coalition of important supporters, the more so since Khrushchev (with some reason) viewed Molotov as a threat to his leadership more generally.

Thus, for example, it would appear to have been Khrushchev, not Molotov, who took the initiative which led to the decision to pull Soviet troops out of Austria and Finland. Referring to his visit to Vienna for his meeting with President Kennedy in 1961, Khrushchev wrote:

> The Austrians were well disposed toward us because after Stalin's death we signed a peace treaty with them and withdrew our troops, which had been stationed on their territory for a long time. The Austrians gave me credit for having played a leading role in the decision to pull out of Austria, and they were quite right. They didn't have any idea what sort of internal struggle had taken place before we signed the peace treaty, and I don't deny it was on my initiative that the correct decision was finally made.[4]

As for Finland, when Khrushchev was in Geneva for the four-power summit meeting in 1955, he 'didn't even suggest the idea of giving up our base in Finland to Molotov because I knew he would disagree'.[5] Instead, he broached the matter with Bulganin and Zhukov and secured their agreement. Both of them accepted that the Soviet base just outside Helsinki was politically damaging (for Soviet-Finnish relations), with Zhukov adding the clinching argument that it was militarily unnecessary and economically costly. Only when he had mobilized his political forces did Khrushchev raise the matter with Molotov who 'put up an obstinate argument' against withdrawal. However, on their return to Moscow 'a brief discussion in the government leadership as well as in the Central Committee of the Party' settled the issue in favour of withdrawal from Finland.[6]

After Khrushchev had survived an attempt by a majority of his Politburo colleagues to remove him from the party leadership (the 'anti-party group' crisis) in 1957, he was able to bring more of his followers into the Politburo; the constraints upon his initiatives in both foreign and domestic policy became weaker while his disregard for collective decision-making bodies and for bureaucratic agencies and norms became more pronounced. If his own account is to be believed, he was personally responsible for making a public apology from Eisenhower for the U–2 flights over Soviet territory a condition of any progress at the 1960 Paris 'summit meeting' on the German question and disarmament. The Soviet delegation, which included the Foreign Minister, Andrey Gromyko, and the Minister of Defence, Marshal Malinovsky, had left Moscow with a relatively conciliatory set of documents, but 'after we were already in the air flying toward Paris', Khrushchev recalled, 'the idea came to me that we should make some basic alterations in the declaration we had prepared for presentation at the outset of the negotiations'. He felt that the Soviet 'reputation depended on our making some sort of protest'.[7]

Khrushchev relates that in the course of the journey he consulted Gromyko who 'agreed' and Malinovsky who 'felt I was absolutely right' and that 'since we hadn't discussed the new declaration with the collective leadership, we immediately transmitted the draft to Moscow for examination by the other comrades' who answered 'right away', giving their 'complete approval to our new position'. Thus, he observes, 'we had left Moscow with a set of documents pointing in one direction, and we landed in Paris with documents pointing in the opposite direction'.[8]

While this rather remarkable story illustrates that it was necessary for Khrushchev to go through the motions of consultation with the leading members of his delegation and, in a still more perfunctory way, with the Politburo, it is much more to the point to see it as an instance of how the need for speed of decision in foreign policy can concentrate a great deal of power in the hands of the *de facto* chief executive. Of course, in this particular case the urgency had been artificially created by Khrushchev. Nothing had occurred since he and his colleagues boarded the plane for Paris which was not known when they were all in Moscow. Whether the change of tack is to be attributed to Khrushchev's well-attested impulsiveness or whether it was a more calculated move inasmuch as he had been uncertain of getting support in the course of less hasty deliberations in Moscow for an approach likely to wreck the Paris talks before they got started must remain a matter for conjecture. In either event, it illustrates both Khrushchev's boldness in asserting his views and his ability on occasion to leave the 'collective leadership' with very little option but to support him.

Numerous other initiatives came from Khrushchev personally and not all were to the liking of his colleagues. The fact that Khrushchev got away with them at the time does not mean that they were unambiguous successes for him; this style of leadership contributed to his downfall in October 1964. One example is the part he played in creating the Cuban missile crisis. On Khrushchev's own admission, the 'idea of installing missiles with nuclear warheads in Cuba without letting the United States find out they were there until it was too late to do anything about them'[9] was his. He had some difficulty in persuading Fidel Castro to accept the missiles and later had trouble in convincing him of the necessity of removing the missiles in the light of the American reaction.[10] Though Khrushchev could make a case for saying that the ultimate Soviet-American compromise made the venture worthwhile, there seems no doubt that the episode weakened his standing within the Soviet leadership, not least in the eyes of the military.[11]

The use that Khrushchev made of his son-in-law, Aleksey Adzhubey, for sensitive diplomatic missions was regarded by his colleagues in the leadership as a serious example of bypassing the appropriate institutional channels. When these missions included a visit to Bonn in the summer of 1964, Khrushchev had created a stick which his opponents were able to use against him. He had raised the suspicion that he was going to do a deal with the West Germans[12] and had complicated Soviet relations with East Germany, especially since Adzhubey had 'spoken slightingly of Walter Ulbricht' in Bonn.[13] Suslov, in his indictment of Khrushchev at the Central Committee plenary session of 14 October 1964, spoke of Adzhubey having 'assumed the role of shadow Foreign Minister' and of his having 'attempted to meddle in diplomatic matters at the highest level, confusing the ambassadors'.[14] A French Communist party delegation to Moscow was told at the end of October 1964 that this was one of the reasons for Khrushchev's removal. 'By-passing elected officials, he entrusted increasingly important missions to members of his personal entourage', Georges Marchais reported.[15]

While there were many reasons why his colleagues had determined to rid themselves of Khrushchev,[16] bypassing Ministry of Foreign Affairs channels had its place in the list. It clearly infuriated the foreign policy establishment in general and the Foreign Minister, Andrey Gromyko, in particular. Though not as yet a member of the Politburo, Gromyko attended the enlarged session of that body when it met on 13 October 1964 to demand Khrushchev's resignation. Seeing things, as Michel Tatu has observed, from the standpoint of his own job, Gromyko went so far as to say to one of his visitors shortly afterwards: 'Why was

Khrushchev overthrown? Because he sent Adzhubey to Bonn, of course'.[17]

Brezhnev's style of leadership was quite different from Khrushchev's. This was partly no doubt because he differed greatly in predisposition and temperament from his predecessor, partly because he had learnt from Khrushchev's mistakes and saw that it would be counterproductive to push his personal views too hard or to bypass important institutional interests, and partly because the Politburo collectively and the major institutional interests (including the military and the KGB), having joined a coalition to remove one General Secretary, were in no mood to be pushed around by another.

It is normal in the Soviet system for a General Secretary to wield more power and influence in foreign policy after he has been in office for some years.[18] One important reason for this is that the General Secretary inherits a top leadership team which he cannot instantly change. In particular, it may take him some years to bring about decisive changes in the voting membership of the Politburo. Brezhnev was certainly no exception to that rule. Though Western governments should have recognized earlier than they did that the General Secretary wielded more power than any other individual within the Soviet leadership, Brezhnev felt it expedient, and perhaps necessary, to allow Kosygin to be the Soviet Union's principal foreign policy spokesman during the second half of the 1960s except when relations with other Communist countries were involved. Thus, Brezhnev was chief Soviet spokesman on Czechoslovakia in 1968[19], but it was Kosygin who had talks with Lyndon Johnson in the USA, with de Gaulle in France and with Harold Wilson in London.

George Brown, the British Foreign Secretary between 1966 and 1968, later confessed: 'When I was in office we never really knew who was the Russian leader.'[20] Henry Kissinger has recalled that 'until well into 1971 all our high-level communications with the Soviet Union were with Kosygin'.[21] Though the fact that Brezhnev held the most powerful post within Soviet politics could scarcely fail to give him an exceptionally important voice in Politburo discussions of foreign policy, Kosygin, as Chairman of the Council of Ministers, was for the first six or seven post-Khrushchev years much more actively involved in high-level talks with foreign leaders; it was only from the early 1970s that he ceded the role of topmost diplomat to Brezhnev.

That 1970–71 marked a turning-point in the degree of attention which Brezhnev devoted to foreign policy in general and to international diplomacy in particular has been remarked by Willy Brandt as well as by Kissinger. Brandt observed:

My four-hour conversation with Leonid Brezhnev on the afternoon of 12

August 1970 was carefully noted by the world at large. Few non-communist visitors from abroad had yet been granted a lengthy interview with the General Secretary. He made a rather wary impression and spent considerable periods of time referring to his written material, whole passages of which he read aloud. But this was clearly the stage at which Brezhnev had resolved – and had been empowered – to take personal charge of important aspects of Soviet policy towards the West. At the time, he and Kosygin struck me as the Kremlin's '1a' and '1b'. A year later Brezhnev's definite and undisputed supremacy could not escape the eye or ear. He was also a master of his material.[22]

Crises in Soviet relations with other Communist countries no doubt played their part in drawing Brezhnev more deeply into the formulation and conduct of Soviet foreign policy. Not only did Czechoslovakia present the Soviet Union with its most serious dilemma in Eastern Europe since 1956, but relations with China deteriorated to the point at which armed clashes between Soviet and Chinese troops took place on the Communist giants' disputed border in 1969. Since East-East relations also had implications for East-West relations, it is hardly surprising that Brezhnev wished to be more fully involved in the conduct of Soviet policy towards the West and *vis-à-vis* the rival superpower in particular. The extent to which China remained a major preoccupation for Brezhnev is attested in the memoirs of those on the American side who dealt with him.[23] More generally, as many Soviet publications were later (indirectly) to bear witness, Brezhnev had a strong desire to be hailed as the architect of détente.

It is, furthermore, hardly coincidental that Brezhnev's enhanced role and greater self-confidence in foreign policy discussions were detected by Brandt and Kissinger only months after Brezhnev had strengthened his position within the Soviet leadership. In April 1971, at the Twenty-fourth Congress of the CPSU, the voting membership of the Politburo was increased from eleven to fifteen. Three of the four new full members (Kunaev, Shcherbitsky and Kulakov) had connections with, and were strong supporters of, Brezhnev.

Brezhnev continued to play the most prominent part in Soviet high-level diplomacy for the remainder of the decade, though in the late 1970s and early 1980s his activity was reduced by failing health and cooling East-West relations. Thus, during the first half of the 1970s, as the Nixon and Kissinger memoirs testify, Brezhnev was the dominant figure on the Soviet side in US-Soviet discussions.[24] He invested much time and prestige in the successful outcome of the Helsinki negotiations which led to the Final Act of the Conference on Security and Co-operation in Europe, signed in August 1975 (even if, in the light of some of the 'Basket Three' proposals contained within the Helsinki Agreement, this could be regarded as at best a Pyrrhic victory).

Brezhnev had already some background in foreign policy when he became party leader in October 1964. He had, after all, been a full member of the Politburo since 1957 and Chairman of the Presidium of the Supreme Soviet from 1960 until 1963. The latter post had given him, as formal head of the Soviet state, his first real taste of international diplomacy. When, however, Brezhnev died in November 1982 and was succeeded by Yuriy Andropov, the Soviet Union had for the first time a General Secretary who came to the post with at least as much knowledge of, and experience in, foreign affairs as in domestic politics. He had moved from the party apparatus to the Ministry of Foreign Affairs in 1953. For most of the next four years he was Soviet Ambassador to Hungary. When he returned to the Central Committee apparatus in 1957, it was with important international responsibilities – as head of the Department of Relations with Communist and Workers' Parties of Socialist Countries.

This was followed by Andropov's fifteen-year stint as head of the KGB – from May 1967 until May 1982 – which, in principle at least, should have made him as knowledgeable about the Western world as he was of the Communist world. There remained, however, an important difference. Whereas his previous post had involved him in travelling frequently to Eastern Europe (and on occasion to China), his new job virtually ensured that when he became General Secretary he would still not have paid a single visit to a Western country. Indeed, Andropov died without ever having been in the West – the only Soviet top leader to have suffered from such a limitation upon his travels. In that respect at least, his successor, Konstantin Chernenko, had an advantage over him, since Chernenko's travels, prior to his succeeding to the General Secretaryship, included visits to Austria (for the Vienna Brezhnev-Carter summit in 1979), Denmark, France and Greece. In other respects, of course, Andropov had a much stronger foreign affairs background than Chernenko.

Andropov indeed, as a member of the Politburo for almost ten years, as a member of the Defence Council, as the recipient of all the information at the disposal of the KGB, and as a party leader who had maintained links with intellectuals with specialist knowledge of international affairs, was formidably equipped to play a more important part in the foreign policy-making process from the very outset of his General Secretaryship than any of his predecessors in that post or his successor. Soviet pronouncements on foreign policy from the first weeks of the post-Brezhnev era frequently bore the mark of Andropov's personal style. He lost no time in getting down to meetings with foreign visitors. During the first eight months of 1983, his schedule included meetings with the West German SPD leader, Hans-Jochen Vogel; the Finnish President, Mauno Koivisto; King Hussein of Jordan; the PLO Chairman, Yasser Arafat; the French Foreign Minister, Claude Cheysson; the distinguished veteran of American-Soviet diplomacy, Averell Harriman; an American trade union leader, William Winpisinger; and a group of nine American Democratic Senators.[25]

That last meeting in August 1983 was, however, Andropov's final one with non-Communist foreigners. Deterioration in his health, of which there had already been some signs, became sufficiently marked to force him to miss the November celebrations of the Bolshevik Revolution and both the Central Committee meeting and Supreme Soviet session held in late December. Though the political promotions announced at the December Central Committee plenum indicated that, even from his sick-bed, Andropov still had his hands on the levers of power, his grave illness could not but dimish his participation in the foreign policy process. Given the authority and power which Andropov had acquired uncommonly quickly, the main effect of his illness on Soviet foreign policy may well have been to make flexibility and new initiatives from the Soviet side more difficult than they would have been with a fully-fit Andropov in charge.

When Andropov died on 9 February 1984 and was succeeded by Chernenko, it was made clear from the outset – as it had been when Andropov succeeded Brezhnev – that the new General Secretary was indeed the top Soviet leader.[26] It was with him that the most important foreign political leaders – including Vice-President Bush, Chancellor Kohl, Mrs Thatcher and French Prime Minister Pierre Mauroy – had meetings when they attended Andropov's funeral. Gromyko was, however, in attendance, and Chernenko did not play as dominant a part in these discussions as Andropov had done fifteen months earlier. As of late March 1984, it can be said that Chernenko has lost no time in building up his domestic authority through the Soviet mass media in which he has been accorded even more extensive coverage and more favourable publicity than was Andropov during the earliest stage of his General Secretaryship. Yet – and this is not surprising, given the differences in background and experience of the two men – he is playing a less prominent part in the conduct of Soviet foreign policy than did his predecessor during his first weeks of office. It must be added that, coming to the General Secretaryship early in an American presidential election year and having no wish to assist in the re-election of Ronald Reagan, Chernenko had no immediate incentives for making spectacular gestures in the vital realm of Soviet-US relations, even should his colleagues in the Politburo be willing to accord him a free hand (which, of course, they would be most unlikely to do).

The Politburo

Since the death of Stalin, the Politburo has been the ultimate collective arbiter of Soviet foreign policy. It is clear that debate on foreign policy issues took place in this forum during Khrushchev's time, though there is some evidence that there was less argument and more monologue (from the chair) after Khrushchev defeated the anti-party group in 1957.[27]

In view of the length of the Politburo agenda, and the extent to which the accompanying papers prepared by the Secretariat embody the results of consultations with the major individuals and institutions involved, approval of documents and actions may often be a formality. Given, for example, the overlap between defence and foreign policy, it is likely that a number of issues will have been virtually settled by the Defence Council before they reach the Politburo. Yet even on arms control proposals, it would appear that the Politburo has the last word. Both in the early and the late 1970s issues were referred back to the Politburo by Soviet negotiators for final decision on what concessions might be made.[28] Indeed, in agreeing to Moscow as a venue for a meeting with Gromyko on SALT II in October 1978, the American Secretary of State, Cyrus Vance, was influenced by his hope that 'the physical proximity of the negotiations to the Politburo might make it easier to get quick and favourable Soviet decisions during the talks.'[29] (On this occasion, Vance was to be disappointed.)

Politburo meetings are usually held once a week, the normal day for these sessions being Thursdays (as with the British Cabinet). There are weeks in which more than one meeting is held and holiday periods in which for several weeks on end the Politburo does not meet at all. Thus, for example, in the period of 259 weeks between the Twenty-fifth Party Congress in 1976 and the Twenty-sixth Congress in 1981, the Politburo met 236 times. In weeks in which it did not meet, direction and continuity in Soviet policy apparently was provided by the Secretariat of the Central Committee which held 250 meetings in that same period.[30]

The composition of the Politburo makes it the most appropriate body to consider the implications of international events and crises, and it is the body to which Soviet leaders who have had meetings with foreign politicians report.[31] Politburo meetings are attended not only by the full members of the Politburo but by the candidate members and by Secretaries of the Central Committee. (As of March 1984 there are twelve full members, six candidate members and five Secretaries other than those already counted because they are also members or candidate members of the Politburo.) Since 1973, when Andropov, Gromyko and Grechko entered the Politburo, the Chairman of the KGB, the Minister of Foreign Affairs and the Minister of Defence have thus been entitled to participate in these meetings, apart from the period between May 1982 when Andropov left the KGB for the Secretariat of the Central Committee and December 1983 when Viktor Chebrikov (KGB chairman since December 1982) became a candidate member of the Politburo. The presence of these three office-holders clearly strengthens the Politburo's suitability to determine foreign policy in terms of relevant institutional representation.

Apart from the General Secretary, who chairs the meetings, there are several others among these top two dozen people with particular foreign policy experience. They include the Chairman of the Council of Ministers who is always a full member of the Politburo. The part played by the incumbent of that office varies from time to time. Kosygin, while never less than important throughout his chairmanship, played a more prominent part in the 1960s than in the 1970s. His successor, Nikolay Tikhonov, though a less substantial political figure than Kosygin, has frequently represented the Soviet Union in talks with foreign statesmen, reporting on these meetings to the Politburo.[32] As formal head of government within the Soviet Union, the Chairman of the Council of Ministers is able to take some weight off the shoulders of the General Secretary. On the strength of the Council of Ministers Chairman's extensive participation in high-level talks, he can be assumed to be, and most obviously was in the case of Kosygin, a significant contributor to Politburo discussion on foreign policy (as well as on the Soviet economy which is, perhaps, his primary concern). Two Secretaries of the Central Committee with a special contribution to make to foreign policy discussion in the Politburo are Boris Ponomarev who is in charge of the International Department of the Central Committee and Konstantin Rusakov who is head of the department responsible for relations with the Communist world. The part played by their departments in the foreign policy-making process will be discussed briefly below.

One innovation of the Andropov General Secretaryship – retained under his successor, Chernenko – has been the publication in the mass media of weekly communiqués on what has been discussed in the Politburo. Needless to say, these are not comprehensive minutes. Nor do they purport to be. They usually conclude by observing that 'the Politburo meeting examined and adopted resolutions on certain other matters to do with the foreign and domestic policy of the Soviet state' or that 'the Politburo meeting also discussed certain other matters concerning the country's internal life and the international situation'.[33] Some matters which must certainly have been discussed in the Politburo receive no mention. Though it is evident that the Politburo was not consulted before a South Korean airliner was shot down over Soviet airspace, with the loss of 269 lives, at the beginning of September 1983, it is equally clear that there must have been Politburo discussion after the event to establish the facts and to determine how the Soviet version of them should be presented to the outside world. But this was too sensitive a topic to figure in the published Politburo communiqués.

Nevertheless, these communiqués provide further confirmation of the fact that discussion of foreign policy occupies an important place on the Politburo agenda. They indicate that among the topics discussed in the Politburo during Andropov's period of office were the situation in the Middle East and the position of the PLO, the Madrid meeting of the Conference on Security and Co-operation in Europe, Soviet-US relations, Soviet-West German relations, Soviet-Greek relations, Soviet-Finnish relations, Nicaragua, the Soviet and Warsaw Pact response to the placing of Pershing and Cruise missiles in Western Europe, Angola, the Geneva talks on nuclear arms limitation, the prospect of an anti-satellite arms race in outer space, Andropov's responses to Reagan's statements, and the further development of economic integration within the CMEA (Comecon).[34]

It is not usual for the published Politburo communiqués to give any indication of the amount of time devoted to a particular item, but the *Pravda* report of 3 December 1983 on the Politburo meeting held two days earlier mentioned that 'a substantial part of the agenda of the Politburo meeting' had been occupied by issues related to 'the consistent deepening of economic, scientific and technological cooperation among CMEA member countries, the coordinating of their plans, and the developing of the system of communications and exchange of information'. The same meeting approved measures which had been under consideration for some time but the finalization of which had almost certainly been demanded by an earlier Politburo meeting in the light of the Korean airliner incident – namely, for the setting-up of 'a unified system of USSR air traffic control'. It appears that in virtually every case where a Politburo member or Secretary of the Central Committee has had an official meeting with a foreign visitor or delegation or has himself represented the Soviet Union abroad, he presents an account of his talks for the information and approval of the Politburo. Thus, at the Politburo meeting discussed above, Nikolay Tikhonov reported on his meeting with Borislav Srebic, Deputy President of the Yugoslav Federal Executive Council; Andrey Gromyko on his talks with the PLO delegation led by Faruq Qaddumi; Mikhail Gorbachev on his meeting with the American businessman, John Chrystal; and Vasiliy Kuznetsov on his meeting with President Koivisto of Finland.[35]

All this suggests that there is an important sense in which the Soviet Politburo in the post-Stalin (and especially post-Khrushchev) period has been the collective leadership it claims to be. Yet within the Politburo, the General Secretary, though stronger at some times than others, has always been more than *primus inter pares* and better placed than any of his colleagues to give a lead. It is worth noting in passing the advantage to the Soviet system of the fact that any General Secretary, even if he has not had the specific international responsibilities of an Andropov, will come to that office with some knowledge of international issues and experience of actual involvement in the highest-level foreign policy discussions merely by virtue of having attended the Politburo over a period of years. That is quite apart from the fact that there is some division of labour in the meeting of important foreigners, so that a potential General Secretary is likely to have taken part in a number of such meetings and to have been briefed accordingly. The contrast between the Soviet leadership and West European governments is not so very great in this respect – except that Soviet leaders do not have to worry about the vicissitudes of competitive elections and the possibility of returning to government only after a lengthy spell in opposition. It is, however, very different from the United States where the President can emerge from Georgia or California with no experience at all of foreign policy-making.[36]

The Central Committee apparatus

It is reasonable to suppose, as noted earlier, that most of the detailed working-out of Soviet policy is done in between, rather than at, Politburo meetings and that much of the Politburo's discussion of foreign policy must consist of approving documents already prepared. (However, any change of policy – such as the Soviet overtures to the West of the early 1970s – clearly involves lengthy Politburo discussion, as do events abroad which assume crisis proportions in the eyes of the Soviet leadership.) Several departments of the Central Committee have a special responsibility for preparing and processing the papers on which Politburo decisions on foreign policy issues are based. The most significant of these are the International Department and the Department of Relations with Communist and Workers' Parties of Socialist Countries. Of these two, pride of place is taken by the International Department which has responsibilities for the entire non-Communist world, including state-to-state relations and not merely the party-to-party relations with non-ruling Communist parties which have sometimes been viewed as the sum total of the department's functions.[37]

The importance of the department is indicated by the political standing of its head since 1955, Boris Ponomarev, who has been a Secretary of the Central Committee since 1961, and since 1972 a candidate member of the Politburo while retaining his Secretaryship. He has, in other words, been attending Politburo meetings for almost a quarter of a century with the right to speak, though not to vote. (As in the British Cabinet, however, voting in the Politburo is exceptional rather than the rule.) The first deputy head of the department, Vadim Zagladin, is a member of the Central Committee.

The Secretarial overlord of both the International Department and the Department of Relations with Communist and Workers' Parties of Socialist Countries (hereafter Socialist Countries department) was for many years Mikhail Suslov. Suslov and Ponomarev worked closely together and were conservative influences in Soviet foreign policy-making. So far as the international Communist movement is concerned, both played exceptionally important roles in deciding what was revisionism and what could be accepted as legitimate development within socialism. Both tended to take a hard line on Yugoslavia (whose 'socialist' credentials were sufficiently suspect in Soviet eyes to bring it at times within the purview of the International Department as well as the Socialist Countries department) even when other leaders, including Khrushchev, were inclined to be conciliatory.[38] The Yugoslav Ambassador to Moscow in the mid-1950s, Veljko Mićunović, noted not only the considerable influence of Ponomarev but also the fact that he had 'a portrait of Stalin in a prominent place in his office two years after Khrushchev made his secret speech'.[39]

The Socialist Countries Department, whose head from 1957 until 1967 was Andropov, is (as of early 1984) headed by Konstantin Rusakov. The importance of the department is indicated by the fact that when Rusakov became its head in 1977, he was accorded the rank of Secretary of the Central Committee. (The fact that he had worked as a personal assistant to Brezhnev from 1972 to 1977 no doubt greatly facilitated his promotion.) It is quite evident that members of the Socialist Countries Department can exert significant influence on Soviet decision-making relating to other Communist states. In visits to Czechoslovakia in 1967 one of the more influential among them heard (and apparently accepted) many of the arguments on the need to replace Antonín Novotný put to him by Czechoslovak Communist Party intellectuals. When Brezhnev, on his visit to Prague at the end of that year, disappointed Novotný by not lifting a finger to help him, it is a reasonable assumption that advice from the Socialist Countries department played a substantial part in producing his memorable parting words to the Czechs, 'It's your affair'.[40] (It is also, however, worth adding that Novotný had had a slightly uneasy relationship with Brezhnev ever since he had questioned the way Khrushchev was removed in October 1964.[41]) In 1968 developments in Czechoslovakia sufficiently alarmed the Soviet leadership to make the Socialist

Countries department just one institutional voice among many on an issue which had become a major preoccupation of the entire political elite.

Papers for the Politburo are processed by the General Department of the Central Committee, which acts as a kind of secretariat (in the narrower sense) for the Politburo and is responsible for the agenda. Since the head of the General Department works especially closely with the General Secretary (from 1965 until shortly after Brezhnev's death the post was held by Konstantin Chernenko), the agenda doubtless gives due prominence to the General Secretary's priorities. It seems certain, though, that the International Department and the Socialist Countries department have easy access to the agenda. The importance of their fields, the standing of the departments and the political authority of their heads make it unlikely that they would be debarred from putting an item on it if they wished to do so. It is probable, moreover, that they make extensive use of this privilege, for there is a strong tendency within the Soviet system to push matters upwards for decision. Since the relevant department of the Central Committee provides most, if not all, of the documentation on which a Politburo decision is based, in many cases such a decision merely allows the department to do what it wished to do in any event. To have the imprimatur of the Politburo for a course of action has the advantage, however, not only of making implementation easier but also of relieving the department of ultimate responsibility should things go wrong.

Since ministers who are not members of the Politburo have no automatic access to the Politburo agenda, but must go through the Secretariat if they wish to have a matter considered at a Politburo meeting, it seems likely that the International Department has wielded a still greater power and influence in foreign policy-making at those times when the Minister of Foreign Affairs has not been a Politburo member. Thus, while the department remains to the present day exceedingly important, it is worth noting that over the past decade it has lost its near-monopoly as channel of international information to the Politburo.

Two other departments of the Central Committee with international responsibilities deserve mention in passing, though they would appear to play a much less significant part in the foreign policy-making process. That is particularly true of the Foreign Cadres Department which approves the appointment of Soviet personnel to posts abroad. The International Information Department, which was created as recently as the late 1970s and is headed by Leonid Zamyatin (a full member of the Central Committee since 1976 and a former director general of the Soviet news agency, TASS, who earlier served for many years in the Ministry of Foreign Affairs) may be of rather more consequence in the policy-making context. While it is concerned with the dissemination of the Soviet view of current international events,[42] with a view to influencing world opinion, rather than with the gathering of information from abroad, its contribution to the wording of Soviet official statements should not be discounted. Since 'words in international relations are', as Jerry Hough has put it, 'a significant part of policy, the department's drafting role may well have an impact'.[43]

The Minister and Ministry of Foreign Affairs

The Soviet Foreign Minister has not always been a member of the Politburo. Gromyko's immediate predecessor, Shepilov, was a candidate member and his predecessor, Molotov, a full member, but Gromyko himself was not even a candidate member from 1957 when he succeeded Shepilov until 1973 when he was accorded voting membership. This is not to say that even in those days he was not an influential figure. Though the Politburo, at the highest level, and the International Department, in more detail, may have set the limits within which he was permitted to operate, it was Gromyko who met more foreign statesmen over a longer period of years than any of his colleagues. His first-hand contacts with Western countries and Western politicians were much greater than those of Ponomarev, and it would have been surprising indeed if his experience and knowledge had been disregarded at the top leadership level.

In fact, even Khrushchev, who at times treated Gromyko roughly, had respect for Gromyko's knowledge and skills, and though the Foreign Minister was by no means as influential in Khrushchev's time as he was to become later, he played, nevertheless, an important part in the formulation and conduct of Soviet foreign policy. When Khrushchev made his famous visit to the United Nations, the Soviet resolution put to the assembly had, naturally enough, been worked out in advance. As Khrushchev noted in his memoirs:

> In matters like this we had a real craftsman in Andrei Andreyevich [Gromyko]. He'd been with the UN since its inception. He really knew his way around the kitchen, so to speak, and he was very useful to us when we had to cook something up of our own.[44]

Though elsewhere in his memoirs, Khrushchev refers to Gromyko 'as a good civil servant who always went by the book' and criticizes him for being willing merely to draft a diplomatic protest concerning American U-2 flights over Soviet territory just before the plane piloted by Gary Powers was shot down,[45] he clearly relied very much on his Foreign Minister's briefings before he met foreign statesmen. Khrushchev's personality was such that he would not allow himself to be seen accepting Gromyko's counsel in public; that is not at all the same thing as rejecting all of his advice in private. Before his American tour, Khrushchev recalled in his memoirs, he had comforted himself with the thought that 'I wouldn't be completely on my own; Andrei Andreyevich Gromyko would be with me', adding:

> I respected Gromyko then, and I respect him now, as a fine Foreign Minister. But I wouldn't be able to start whispering questions back and forth with him in the middle of my talks with Eisenhower. I'd been very disdainful of the way Eisenhower had let Dulles shove notes in front of him all through our negotiations in Geneva, and I didn't want to do the same sort of thing myself.[46]

Under Brezhnev, Gromyko's influence grew and when he joined the Politburo in 1973, it is likely that he not merely enhanced his own power and authority but increased the standing and influence of the Ministry of Foreign Affairs. Just as in Whitehall, ministries like to see their political head in the Cabinet, since this strengthens their departmental bargaining position, so it would appear that in the Soviet Union the tiny minority of ministries whose head is in the Politburo (at present this applies only to the Ministry of Defence and the Ministry of Foreign Affairs, though the KGB – a quasi-ministry – is headed by a candidate member) possess significantly greater political authority than those ministries not represented in the highest policy-making body.

A member of the Politburo has the right to put a matter on the Politburo agenda. Thus, through Gromyko, senior officials in the Ministry of Foreign Affairs were now able to make their own views known to the Politburo. Though it is likely that Gromyko was frequently called into Politburo meetings before he became a member, a non-member must speak when he is spoken to, whereas a full member can speak with weight and authority on his own subject, not least when he knows it as well as Gromyko does.

An interesting example of the enhancement of the Ministry of Foreign Affairs' influence is given by Franklyn Griffiths. The international section of the Central Committee report delivered by the General Secretary to party congresses is naturally a party, rather than a governmental, responsibility, and the International Department of the Central Committee coordinates the preparation of the preliminary draft, though the General Secretary's 'personal advisers are also in a position to commission special contributions that may be incorporated at some point in the drafting process'.[47] Yet a major contribution to the international report presented to the Twenty-fifth Party Congress in 1976 was made by the Department of General International Relations of the Ministry of Foreign Affairs, while the Institute of World Economy and International Relations (which had been responsible for the corresponding section of the report to the Twenty-fourth Congress five years earlier) was 'relegated to a primary concern with economic matters'.[48] This is related, quite convincingly, by Griffiths to 'the growth of the Foreign Ministry's authority following the elevation of A.A. Gromyko to the Politburo in 1973. . . .'[49]

During the last few years of Brezhnev's life, Gromyko's influence developed further, given that Brezhnev's health was such that he no longer retained the detailed grasp of the issues which he had displayed in the early and mid-1970s. At the Soviet-American summit at Vienna in June 1979, he had to rely on Gromyko in his talks with Carter in the way Khrushchev had been determined to avoid in his meetings with Eisenhower. That much seems clear, even though there are differences of emphasis in the accounts of the meeting produced by leading American participants. Former President Carter observes in his memoirs that 'there was never any doubt that Brezhnev was in charge', but he adds that Gromyko was always close by, 'speaking up frequently and forcefully whenever he seemed inclined to do so' and taking 'a much harder line on almost every subject than anyone else'.[50]

Zbigniew Brzezinski, somewhat in contrast, writes:

> When Carter met alone with Brezhnev, Brezhnev – as Carter later told me – seemed unable to cope with a direct and informal discussion. His translator had a file next to him, with different topics indexed, and he would reach into the file, pull out an appropriate piece of paper, and Brezhnev would read his response to Carter's comments from the piece of paper.[51]

Brzezinski goes so far as to describe Gromyko as 'clearly the dominant figure on the Soviet side'. In the sessions in which the American National Security Adviser participated, Brezhnev deferred a great deal to Gromyko who would 'whisper instructions to him in a quiet but firm voice'. Brzezinski had the advantage over Carter that he could understand Russian and so is able to record that Gromyko would sometimes tell Brezhnev, 'No, don't agree to this', or point to Brezhnev's script and tell him where to read and at what point to stop.[52]

High as Gromyko's standing was within the Soviet leadership in the late Brezhnev years, it became still higher on the latter's death. Andropov, Ustinov and Gromyko clearly had a good working relationship, and though there are conflicting reports on the positions taken by the various Politburo members on the succession to Brezhnev, all accounts put Gromyko on Andropov's side.[53] That the esteem was mutual was strongly suggested in March 1983 when Gromyko's formal political standing was enhanced by his appointment to be a First Deputy Chairman of the Council of Ministers while remaining Minister of Foreign Affairs. The other two First Deputy Chairmen, Ivan Arkhipov and Geydar Aliyev, do not head any particular ministry, but have inter-departmental responsibilities. It is possible that Gromyko's promotion was not only a signal of his greater political authority but also marked an extension of his coordinating role in foreign policy. The fact that, though in his mid-seventies, he was four years younger than the head of the International Department, Ponomarev, and that, though five years older than the last General Secretary, he was physically much fitter than Andropov (who had from the previous month, as the medical communiqué after his death a year later was to reveal, begun to receive treatment on a kidney machine) adds plausibility to such conjecture.

The disparity between the experience and knowledge of international affairs of Gromyko, on the one hand, and Chernenko, on the other, means that, health permitting, Gromyko is likely to enjoy still more authority and influence in the making of Soviet foreign policy during the period of Chernenko's leadership than at any other time in his career. There is no reason to suppose that personal relations between Gromyko and Chernenko are particularly close, but given that by this time Gromyko is a considerable figure in the Politburo in his own right and that such expertise as Chernenko may possess does not lie in foreign policy, that need not prevent the establishment of a *modus operandi* whereby the leading role in day-to-day foreign policy-making is, in fact, played by Gromyko. The health proviso is, of course, an important one when the discussion concerns the relationship between two men in their seventies.

So long as Gromyko continues as Foreign Minister, the Ministry of Foreign Affairs is likely to retain its enhanced institutional standing. It is of some consequence that Gromyko outranks the long-standing head of the International Department of the Central Committee, Boris Ponomarev.[54] Though both the International Department and the Ministry are likely to remain key institutions in Soviet foreign policy-making, their precise relationship when their present elderly heads depart may depend to no small extent on the relative political standing of those who fill the shoes of Gromyko and Ponomarev.

* * *

A fuller account of the Soviet foreign policy-making process would include consideration not only of those institutions discussed in other chapters of this book but of the role of the personal assistants (*pomoshchniki*) of Soviet leaders – in particular, of successive General Secretaries – and the inputs of the Soviet Union's numerous policy-oriented research institutes. Such a task is well beyond the bounds of a chapter of moderate length, but if one takes the case of Andropov's personal aides, it is worth noting that at least three of them had foreign policy backgrounds.

The most experienced among them was Andrey Aleksandrov-Agentov (usually referred to in the Soviet press now simply as A.M. Aleksandrov) whom, in spite of his long association with Brezhnev, Andropov chose to retain. Aleksandrov was at Brezhnev's side throughout his meetings with Western leaders (including three American Presidents) during the 1970s. He spent over twenty years with TASS and the Ministry of Foreign Affairs before joining the staff of the Presidium of the Supreme Soviet in 1961 (which gives him links also with Chernenko who headed the Presidium's secretariat at that time and who, not surprisingly, chose to retain Aleksandrov's services when he succeeded Andropov as General Secretary). When Brezhnev returned to the Central Committee Secretariat in 1963, Aleksandrov went with him, and served throughout his entire General Secretaryship as one of Brezhnev's personal aides. At the Twenty-sixth Party Congress in 1981, he became a full member of the Central Committee which enhanced his political standing beyond that normally associated with a *pomoshchnik*. Possibly because of the high political status he had thereby attained, but more probably because he valued Aleksandrov's abilities, experience and 'institutional memory', Andropov retained his services, even though a General Secretary may be assumed to have a free hand in the choice of his personal aides, as distinct from occupants of 'elective' posts such as members of the Politburo and Secretaries of the Central Committee. It would be surprising if Aleksandrov, who is second only to Gromyko in experience of 'summit meetings' among those still active in Soviet politics, did not exert some influence and perhaps a greater influence on Chernenko than on the two previous General Secretaries whom he served.

Aleksandrov's expertise is on Western countries, particularly the Federal Republic of Germany and the United States. Among the *pomoshchniki* to the General Secretary brought in by Andropov were two people with knowledge of Communist countries who also had long associations with him, namely Viktor Sharapov and Pavel Laptev. Sharapov (who, interestingly enough, has been retained by Chernenko) and Laptev worked for Andropov in the Socialist Countries department of the Central Committee when he headed that department. Sharapov was at that time a specialist on China and Laptev on Albania. Evidently they retained their links with Andropov after he moved to the Chairmanship of the KGB, for they jointly edited a volume of his speeches published in Moscow in 1979. As this suggests, they doubtless served Andropov in a general capacity and not only as experts on 'socialist countries'. Advising Andropov on Albania would, after all, scarcely have been a full-time job!

There is a broader community of foreign policy influentials, many of whom are to be found in the leading research institutes in Moscow but also, for example, among journalists. Thus, one would wish to include in these ranks Aleksandr Bovin, the political correspondent of *Izvestiya*, a frequent broadcaster and traveller, and a former head of Andropov's group of consultants in the Socialist Countries department of the Central Committee in the mid-1960s. His *Pravda* counterpart, Yuriy Zhukov, is prominent as a propagandist, and he was a member of the Soviet group led by Chernenko which took part in discussions with a West German SPD delegation led by Hans-Jochen Vogel.[55] Bovin was more likely to have had the ear of Andropov. His visit to China in February 1983 was, in all probability, as much concerned with taking political soundings as with journalism.

Among the policy institutes, the two most important in relation to Soviet foreign policy are the Institute of World Economy and International Relations (headed by Nikolay Inozemtsev from 1966 until his death in 1982 and since 1983 by Aleksandr Yakovlev) and the Institute of the United States and Canada (headed since its foundation in 1967 by Georgiy Arbatov). The fact that both Inozemtsev and Arbatov became candidate members of the Central Committee in 1976 and full members in 1981 indicates the policy relevance of these institutes as well as the political standing of the individuals. Though both institutes are attached to the Academy of Sciences of the USSR, their members accept assignments from, and may exert influence through, the Central Committee, especially its International Department. There is evidence that the directors of these institutes have access to the Politburo and to the General Secretary. Arbatov, for example, accompanied Brezhnev on his visit to the United States in 1973. And as another former head of Andropov's talented group of consultants who served him in the Socialist Countries Department of the Central Committee (a group which, as noted earlier, was also headed at different times by Bovin and Burlatsky), he almost certainly had access to Andropov when the latter was General Secretary. So far, moreover, he has retained his prominence under Chernenko. Among those present at the meeting between Chernenko and Vogel discussed above were Arbatov and the IMEMO director, Yakovlev. Thus, the assessment of the long-serving and highly capable Soviet Ambassador to the United States, Anatoly Dobrynin (as reported by Zbigniew Brzezinski) of Arbatov as 'a man of no standing and little influence'[56] seems wide of the mark. It is more revealing of personal and institutional rivalries within the Soviet foreign policy establishment than about the USA Institute and its director.

Within the community of those professionally interested in foreign policy, including journalists as well as academics, differences of view may frequently be detected. The various elements within the Soviet *leadership* are very successful at displaying collective solidarity both *vis-à-vis* their own society and *vis-à-vis* the outside world. But in fact the Soviet system as a whole and the Communist Party of the Soviet Union in particular do not possess that monolithic unity attributed to them both by Soviet propagandists and the most anti-Soviet propagandists. Even when there are differences behind the scenes and between the lines, it is an advantage for the Soviet Union, in the conduct of its foreign policy, that the Politburo can produce a united public front. Yet, in the pronouncements of Soviet commentators as well as in the more specialist Soviet literature on foreign countries and on international relations, diversity of view is to be found.

Thus, for instance, two different reactions are discernible to the shift in British foreign policy from the autumn of 1983, given additional publicity after the succession of Chernenko to the General Secretaryship in February 1984, whereby a somewhat greater emphasis has been placed by the government, and by the Prime Minister personally, on increasing East-West contacts and on improving British relations with the Soviet Union and Eastern Europe. Referring to Mrs Thatcher's reported view that arms control should not bear the entire brunt of promoting East-West relations and that there was a need for broader understandings and more regular contacts on regional issues which would create a better context for arms control agreements, the Soviet commentator, Stanislav Kondrashov, used the term 'disconcerting' on Moscow television on 26 February 1984 to describe the position that 'arms control is too narrow a field to bear the whole burden of East-West relations'. Kondrashov added: 'It is hard to view such a position as constructive. Regional issues, for all their importance, cannot make up for the absence of progress – more than that, a moving backwards – in such an important field as arms control.'[57] In contrast, Aleksandr Bovin, who is also a frequent participant in Soviet television discussions but on this occasion was being interviewed by Prague radio, evaluated the same position of Mrs Thatcher positively. Speaking on 2 March, he saw a manifestation of 'one of the aspects of the positive change in British policy' in the view attributed to Mrs Thatcher that to conduct talks 'always from the viewpoint of our military interests and to concentrate in these talks solely on the topic of military confrontation between our two sides, means staying permanently at an impasse'.[58] It is a reasonable assumption that differences of opinion within the community of foreign policy influentials in the Soviet Union which can surface in such a way in public are expressed all the more clearly and frequently when the discussion is behind closed doors.

Conclusions

The foregoing survey is of necessity too brief to do justice to a series of major institutional and individual participants in Soviet political life. The main general point to emerge is that the structure of power and influence within the foreign policy-making process is by no means unchanging. Generalizations to the effect that the entire process is at all times dominated by the General Secretary, or by the International Department of the Central Committee, or by the military, or by the KGB are profoundly suspect. The weight of different institutional actors has varied over time and the influence exerted by particular individuals, whether General Secretaries or Foreign Ministers, has also been far from constant, even in the course of their incumbency of the same office. Thus, as noted earlier, Brezhnev played a more important role in Soviet foreign policy-making in the mid-1970s than in the mid-1960s and Gromyko's influence and authority were significantly greater in the early 1980s than in the early 1960s, though formally both men were holding the same post in the later of the two periods mentioned as they held in the earlier.

The institutional structures which provide the framework of Soviet foreign policy are very strong and yet a General Secretary may at times make his personal views prevail over them. Stalin did so to an unequalled degree, but the period of 'high Stalinism' (roughly the last twenty years of Stalin's life) is, fortunately, no guide to the realities of post-Stalin politics. More to the point is the example of Khrushchev who, without resorting to terror against his opponents, was able to impose his will on the various bureaucratic agencies to a surprising extent, even if those who manned these agencies had the last laugh. Clearly, in the interaction between individual Soviet politicians and institutional structures, there is always scope for a forceful and capable individual who disposes of considerable patronage to affect policy outcomes. A General Secretary with the necessary experience and abilities is, in principle, in a particularly strong position to do so, even if, in practice, particular General Secretaries have at times been heavily reliant on the Minister of Foreign Affairs. If emphasis on such variation makes the Soviet foreign policy-making process seem less straightforward and preordained than it is often assumed to be, it underlines the need for detailed and continuing Western scholarship in this field which has been comparatively neglected – not least in Britain.[59]

Notes

1 T.H. Rigby, *Lenin's Government: Sovnarkom 1917–1922* (Cambridge, Cambridge University Press, 1979), p. 112.

2 Stalin assumed the rank of Chairman of the Council of People's Commissars in 1940. On the renaming of that body in 1946, he became

Chairman of the Council of Ministers. During the war he also accumulated the titles of Commissar (later Minister) of Defence, Marshal of the Soviet Union and Generalissimo.

3 *Khrushchev Remembers: The Last Testament*, translated and edited by Strobe Talbott (Vol. 2 of Khrushchev's memoirs) (London, Andre Deutsch, 1974), pp. 356–7.

4 Ibid., p. 493.

5 Ibid., p. 223.

6 Ibid., p. 224.

7 Ibid., pp. 450–1.

8 Ibid., pp. 451–2.

9 *Khrushchev Remembers*, translated and edited by Strobe Talbott (Vol. 1 of Khrushchev's memoirs) (Boston, Little, Brown, 1970), p. 493.

10 *Khrushchev Remembers*, pp. 488–505; *Khrushchev Remembers: The Last Testament*, pp. 509–11, esp. p. 511. For confirmation of the latter point, see the account of Fidel Castro's 1975 conversation with George McGovern in Arthur M. Schlesinger, Jr., *Robert Kennedy and His Times* (New York, Ballantine Books, 1979), p. 537.

11 Carl A. Linden, *Khrushchev and the Soviet Leadership 1957–1964* (Baltimore: Johns Hopkins Press, 1966), pp. 146–73. See also Arthur M. Schlesinger, Jr., *Robert Kennedy and His Times*, p. 571.

12 Robin Edmonds, *Soviet Foreign Policy: The Brezhnev Years* (Oxford, Oxford University Press, 1983), pp. 36–7.

13 M.A. Suslov, cited by Roy Medvedev, *Khrushchev* (translated by Brian Pearce, Oxford, Blackwell, 1982), p. 238.

14 Ibid.

15 Michel Tatu, *Power in the Kremlin: From Khrushchev's Decline to Collective Leadership* (translated by Helen Katel, London, Collins, 1969), p. 389.

16 See, for example, Medvedev, *Khrushchev*, pp. 237–44.

17 Tatu, *Power in the Kremlin*, p. 389.

18 For elaboration of this point, see Archie Brown, 'The power of the General Secretary of the CPSU', in T.H. Rigby, Archie Brown and Peter Reddaway (eds.), *Authority, Power and Policy in the USSR* (London, Macmillan, 1980), pp. 135–57; and Archie Brown, 'Leadership succession and policy innovation', in Archie Brown and Michael Kaser (eds.), *Soviet Policy for the 1980s* (London, Macmillan, 1982), pp. 223–53.

19 See Zdeněk Mlynář, *Night Frost in Prague: The End of Humane Socialism* (translated by Paul Wilson, London, Hurst, 1980); and Jiri Valenta, *Soviet Intervention in Czechoslovakia, 1968: Anatomy of a Decision* (Baltimore, Johns Hopkins Press, 1979).

20 George Brown, *In My Way* (Harmondsworth, Penguin, 1972), p. 247.

21 Henry Kissinger, *White House Years* (Boston, Little, Brown, 1979), p. 796.

22 Willy Brandt, *People and Politics: The Years 1960–1975* (translated by J. Maxwell Brownjohn, London, Collins, 1978), p. 334.

23 See, for example, Henry Kissinger, *White House Years*; Henry Kissinger, *Years of Upheaval* (Boston, Little, Brown, 1982); *The Memoirs of Richard Nixon* (New York, Grosset and Dunlap, 1978); Jimmy Carter, *Keeping Faith: Memoirs of a President* (New York, Bantam Books, 1982); and Zbigniew Brzezinski, *Power and Principle: Memoirs of the National Security Adviser 1977–81* (London, Weidenfeld and Nicolson, 1983).

24 See Kissinger, *White House Years* and *Years of Upheaval*; Nixon, *The Memoirs of Richard Nixon.*

25 See Jonathan Steele and Eric Abraham, *Andropov in Power: From Komsomol to Kremlin* (Oxford: Martin Robertson, 1983), pp. 3–4 and 174–204.

26 On the transition, see Archie Brown, 'The Soviet succession: from Andropov to Chernenko', in *The World Today*, April 1984, pp. 134–41.

27 See *Khrushchev Remembers: The Last Testament*; Medvedev, *Khrushchev*; Linden, *Khrushchev and the Soviet Leadership 1957–1964*; and Tatu, *Power in the Kremlin.*

28 David Holloway, *The Soviet Union and the Arms Race* (New Haven and London, Yale University Press, 1983), p. 109; Strobe Talbott, *Endgame: The Inside Story of SALT II* (New York, Harper Colophon, 1980), pp. 209, 214.

29 Talbott, *Endgame*, p. 217.

30 L.I. Brezhnev, *Otchetnyy doklad Tsentral'nogo Komiteta KPSS XXVI s' ezdu Kommunisticheskoy partii Sovetskogo Soyuza i ocherednye zadachi partii v oblasti vnutrenney i vneshney politiki, 23 fevralya 1981 goda* (Moscow, Politizdat, 1981), pp. 79–80.

31 See, for example, *Pravda*, 15 October 1983; 29 October 1983; 5 November 1983; and 12 November 1983 (all p. 1).

32 See, for example, *Pravda*, 3 December 1983, p. 1, and 24 December 1983, p. 1.

33 See, for instance, *Pravda*, 26 November 1983, p. 1, and 10 December 1983, p. 1.

34 *Pravda*, 21 January 1983; 29 January 1983; 2 April 1983; 15 April 1983; 20 May 1983; 11 June 1983; 9 July 1983; 27 August 1983; 8 and 29 October 1983 (all p. 1).

35 *Pravda*, 3 December 1983, p. 1.

36 The West European-American comparison has been interestingly elaborated by Fyodor Burlatsky, a prominent Soviet scholar who was a member (and for a time head) of Yuri Andropov's group of consultants in the Central Committee apparatus in the first half of the 1960s. Writing in September 1983, Burlatsky makes the contrast not only between heads of executive in the two continents but also between the broader circles of people with foreign policy responsibilities. He argues that 'the mechanism of formation of the political leadership of the USA is greatly deficient in comparison with the analogous mechanism in the countries of Western Europe' and holds that the leading political figures of Western Europe, regardless of their political orientation, have, as a rule, knowledge of international problems, and are 'not novices'. See F.M. Burlatsky, 'Nekotorye voprosy teorii mezhdunarodnykh otnosheniy', *Voprosy filosofii*, no. 9, 1983, pp. 36–48, esp. 46–7.

37 Leonard Schapiro, 'The international department of the CPSU: key to Soviet policy', *International Journal* (Toronto), Vol. XXXII, no. 1, Winter 1976–7, pp. 41–55. I am in agreement with Schapiro's rejection of the narrow view of the International Department's functions, but his attribution of minimal significance to the Ministry of Foreign Affairs (even after Gromyko's promotion to the Politburo) is different from the interpretation offered in this chapter.

38 Veljko Mićunović, *Moscow Diary* (translated by David Floyd, London, Chatto and Windus, 1980), esp. pp. 64, 233, 288, 365, 385–6.
39 Ibid., p. 386.
40 Mlynář, *Nightfrost in Prague*, p. 71.
41 Ibid., pp. 70–71.
42 Thus, for example, Zamyatin appeared alongside Marshal Nikolay Ogarkov and First Deputy Minister of Foreign Affairs, Georgiy Kornienko, at the press conference held in Moscow on 9 September 1983 to give the Soviet version of events leading up to the shooting-down of the Korean airliner on 1 September.
43 Jerry F. Hough, 'Soviet policy-making toward foreign communists' in *Studies in Comparative Communism*, Vol. XV, no. 3, Autumn 1982, pp. 173–4.
44 *Khrushchev Remembers: The Last Testament*, p. 481.
45 Ibid., p. 444.
46 Ibid., p. 374. Gromyko's formidable knowledge and skills have also gained the respect of many Western politicians who have dealt with him. See, for instance, Cyrus Vance, *Hard Choices: Critical Years in America's Foreign Policy* (New York, Simon & Schuster, 1983), p. 18.
47 Franklyn Griffiths, 'Ideological development and foreign policy', in Seweryn Bialer (ed.), *The Domestic Context of Soviet Foreign Policy* (London, Croom Helm, 1981), p. 20.
48 Ibid.
49 Ibid.
50 Carter, *Keeping Faith*, p. 276. The Soviet negotiating team, apart from Brezhnev and Gromyko, included Ustinov and Chernenko.
51 Brzezinski, *Power and Principle*, p. 343.
52 Ibid.
53 See, for example, Zhores Medvedev, *Andropov* (Oxford: Blackwell, 1983), p. 112; Steele and Abraham, *Andropov in Power*, p. 151; and Brown, 'The Soviet succession; from Andropov to Chernenko', p. 136.
54 The latest indication of the comparative standing of the Soviet leaders is provided by the order in which they delivered the addresses to their constituents prior to the Supreme Soviet election of March 1984. These were given in ascending order of importance. The rank order revealed put Gromyko in fifth place in the leadership (after Chernenko, Tikhonov, Gorbachev and Ustinov) and Ponomarev in eighth equal position (after Grishin and Romanov and alongside Shcherbitsky and Solomentsev). See *Pravda*, 25 February–3 March 1984.
55 *Pravda*, 13 March 1984, p. 1.
56 Brzezinski, *Power and Principle*, p. 153.
57 BBC Summary of World Broadcasts, SU/7578/A1/1, 28 February 1984. The starting-point of Kondrshov's remarks was the report by Richard Davy, 'Thatcher lays down détente guidelines' in *The Times*, 16 February 1984, p. 7.
58 BBC Summary of World Broadcasts, SU/7584/C/5, 6 March 1984.
59 Though Soviet studies, as an area of scholarship, are generally (and rightly) considered to be rather strong in Britain, only a tiny proportion of the scholars engaged in them work on aspects of Soviet foreign policy (whether content or process).

14 Conclusion: The Implications for Foreign Policy

Curtis Keeble

Ideology and power

In the last year of the Brezhnev regime, after a lunch with Soviet guests in our Embassy in Moscow, the discussion turned to the conservatism of the Orthodox church. 'Well,' I said, 'There's nothing wrong with conservatism' and, pointing across the river to the golden domes of the Kremlin, I added, 'There are plenty of good conservatives over there.' 'Yes, indeed,' commented one of our guests, a Soviet citizen of some distinction, 'Conservatism and dogma, the twin pillars of the Orthodox Church and the Soviet state.' I often think back to that conversation when faced with the doctrinaire rigidity of Soviet policy.

Now, in twelve separate studies, we have examined various aspects of the Soviet domestic scene, in an attempt to identify those essential characteristics of the Soviet Union which form the roots from which its foreign policy springs. As our studies progressed, we were all conscious that the constraint of space was forcing us into compression, simplification and omission. This state, greater in land surface than the United States, China and India put together, with twenty-two national groups each more than one million strong and a host of smaller ones, is all held in a tight central administration by a single party based on a single political ideology, but it does not lend itself to easy characterization in a few clean strokes. The picture is probably more accurate if we let the inconsistencies stand than if we try to iron them out. Moreover, given that the individual contributions are already heavily condensed, to summarize them is to risk ending with no more than that collection of platitudes which forms the substance of so much contemporary discussion of the Soviet Union. Yet, if our studies are to be relevant to Western policy, we need to bring together the threads of the earlier chapters and assess the ways in which the nature of the Soviet state may be reflected in its foreign policy. Only on this basis is it realistic to explore the kind of relationship which a Western democracy can reasonably expect to sustain with the Soviet Union. That is the purpose of this final chapter.

Few people would suggest that Soviet policies always have their source in Marxist-Leninist theory, but it is in terms of this body of theory, elaborated and codified by its guardians in the party throughout the whole history of the Soviet state, that they must be argued and presented. Soviet writers see Marxism-Leninism as the ideological foundation on which is erected a 'principled' Soviet foreign policy, different in character from that of non-socialist states. Up to a point they are right. There is a certain qualitative difference between the international conduct of those states that regard a codified ideology as the basis of foreign policy and those that follow a more empirical line. If policy is formulated in Marxist-Leninist terms by officials who have to act as though they believe that there is a scientific accuracy to the theory, the pressure is strong to fit the world into the ideological stereotype and formulate the stereotype solution. In any analysis, the use of a particular method of argument is a constraint on the solutions which can emerge. In a state where Marxist-Leninist indoctrination is all pervasive, where Marxism-Leninism is the language of political discourse and where all decisions have to be justified in Marxist-Leninist terms, Soviet policy-makers are subject to a constraint which is not always fully perceived from the West. As a result of it, the policy which emerges is that of the tram, not of the bus. The lines are laid down and parallel with them runs the power. There are curves, there are points, there are possibilities of switching from one track to another, but those possibilities are constrained by the system, limited in scope and not easily extensible. Collision will produce a major hold-up.

Yet it would seem that the theory requires a pre-supposition of collision. 'The world outlook and class aims of socialism and capitalism are opposite and irreconcilable'[1] wrote Brezhnev. He was echoing Lenin, who, arguing that the international system of states was characterized by the struggle between socialism and capitalism, wrote, 'If we lose sight of this, we shall not put a single question correctly, even in the remotest corner of the world.'[2] A contemporary Soviet commentator, Lebedev, is only one of the host who make the same point. 'The struggle between two systems, forming the axis of international life, conditions not only the foreign policy of states with different social structures but also the development of the whole system of international relations.'[3] In one form or another this basic tenet underlies all Soviet foreign policy. We delude ourselves if we believe otherwise. But if a dogma is to serve as the basis for the government of a state it must have its built-in escape clauses. For it is by the power of the state that those who preach the dogma survive, and it serves them little if the purity of the dogma survives only in the ruin of the state.

So Brezhnev used to assert that Marxism-Leninism was not a dogma, but a 'guide to action', and the younger Gorbachev took the same line: 'Leninism is not a collection of congealed dogmas and ready made recipes, but a theory and method of dialectical thinking and analysis.' There is in fact within the party, some room for different trends in the development of Marxist-Leninist theory and its application to practical policy. There is also room for tactical flexibility. Lenin can be cited as the authority for this, as, indeed for all else: 'We learnt to be flexible, to change our tactics quickly and sharply, taking account of changes in the objective conditions, choosing a different course to our goal if the former one showed itself inappropriate or impracticable at some given time.'[4] Like most religions, Marxism-Leninism has enough precepts to justify virtually any conceivable course of policy and where a long-term Soviet goal or an overriding Soviet interest require tactical flexibility, it can go a long way. A doctrine which with no audible hiccup can swallow the pact with Hitler can comfortably accommodate the combined strategic requirements of the imperial legacy of Russia and the contemporary demands of the socialist community. We have seen substantial adaptation and indeed reversal of policy in the conclusion of the Austrian State Treaty and the resolution of the Cuban missile crisis. We have seen a measure of flexibility in the final stage of the Madrid CSCE Review Conference. At a technical, but nonetheless politically significant level, we saw some flexibility in the later stages of the Law of the Sea negotiations. Yet, for all this, changes of course are not easily or quickly attained in a system which is ideologically based and centrally controlled and which lacks an effective machinery for the generation and advocacy of heterodox policies.

It would be idle to suppose that matters will change substantially in the future. The ideology will not be abandoned. With the passage of years we can expect it to inhibit rather than to inspire policy, and with the demonstration of its irrelevance to the pressing problems of the day, we can expect to find it progressively less useful as a guide to developments. But those who have been reared in it, cynical though they may be about it, will not escape its influence. The inherent inflexibility and doctrinal hostility will last for many decades yet, and will demand a corresponding tenacity and firmness on the part of those in the West who have to deal with the Soviet Government.

Russian history and Marxist-Leninist philosophy coincide to produce an obsession with power, both political and military, internal and external, which may perhaps legitimately be called a national instinct. What Lenin understood was, above all, the manipulation of power and today the Soviet leadership look at foreign policy in terms of a 'correlation of forces', a correlation in which, on the Soviet side, they rely upon military power plus socialist doctrine. 'The source of the power and authority of socialist foreign policy is, above all, the might of the Soviet state and the advantages of the socialist system.'[5] The socialist system may be a doubtful prop, but the need to sustain it represents a major policy input. So it is that two principal threads of contemporary Soviet foreign policy begin to come together. Professor Seton-Watson has drawn attention to the 'either-or fallacy' of seeing ideology and security as alternative motive forces for Soviet policy. I would go further. The mantle of Marxism-Leninism has been slipped smoothly over the imperial heritage, shaping itself to the broad shoulders on which it rests. We have to deal today with a power which, over the centuries, has sought security against the threat and the reality of invasion across open land frontiers by the constant extension of its power into areas beyond those frontiers. Having done so, it has found the need to secure tranquillity within areas newly brought under control as well as stable, compliant administration in those adjacent to the imperial frontier. Not that the craving for security has been the sole motive force. The great periods of Russian expansion were characterized by a drive to the East, the South and the West – and, for that matter, to the North too – for which the sheer urge of power must be seen as a motive at least as powerful as the need for security. So it was when the imperial legacy was taken over by the Soviet state and the Tsarist policy replaced by Leninist. There was little reason to be surprised at the way in which the Soviet army was used to establish and to sustain control over Eastern Europe, or, more recently, over Afghanistan. The objective factors of geo-politics and imperial management must in many respects determine the course of Soviet policy as they did the course of Russian policy.

Yet to see contemporary Soviet policy simply in terms of an adaptation of Russian imperialism is as misleading as to see it simply in terms of Marxist-Leninist doctrine. The doctrine does of course provide a convenient justification for the use of Soviet power outside the boundaries of the Soviet state. Soviet theorists do not need to advocate the export of revolution and indeed they firmly disavow it. It is enough for them to proclaim the scientific inevitability of revolution and to analyse any situation of conflict in terms of a struggle between socialism and capitalism, in which socialism must win unless it is frustrated by the forces of reaction. It is classic Soviet doctrine that the imperialist powers seek to 'arrest the onward march of history' by the 'export of counter-revolution'. If 'socialism' triumphs, the logical consequence is the addition of a new area to the 'socialist community'. If, on the other hand, this natural course of events is interfered with, the 'peace-loving policy of the Soviet Union' requires action to 'promote . . . the triumph of the new and revolutionary over the old and obsolete'.[6] At the level of socialist theory it all fits very tidily into place as a justification for the external development of Soviet political and military power.

It is easy enough to set out a case based on quotations such as these to demonstrate how they are applied in practice, for instance in the way the official Soviet chronology of international events notes for August 21 1968 'Entry into Czechoslovakia . . . of Soviet military units . . . to help the working people of that country safeguard their revolutionary achievements against encroachments by internal and external enemies of socialism'; to point to Soviet policy in relation to situations of conflict in the third world, and to conclude that we are faced with a peculiarly malevolent and expansionist conjunction of historical tradition, doctrinal precept and brute power. In various forms an analysis on these lines inspires much current thinking about the conduct of relations with the Soviet Union. It contains much that is correct. In these discussions about the domestic roots of Soviet policy we have, however, questioned whether as an analysis it is adequate.

If the foreign policy decisions of the Soviet leadership reflect their estimate of the power of their state and their ideology, what is that estimate likely to be? After sixty-seven years of Soviet rule, how stable and how strong is the Soviet state? Patriotism may be an old-fashioned word, but the loyalty of the Russian to his country and its rulers is a powerful force. Such direct observation as is possible for a foreign observer suggests that an innate Russian patriotism has, to a significant extent, been transformed into a Soviet patriotism. The Soviet Union is not some wholly artificial creation and the Russian heritage has been carefully cultivated by the Soviet state. In the battle of Kulikovo on 8 September 1380, Prince Dmitri threw back the Tartars and established the supremacy of Moscow. In 1980 the six hundredth anniversary of Kulikovo was the subject of much official celebration. From Kulikovo through Borodino to Stalingrad and the eventual victory in the 'Great Patriotic War', most of today's Soviet citizens see a continuing tradition of which they feel themselves a part. So, in having harnessed the historical element of Russian patriotism to the Soviet state, the leadership may feel reasonably content. They have, moreover, had some success in establishing the forces of 'imperialism' in the popular mind as the external foe, in a direct line of descent from all those who through the centuries ravaged Russian soil. The emotional scars of war are much traded on by the propagandists, but they are real. It is scarcely surprising that with 1941 still alive in the memory of the older generation and the Allied intervention of 1918 embedded in the folk memory, the current Soviet line about the dangers of American militarism and the threat posed by NATO weapons systems in Western Europe should find a certain resonance among the Soviet public. So too can the

Chinese threat be conjured up to awaken ancient fears. Although we may expect the ideological drive of Soviet policy to continue to weaken, the influence of old style Russian patriotism is likely, if anything, to increase. The signs are already there and the more tense the international scene, the stronger this factor will become.

Social problems

When we turned to an examination of Soviet society and the Soviet economy, we saw more reason for concern on the part of the leadership. The pattern was, however, by no means consistent. Our study of Soviet society produced a double image. On the one hand, we found little to suggest that the stability of the Soviet state was itself under immediate threat. On the other, we saw massive evidence of a corrosive malaise in society. Much has been written about the consequences of the change in the population structure as a result of the difference in birth-rate between the Russian and the Central Asian peoples of the Soviet Union, a change, the effects of which already apparent, could within a few decades become dramatic. Yet, while this poses social and economic problems, it was Alastair McAuley's view that there is not today in the Central Asian Republics a serious menace to stability in classic 'nationalist' terms. The menace may, however, develop if the regime fails to solve the economic and social problems of the region. It may also develop in those other republics, the Baltic states, the Ukraine, Georgia and Armenia, where the political focus of dissident nationalism is always latent. It must, in this multi-nation state, be a constant source of concern and in various specific ways it is a constraint on foreign policy. There were, within the group, differing views on this issue. Certainly, nationalism in the Baltic states has been a constraint on any post-Helsinki easing of external contacts and the potential risk of Central Asian nationalism a constraint on relations with the Muslim world. These specific factors aggravate the natural inclination of the regime to nervous hostility externally and repression internally, but are not such as to constitute, in our view, a major inhibiting factor in terms of the leadership's assessment of the power at its disposal.

It was when we considered the other aspects of the social structure of the Soviet Union today that the picture became substantially more complex and, for the leadership, less reassuring. David Lane makes the point that this is a changing society; one which, in the process of modernization, is becoming more differentiated. The significance of this differentiation, for a political system derived from elementary concepts of a relatively primitive social structure, should not be underestimated. Within a lifetime, the Soviet Union has moved from Lenin's society of workers and peasants to a substantially more complex structure, in which the top strata of those with a vested interest in the system of government have been broadened and strengthened, but, in which, beneath them, the underlying strata are beginning to show the fissile characteristics of a more sophisticated state. Our discussions endorsed David Lane's judgement that internal changes in population and social structure do not seem likely to lead to serious problems of political legitimacy. Indeed, one may say that the Soviet Union need not be seen as an inherently unstable society. That said, the social problems are profound, the system is essentially brittle and the strains upon it are severe. Central to them is the problem of the relevance and effectiveness of the party's philosophy. There is no doubt that one of the characteristic features of the Soviet Union today is the prevalence of cynicism about the party's ideology and disillusionment about its ability to make the state function in a way which will meet the more complex economic and social requirements of contemporary society. The Central Committee report to the Twenty-sixth Party Congress in 1981 contained a section entitled 'Strengthening the Material and Intellectual Foundations of the Socialist Way of Life and the Moulding of the New Man'. In the 'moulding of the new man', said Brezhnev, 'we are faced with quite a few problems'. Later, dealing with the party's ideological work, he complained of the 'general verbiage' which made people switch off the television or set aside the newspaper, and he reminded his audience that it was one thing to address people who were inadequately trained and had little education, but another to speak to the present-day Soviet citizen. Not only are those who ought to be the 'new men' – or at least the parents of the 'new men' – cynical about the ideology. They are depressingly like the old Adam of Tsarist Russia in their addiction to vodka, in their corruption where they have access to the levers of power – levers which in a socialist state are multiplied in number and enhanced in effect by the full scope of the state's power – and in their disinclination to work harder than is necessary to secure their daily bread. While Oblomov is still in his bed, the young are becoming more inclined to ask awkward questions and are showing a taste for some of the frothier manifestations of Western society. The symptoms of social stress are visible in the pattern of abortion and divorce.

This is not necessarily the pattern of a society which is disintegrating, but it is evidence of a malaise which can sap the power base and, with that, the self-confidence of the party. It necessitates remedial action. This action is in essence domestic, but it has a direct effect on foreign policy, in that it incorporates an enhancement of that internal repression which, more than any other characteristic of Soviet domestic policy, aggravates relations with the West. All this has been made apparent in the policies pursued since Brezhnev's death. At the first Lenin's birthday celebration after Andropov took over, the keynote speech was given by Gorbachev, still in his fifties and representative of the younger generation of Politburo members. It was, *inter alia*, a call for moral revival: 'We cannot assume that the young will automatically take over the legacy of the ideas and morals of their mothers and fathers. . . . We live in conditions of the bitterest ideological confrontation. . . . There is no place in our society for illusions of permissiveness and impunity.' Calls for an improvement in the ideological work of the party, for greater discipline and for higher moral standards, have been a feature of recent party pronouncements. Alongside the attempt to revitalize the economy, a reform of the educational system was one of the few initiatives of the brief Andropov regime, and it is interesting that it was introduced by Chernenko. The aim was not just to instil knowledge, but, as the Central Committee put it, to increase vigilance against imperialist attempts to take advantage of the 'lack of political sophistication among the young'.[7] Soviet citizens, they proclaimed, must be educated to be citizens of a socialist society, active builders of communism, with all the inherent qualities this required.

It is one thing to kindle and to sustain the enthusiasm of those who make a revolution. It is another to rekindle enthusiasm in a generation which has lost it. The regime have, no doubt, few illusions about the difficulty of the task which confronts them and they can scarcely be optimistic about their chances of success. Many of the values they seek to inculcate would have commended themselves to a Victorian Methodist – hard work, sobriety, honesty, respect for society and even for the family. The problem lies less in the values than in the philosophy to which the party tries to harness them.

If, as we have noted, Soviet foreign policy claims to derive its strength in part from the power of the state and in part from the socialist philosophy, then in so far as the latter is weakened, the need to rely upon the former is, if anything, enhanced. Current Soviet policy is consistent with an awareness of this. The call for vigilance against imperialist moral subversion requires an intensified campaign against any who may be seen as its agents within the Soviet Union – the Helsinki monitoring groups, the dissenting intellectuals and that alternative focus of loyalty, the Church. It requires a direct effort to block Western influence by measures such as the jamming of radio broadcasts. Against the background of Sir John Lawrence's chapter on the growing strength of religion in the Soviet Union, it was revealing to see Pravda find it appropriate to begin a leading article[8] on the need for better atheist propaganda with the double-edged affirmation that religion would disappear in step with the development of socialism. A few weeks later,[9] it was the writers who were being exhorted 'in a situation of bitter opposition of two world systems' to 'uphold the Soviet way of life' and 'unmask the intrigues of the enemies of peace'. The note of concern is apparent. Despite the barrage of internal and external propaganda, there is a sterile defensiveness to Soviet policy in international contact at the personal and cultural level and perhaps even some sign of a lack of self-confidence in the relationship with non-ruling Communist parties in other countries. At the same time, the emphasis upon the Soviet armed forces as the guardians of the Soviet state and the international socialist community is clear. 'Surrounded by the love of the whole people and the care of the Communist Party and the Soviet state, the armed forces of the Soviet Union vigilantly safeguard the peaceful life of the Soviet people, of the whole community of fraternal socialist countries.'[10] With the domestic power base of the Soviet Union affected by cynicism and systemic inefficiency and the external power ratio prejudiced by the failure of the attempt to prevent the NATO deployment of Cruise and Pershing missiles, we must expect a determined effort, internally and externally, to redress the balance. Yet existing adverse internal trends are likely to be intensified. The social malaise is likely to deepen as the regime fails to satisfy the material or spiritual needs of the new generation. The internal and external decline of the ideology will continue, making both internal discipline and external force the more necessary if power is to be sustained.

Economic problems

The spread of cynicism among the younger generation about the party and its philosophy may be potentially the most serious problem confronting the leadership, but the inefficiency of the economy is probably the one to which the greatest current effort is being devoted. The potential strength and practical problems of the economy are linked at every point to the power and the doctrine of the Soviet state. The strength is essentially that of the natural resources which give this country a unique potential for self-sufficiency – not total, but very substantial – at the superpower level. It is a potential of which the leadership are fully conscious, and it does much to colour their thinking. By way of illustration we included a chapter on Siberia, which, with its oil, gas, coal, iron, timber, copper and much more, is a powerful psychological and practical symbol of Soviet resources. Yet, despite all the resources of Siberia, all the grain of the Ukraine and the cotton of Central Asia, despite all the potential economic power within their grasp, the leadership are fully aware that their economy, as at present organized, is failing to meet the full needs of the state.

The system can make impressive achievements when it marshals the full resources of the state in the attainment of an overriding objective, be it the re-equipment of the forces after 1941, the creation of a nuclear strike capability, the rural electrification programme, the provision of basic modern housing or the space programme. It is able today to meet the equipment requirements of the armed forces, but it is not able to produce and distribute the necessary total flow of goods at a sufficiently high level of quality to meet this objective, while at the same time providing adequately for the Soviet consumer and supporting Soviet foreign policy. So, in the essentials of its economic policy, the leadership is brought back again to the twin bases of its policy, power and doctrine. If the people are discontented they are the more likely to question the doctrine and weaken the system. If the armed forces go short, the physical power of the state will be prejudiced. And the price of remedying economic deficiencies may be the system itself.

The primary task of the economy, as defined in the current five-year plan, is to 'ensure the further improvement of the Soviet people's well-being'. Throwing away the jargon at his last Party Congress, Brezhnev put the problem in these terms: 'What we are discussing – food products, other consumer goods and services – are part of the everyday life of millions upon millions of people. People go to shops, canteens, laundries every day. What can they buy? How are they welcomed? How are they spoken to? How much time do they spend on all sorts of household chores? It is on the strength of how these problems are solved that people largely judge our work. They judge it strictly, exactingly.' Everyone who has lived in the Soviet Union knows that, implicit in the question, is the answer. The people are not satisfied. In their dissatisfaction lies an element of considerable significance for the future development of the Soviet state. For half a century or more the basic and urgent needs of a rather simply structured society could be met with reasonable adequacy by the application of centrally controlled resources. Now, as a more complex society develops more complex requirements, the inherent inadequacy of the economic system is becoming ever more cruelly exposed, not least by the growing recourse to a secondary 'black' economy. For the older generation the state's achievements in terms of the housing programme brought a substantial and demonstrable improvement in living standards, but now a younger generation takes those achievements for granted and is bitterly critical of the failings. So the existing social strains are intensified, the questioning of the doctrine grows and the ultimate power of the party is eroded.

However, while the well-being of the people is defined as the primary task of the economy, the first charge upon the economic resources of the state is the defence programme. The central planning system may be inefficient in meeting consumer needs, but it is essential and effective in ensuring that the armed forces secure the equipment they require and, if, in a tense international situation, the consumer has to tighten his belt, he will do so. The need to make available the resources required by the forces does, however, begin to impose a certain pressure so to manage the foreign policy of the state as to contain those requirements.

There can be little argument that the problems of the economy are inherent in the system of centrally planned state control. The symptoms are various – managerial inefficiency, insensitivity of reaction to demand, inflexibility, poor quality, poor distribution and a deplorable service sector. The list could be longer. The point is that an effective solution requires radical change in the system, yet to effect such change would be to cast aside a central element of the structure of the state, with the risk of further disintegration and also of direct prejudice to the claims of the defence sector and of all those whose personal position is bound up with the present system. Lenin had the courage to introduce a New Economic Policy, but Khrushchev failed when he tried to effect a radical shake-up of the system and in the last thirty years, while the problems have multiplied, the remedies have rarely gone beyond a mixture of exhortation and tinkering. David Dyker, Alan Smith, Alec Nove and Edwina Moreton have, in their separate studies, analysed different sectors of the economy and shown how, in each, the leadership's freedom of manoeuvre is limited by the constraint of the system. Now, under Chernenko, a new commission is to try yet again. The fact that it is headed by Gorbachev, who must be the strongest contender for the succession, suggests a readiness for drastic action, yet it must still be questionable whether there are any measures which, in a state the size of the Soviet Union, can introduce the necessary economic stimuli without at the same time transforming the character of the state. To do so would be to move into uncharted waters, with great potential for gain and for loss so far as the leadership are concerned and, indeed, in terms of Soviet foreign policy.

In considering the economic roots of Soviet foreign policy we have, however, taken the economy essentially as it is. The first of the direct inputs which one may note is the self-confidence which stems from the size of the country's resource base. There is a certain sense that, no matter what troubles may befall the Soviet Union, it has the sheer size and the materials to be invincible. Allied to this is the fact that there is no overpowering drive to secure access to new sources of strategic materials. There are, as we have noted, factors making for expansion, but economic pressure is not one of them. Indeed, in a sense, the economy works in the opposite direction. The leadership's inability to develop it to the full means that policy is constrained by a lack of deployable, as compared with potential, resources. There is thus a need to contain the economic cost of existing commitments and to weigh carefully the cost of new ones. Imperial policies contain a nice balance of gain and loss. In the early stages, gains of territory and power bring a material as well as a psychological boost to the centre, a return which a leadership may judge sufficient to justify the cost. Later, as the expansionist zeal diminishes and the economic burden of client states increases, the balance begins to look different. Cuba is estimated to cost the Soviet Union the equivalent of some $4bn each year. There must have been occasions in recent years when the Governor of the Soviet Central Bank, contemplating the depletion of his foreign exchange reserves as a result of grain purchases, begrudged the cost of support for Cuba. No doubt the Politburo judgement was that the price was worth paying, or, at least, that a refusal to pay it would have raised unacceptable doubts about the Soviet Union's ability to sustain its allies. Andropov himself, however, in his speech at the June 1983 Plenum of the Central Committee, made clear the limitation upon Soviet ability to help even those countries 'in the ex-colonial world which have chosen a socialist orientation'. 'It is', he said, 'one thing to enunciate socialism as an objective, but another to build it.' The socialist countries 'are rendering them aid in the field of politics and culture, and are promoting the strengthening of their defence. We assist also, within our capabilities, their economic development. But, in essence that development, like the entire social progress of these countries, can of course result only from the labour of their own peoples and the correct policy of their leaderships.'

Within the socialist community of Eastern Europe the requirement for the maintenance of political and military control must be the dominant factor, and it must be held to justify some economic cost, but that cost needs to be contained and where possible offset by an economic as well as a political return. To this end, it has been in the Soviet interest, while developing a Soviet dominated economic integration, to permit a relatively wide degree of latitude to the CMEA members in the development of their own economies, including trading links with the West. The experience of Poland showed that, in economic as in political terms, those countries did so at their own risk and that, at the end of the day, solvent or not, they would have to accept the Soviet strategic requirement.

We conclude that the constraint of the Soviet economy will compel the leadership to contain the cost of overseas commitments and to deploy resources in close relationship to the strategic importance of the area concerned – although the resources of the printing and arms industries make it easy to pursue relatively lavish policies in the supply of somewhat dated dogma and weapons.

It may in this context be relevant to note that the low productivity, to which David Dyker draws attention, is reflected in a chronic manpower shortage. It is normal to employ the armed forces on civilian tasks in an attempt to remedy some of the more critical deficiencies. If the real or perceived needs of the Soviet Union require them to be used for military purposes there will be no hesitation about leaving the civilian economy in the lurch, and it must not be supposed that civilian needs will be allowed to detract from the defence effort, but the labour shortage must tend to enhance those other factors that militate against external adventure.

In terms of relations with the industrialized Western countries, the weaknesses of the Soviet economy provide an interesting link with foreign policy, but one which is substantially more complex than is sometimes assumed. In a world where the use of armed force by one major power against another carries with it the risk of mutual annihilation, there has been an urgent and largely ineffectual search by the Western nations for some alternative sanction by which to prevent the arbitrary violation of accepted international standards. Inevitably this has led to recourse to economic sanctions. Alan Smith's paper indicates some of the problems which this has involved. The conclusion one may draw is that the weakness of the Soviet Union in certain specific areas of technology combined with more fundamental failings in agricultural policy have led to a situation in which some potential for economic pressure may exist. The very deficiencies of the Soviet economy can, however, be exploited politically against the West, and this has been well understood by the Soviet leadership since the earliest days of the revolution. The linkage of trade and politics, which was seen in one aspect in the period of détente and in another during the Afghan and Polish crises, can be traced back to the Genoa conference in 1922. Lenin welcomed the conference as an opportunity 'to bargain for the most proper and most advantageous and politically suitable terms for trade'. 'We should', he said, 'without concealing our communist views, confine ourselves to a brief and passing mention of them (for instance, in a subordinate clause)'. But at the same time there was the political objective: 'Everything possible and even impossible should be done to strengthen the pacifist wing of the bourgeoisie . . . to disunite the bourgeois countries that will be united against us at Genoa.'[11] Sixty years on, in a time of economic recession, the Soviet Union showed once again, over the Siberian pipeline, how the shortcomings of its own technology may still serve as a political lever to prise apart its Western opponents. It may, in the context of external economic policy towards the West, be appropriate also to mention Soviet shipping and aviation policy as an area where commercial and strategic interests are closely aligned and where the state monopoly can be effectively used to pursue Soviet interests. This is, in fact, an area where the Soviet Union, operating in an environment not under its own control, has achieved remarkable success in exploiting Western laxity and may, by its consequent over-extension, have placed itself in a situation of some vulnerability.

We can thus see Soviet foreign policy influenced in four ways by Soviet technological weakness: (i) to acquire overtly or covertly Western technology; (ii) to negotiate for a containment of the more sophisticated areas of competition in defence technology; (iii) to stabilize the relatively favourable present balance of weaponry; and (iv) to create disunity between the Western powers. In all this, the Soviet leadership has room for tactical manoeuvre, for a balancing of political and economic objectives, and for flexibility in attaining them. At the same time we may expect – and this is crucial for Western policy – no yielding to economic pressure where strategic essentials are judged to be at stake.

Foreign policy formation

Foreign policy is the product not of a mathematical balancing of different factors, but of the separate and collective will of individuals and institutions in the application of available resources. As the final sections of our study show, that collective will is, in the Soviet Union, in respect of the major issues of peace and war, the will of the central, supreme leadership of the party. Our group agreed with Malcolm Mackintosh's contention that it is wrong to assume, at this level of decision-making, a separate and distinct military voice. It would be more accurate to see the military as the guardians of that ultimate power by which the party and the state are preserved, a sector of society which can virtually dictate the resources it requires, but not the use to which they are put. We cannot say that there will not in the future be a trial of strength between the military and political leadership. All we can say is that we do not believe it exists now and that the institutional structure is such as to militate against it in the future.

In fact, if there is one dominant characteristic of the institutional structure it is that the much vaunted 'democratic centralism' sharply accentuates not merely the unity of control but also the rigidity of policy. Here we come back to the twin pillars, conservatism and dogma. It is not that there is no debate about policy. It is rather that, at all levels, within the institutions of the Soviet state, cautious conformity is likely to produce moderate reward with minimal risk, while dissent will sharply increase the risk, with little likelihood of compensating reward. The institutions are concerned either with the implementation of centrally determined policy, or, in the case of those that are responsible for policy formulation, with the pursuit of Soviet interest by the application of doctrinal precedent and accepted practice. It is the nature of bureaucracy to be secretive. In this respect, Soviet bureaucracy, building upon a long Russian tradition, excels. Reinforcing bureaucratic secrecy with priestly dogmatism, it ensures that policy is determined within the responsible organizations by processes largely obscured from public view, and communicated to the people only for approbation and implementation. Archie Brown rightly points out that the Soviet Union is not the monolith portrayed by its propagandists or its critics. There is indeed the possibility of public, licensed, criticism of official shortcomings and misdemeanours through the press and the party organs, and there is, for the *cognoscenti*, even some public debate about policy. Yet Soviet policy is inherently more rigid than that of Western democracies, and the secrecy which surrounds foreign policy formation is itself a factor in determining the substance of that policy. By largely eliminating the possibility of public challenge, it powerfully reinforces continuity, and to that extent, incidentally, makes Soviet foreign policy more predictable. This can be a source of strength to the Soviet Union, but it can also produce those harmful genetic consequences which can attend any excessive inbreeding.

Against this background, the course of Soviet foreign policy in recent years ought to have given us little cause for surprise. Our problem in predicting it has been essentially a problem of understanding from a Western viewpoint the Soviet evaluation of the factors in any international situation. If we give only the most cursory glance to those instances in which the Soviet Union has done most to affront international opinion, the occupation of Afghanistan, the repression of the Solidarity movement in Poland, the shooting down of the Korean airliner and the repression of dissenting opinion within the Soviet Union's own borders, the pattern has shown certain consistent features. It was the occupation of Afghanistan which, more than any other single event, marked the watershed between the years of detente and the current period of tension. In that act the motive forces of history and ideology, power and insecurity came together. Ideologically, the 1978 Revolution in Afghanistan had, in Brezhnev's words, brought a qualitative change in the relationship with the Soviet Union. Historically, it had advanced a stage further the old Russian drive into Central Asia. When it seemed that the revolution was in danger, the only doctrinally permissible explanation was a foreign-inspired counter revolution and this, ideologically, placed a 'duty' on the Soviet Union to 'assist' in its suppression. Failure to sustain the revolution might, it could be argued in the Politburo, set a precedent for the decay of the socialist community and even carry with it the risk of infection in the Muslim Republics of the Soviet Union. The Soviet power instinct called for the use of massive military force and it was calculated that, with no risk of armed involvement by the United States, the operation carried no risk to Soviet security. In several respects the Politburo miscalculated. The Afghan resistance was tougher and longer lasting than had been expected and so too was the international condemnation. But once committed, it was not in the Soviet nature to contemplate withdrawal, despite the damage to wider Soviet interests. The fact that the occupation took place and the fact that it was sustained were not just a matter of tactical misjudgment. They were a reflection of the nature of the Soviet state, its ideology and its policy-making processes. In the case of Solidarity there was again, and more seriously, the fear of a crumbling of the ideological empire and again the historical obsession, in this case with the threat to security across the Polish plains. Control had to be re-established. The case for military action must have been powerfully argued. The fact that in the event the action was taken by the Polish, not the Soviet, army reflected not only Soviet policy but also Polish realities. Above all it reflected Soviet caution in a situation where direct military intervention could have led to an escalation with unpredictable consequences for the Soviet Union itself. The two cases of Afghanistan and Poland illustrate well both the relevance of the domestic factors, and their limitations as a basis for the full understanding of foreign policy. By contrast, the shooting down of the Korean airliner showed typical features of Soviet policy in a situation which was at the crucial stage dealt with in essentially domestic terms – the deep insecurity, the bureaucratic inflexibility, the brutal use of power and the dogged justification of the unjustifiable. So it has been with the treatment of internal dissent. At a time when the Soviet leaders were beginning to be aware of the extent of disillusion with the ideology, there can have been little opposition within the Politburo to the adoption of measures to discipline those whose dissent might weaken the ideological power base and with it the very legitimacy of the party.

It is interesting also to examine Soviet conduct in crises which did not, or need not, directly involve the Soviet Union. The Iranian Revolution destroyed a strong point of American influence on the periphery of the Soviet Union and an attempt was made by Soviet theorists to interpret it as an early stage of a revolutionary process which, in due course, would be succeeded by the true socialist revolution. Up to that point there was a net gain to Soviet interests in terms of the correlation of forces, but when the American hostages were seized, the Soviet Union could not bring itself to take an objective view. It made only the most perfunctory reference to the impropriety of such action and did its best to exploit the situation to the disadvantage of the United States. In the process it no doubt contributed to the election of President Reagan and substantially prejudiced its own wider interests, without in any way further advancing its position in the Muslim world. It was an interesting example of an uncovenanted bonus mishandled through obsession with a false doctrinal interpretation. When the Falklands invasion took place, Soviet ideology required that Argentina should be seen as resisting British colonialism, yet Russian instinct was perhaps better expressed by the person who commented, 'Of course if it had been ours we would have had enough troops there to ensure that they did not start it.' The exploitation of unrest in Central America has shown the old ideological imperialism at work whenever the circumstances are favourable, yet tempered now by a greater degree of caution. There is a readiness to supply arms and training, but a noticeable and natural preference to work through proxies. In the Middle East similar characteristics are apparent, the risks of direct involvement seem to be well understood and caution has so far prevailed. In the field of arms control we have seen the balancing of economic and military considerations, of the need for stability and the determination never to yield an advantage once gained. It has been a trial of Soviet instincts, not least in the decision to break, which threw considerable light on the Soviet evaluation of the potential political bonus and economic penalty. In the handling of relations with China we have perhaps now begun to see Soviet interest gaining the upper hand over ideology.

At many points in this final chapter I have found myself echoing the chill realism of Professor Seton-Watson's opening essay. We do not help the attainment of a sound relationship with the Soviet Union if we close our eyes to the less appealing sources from which its policies stem. Some of those sources are profoundly alien to us and in conjunction they can be profoundly dangerous. Yet they need to be seen in the context of the Soviet Union as it is today and balanced against the evidence of the chapters on economic and social questions on the deep-seated internal problems with which the Soviet leadership must grapple. Virtually no meeting of the Politburo takes place without foreign policy on the agenda, but the questions which, most of the time, loom largest for the Soviet leadership are those concerned with the internal administration of the country. In the Soviet Union the whole functioning of industry, trade and agriculture is a direct governmental responsibility, and there are, as we have seen, few areas of economic or social policy that are not giving serious cause for concern. The capitalist foe is useful as a distraction and the ritual struggle against him must be sustained, but there can be scarcely any significant area in which external adventure will not aggravate rather than ease the internal problems. What is more, there are significant areas in which, both directly and indirectly, a reduction of international tension could ease, if only marginally, the problems of resource allocation and technological development.

In recent years we have seen the historical and ideological legacy of expansion and conquest sustained with brutal determination up to the very limit of the 'socialist community' and a new wave of internal repression initiated, albeit still well short of the excesses of the Stalin era. Yet more and more the Soviet Union has presented the image of a cautious, unadventurous society, a society with waning faith in its ideology, a society whose stability testifies more to a lack of dynamism than to any positive faith, an imperial power extended up to and probably a little beyond the practical limit of its capacity, a state hostile to most of the ideals of the Western democracies, but with a need – which one hopes is perceived by its leaders – for stability in its relations with them. The situation is not one which we can view with any complacency, since if the correlation of forces is perceived by the Soviet Union to have changed to its advantage, by virtue either of its own success or a weakening of Western will, the Soviet Union would be correspondingly encouraged to take advantage of this. It is, however, a situation in which the West, if it knows its own mind, has relatively greater room for manoeuvre.

If there is a time for major changes of Soviet policy, it is with the advent of a new leader. Our own assessment of the internal scene in the Soviet Union would appear to reflect the thoughts of a number of Russians and there was, in Brezhnev's closing years, a remarkable revival of the nostalgia for Stalin. There was a moment, when Andropov came to power, at which one felt a certain new briskness to government, a briskness in the repression of dissent, a briskness too in the dismissal of incompetent ministers and venal officials and in the attempt to enliven the economy. Now, with Andropov replaced by Chernenko, these policies are being pursued, but there is little expectation of a new impulse. The objective factors which we have identified are all there, with all their implications for policy, but, in so far as there is any indication of the new leader's style, it suggests the negative and the cautious rather than the enterprising and risky, at home as abroad. The doctrinal hostility will continue. The Soviet Union may need stability, but if, without significant cost or significant risk, an international situation can be manipulated in such a way as to damage Western interests, this will be done. The avoidance of any risk of armed conflict with a nuclear power will, however, continue to take priority in any situation where the security of the Soviet Union is not directly threatened. The guard will be strong on the ideological frontier, as on the military. There will be a strong incentive to stabilize the military balance, if this can be accomplished at the present level of Soviet advantage in certain sectors.

Détente may again be fashionable. It is a policy which has been much discussed, but, in its essentials is very simple. As we have already noted, Soviet foreign policy is based on the concept of an irreconcilable conflict between socialism and capitalism, but if that conflict were interpreted in terms of armed conflict between states there would be excessive risk to the Soviet state. It is therefore necessary in Soviet theory to provide for a situation in which states representative of the two systems coexist and to minimize the risk of military conflict between them. In such a situation, it is held, socialism will triumph because of its own scientific inevitability. The essence of Soviet détente policy is therefore to stabilize the relationship with the principal capitalist powers in such a way that war is avoided, maximum advantage is obtained from capitalist trade and technology and complete latitude is left for the spread of socialism by means which do not carry the risk of armed conflict with a major power. Détente never meant and was never intended to mean abandonment of the essential conflict. It was therefore never a recipe for an easy relationship, but if we are confident that Marxist-Leninist doctrine is fallible, it can be a recipe for a safe one. The Soviet leadership may well see the adoption of a more conciliatory posture as a means of controlling the burden of external commitments and, in particular, the burden of military expenditure, while concentrating its efforts on internal social and economic problems. In order to realize these gains the leadership would be ready to pay some price. There are common interests, for instance in nuclear non-proliferation. As interest overrides ideology, there could be room for a certain measure of understanding with the West in formal terms on questions of arms control and possibly, in implicit rather than explicit form, on the reduction of tension in areas where mutual military involvement could carry a greater risk of accidental conflict than either side would wish. There is mutual advantage to be derived from trade and from a whole range of cultural and scientific contacts. It would, however, be folly to place on any détente policy a load greater than it can carry. At best it will permit the containment of tension at a safe level, a development of advantage to both sides, but it will not permit its elimination. On the Western side an essential requirement for a détente policy is a commitment to the defence of Western values at least as strong and as effective as the commitment by the Soviet Union to the spread of its own variety of socialism. In conditions of détente the ideological struggle may indeed be the sharper and with it are certain to arise secondary tensions, for instance in Eastern Europe, which will require cool and dispassionate assessment if they are not in turn to generate new risks. If it is correct that the Soviet Union is already strained militarily, economically and socially, at the full extent of its imperial power, the coming decades are likely to see the gradual decay of that power, a process which, if mishandled, can be as dangerous as the period of its accretion. At such a time the case for closer contact at all levels and better understanding of the motivation of Soviet policy by the West can scarcely be denied.

It is always tempting and frequently misleading to extrapolate direct from a perceived current political scene. The safe prediction is probably that the slowing down of the momentum of the Soviet Union will continue and that social and economic pressures will produce a progressive weakening of the ideology. But those who in the past have underestimated the resilience of the individual Russian and of the Soviet state have paid dearly for their error. If we look beyond Chernenko, the potential for policy change may be greater than normal, since the old guard will virtually have disappeared and new, relatively unknown men will be in charge at all levels. The change could equally well be for better or for worse. The next General Secretary will have risen through the party machine and have been largely moulded by it. He, like his predecessors, will probably play safe. But this remarkable country has produced leaders of frightening and erratic power. The country which produced Ivan the Terrible, Peter the Great and Stalin could produce another giant of good or evil. The odds are heavily against it. The heroic days are probably gone. Those who yearn for a new Stalinist era are likely to remain disappointed and we may be spared its consequences. But with each shuffle of the leadership pack there must be a chance, however slender, that it will produce a man with the will and the ability to realize and utilize the vast potential power of the Soviet state and the Russian people in ways which we cannot easily foresee.

My guest may have been right in seeing conservatism and dogma as the twin pillars of the Soviet state, but alongside the shrewd, hard-bitten instinct of the Russian peasant there is a wild, irrational element in the Russian soul, and if we are looking for the roots of policy we should not forget that one is buried deeply there. Indeed, I would end this set of studies not with the leaders, the institutions or the policies of the Soviet state, but with its people, for it is on them that the whole edifice rests and it is in the last resort they who will determine its evolution. One should beware of inferring too much from one's limited contacts with a small number of Soviet citizens, but I would consider it just as misleading if I were to leave out of a final evaluation of the Soviet state the warmth, the friendliness, the human strengths and weaknesses, the mixture of indolence and industry, of passion and quiescence, the basic decency of the individual Soviet citizens whom I knew, as if I were to disregard the more easily identifiable and calculable characteristics of the governmental and party machine. The Communist Party of the Soviet Union has moulded the state to conform to its ideology, but it has signally failed so to mould the people. If the day is to come when the Soviet Union will act as a partner rather than an adversary in the community of nations, it will surely be when the policies of the state come to reflect more its people than its ideology. The way in which the people of the Soviet Union will determine the evolution of their state will be their own, but their perception of the West and its purposes may not be irrelevant. It may even, ultimately, perhaps be as valid a root of policy as was the perception by a German philosopher of the economy and society of Victorian Britain. One may legitimately hope that what the Soviet people will perceive will be a society capable of meeting human aspirations in ways of which Soviet socialism is manifestly incapable and showing realism and patience in its policies.

Notes

1 L.I. Brezhnev, *Following Lenin's Course* (Moscow, Progress, 1975), pp. 94–5.
2 Lenin, *Collected Works*, Vol. 41, p. 242 (as quoted in Lebedev, *Veliki Oktyabr*, Moscow, Nauka, 1978).
3 Lebedev, *Veliki Oktyabr*, p. 19.
4 Lenin, *Collected Works*, Vol. 44, p. 151.
5 A.A. Gromyko and B.N. Ponomarev, *Soviet Foreign Policy* (Moscow, Progress, 4th edn. 1981), p. 11.
6 Ibid., p. 22.
7 CC Draft decree on educational reform 4/1/84.
8 *Pravda*, 14 December 1983.
9 *Pravda*, 3 February 1984.
10 Gorbachev, 23 April 1983, Lenin anniversary address.
11 Draft Decision on the Tasks of the Soviet Delegation at Genoa, Lenin, 24 February 1922.

Index

Subject entries refer to the Soviet Union unless they contain a reference (actual or implied) to other countries.